MW00473176

The Songs of Degrees

Stephen Kaung

The Songs of Degrees

New York • Christian Fellowship Publishers, Inc.

Copyright © 1970
Christian Fellowship Publishers, Inc.
New York
All Rights Reserved

ISBN 0-935008-33-0

Available from the Publishers at:

11515 Allecingie Parkway
Richmond, VA 23235-4301

PRINTED IN U.S.A.

PREFACE

During the spring and summer of 1963 a number of the Lord's children in the city of New York were greatly profited by a special sequence of ministry from God's Word. Our brother Stephen Kaung, formerly of Shanghai, China, delivered a series of messages on the theme: the ascent of the soul, how a child of God moves by successive steps and stages from where he is at the beginning of his Christian life to where he ultimately ought to be in terms of his spiritual union with God. So rich were these studies that increasingly since then there has been the thought that someday these spoken words should be converted to the printed page, that the children of God elsewhere might also benefit from this ministry and so learn to walk more closely with the Father and with their brothers and sisters. What follows in these pages constitutes the fulfillment of that desire and the discharge of that burden.

The soul's ascent as a concept is itself nothing new. Deep and serious Christians throughout the centuries have devoted many volumes to this highly subjective subject. But to our limited knowledge no one has ever before represented the ascent to God by means of the series of Old Testament psalms known as the Songs of Degrees. Our brother has likened these fifteen Songs to a spiritual ladder possessing fifteen rungs divided into three broad stages of spiritual development. Weaving together this set of psalms into a remarkably integrated pattern of Christian experience, the author takes the believer on a spiritual journey filled with searching lessons for him to learn and not too easy steps to ascend, but none of which the pilgrim who is serious with God can afford to miss. Moreover, unlike most others who have only stressed the personal side of the Christian's pilgrimage, the author brings into view in addition its corporate aspect. For he finds running through the Songs as a whole a *collective* sentiment, an expression of concern on the part of each psalmist not only for himself but for all Israel too. Not merely the individual believer's growth is seen but the building up of the true Israel of God—the body of Christ—is also brought into focus.

Yet beyond considerations of treatment and scope, this observer in particular felt the impact of something else which, if not everywhere explicit, was nonetheless implicit throughout this special series of studies. Not only *is* there a way for unholy man to rise to a holy God—a fact which alone would have been enough to leave the Queen of Sheba awestruck (1 Kings 10.5)— but the *way itself* is equally a breathtaking thing to behold. Let the believer find inspiration and encouragement in the fact made clear in the pages to follow: That despite the impression one may sometimes have that his spiritual walk is at times marked by a seemingly unconnected, rambling and incoherent pattern of experiences, there nevertheless belongs to the Christian life *taken as a whole* an order and a timing, a balance and a symmetry, a unity and a harmony which when seen and felt and known in the depths of one's being takes one's breath away indeed! The way is possessed of such a singularly sublime quality that if we see it it ought to attract us the more towards God and, notwithstanding the manifold difficulties, impel us on our journey. What a sense of direction, what a feeling of spiritual well-being, what a sense of fulfillment and destiny this can beget in every believer, and most particularly the young in Christ who are just now beginning their ascent. If we could but apprehend this Way, and *submit* to it with a gladsome heart, our walk before the Lord—both singly and together—would be marked by far less bewilderment, far less discouragement and far less waywardness and unbelief.

May this book which now goes out be used by the Lord to enlighten and encourage those who, never having begun their ascent, may have hesitated out of ignorance as to the true and glorious character of the Way. But may it additionally strengthen and keep those who *are* on the Way from digressing into easier or shallower or even alien paths.

—The Editor

New York
October 1969

Editor's Note

A word should be appended regarding the sources for the material found in the following pages. They are three in number. First, the introductory Chapter and the Chapters covering Steps One through Thirteen were originally messages in English which Mr. Kaung delivered in New York during the period indicated elsewhere. As part of another series, the concluding two Steps were spoken in Chinese by our brother in early 1964 before a group of the Lord's people in Manila, Philippines. These have been translated into English for incorporation into this book to make the work complete. Second, as an added enrichment to the entire volume, our brother kindly loaned to the editor his set of private preparatory notes containing many gold nuggets scattered throughout, a sizeable number of which never found their way into the messages subsequently spoken but now included here. And finally, it should be mentioned that for background material concerning each of the Songs of Degrees, our brother leaned considerably upon Charles Spurgeon's comprehensive work on the Psalms, *The Treasury of David.*

CONTENTS

Scripture quotations are from the
Authorized (King James) Version
of the Bible
unless otherwise indicated.

Father, see this living clod,
   This spark of heavenly fire,
See my soul, the breath of God,
   Doth after God aspire:
Let it aye to God ascend,
   Till I my Principle rejoin,
Blended with my glorious End,
   And lost in Love Divine.

Lord, when Thou from me hast broke
   The power of outward sin,
Burst this Babylonish yoke,
   And make me free within;
Bid my inbred sin depart,
   And I Thy utmost word shall prove,
Upright both in life and heart,
   And perfected in Love.

God of all-sufficient grace,
   My God in Christ Thou art;
Bid me walk before Thy Face,
   Till I am pure in heart;
Till, transformed by faith Divine,
   I gain that perfect Love Unknown,
Bright in all Thine image shine,
   By putting on Thy Son.

Father, Son, and Holy Ghost,
   In council join again,
To restore Thine image lost
   By frail, apostate man;
O might I Thy form express,
   Through faith begotten from above,
Stamped with real holiness,
   And filled with perfect Love!

—CHARLES WESLEY, 1707-1788

The Ascent
of
THE SOUL

The Ascent of the Soul

Brethren, I count not myself to have apprehended: but this one thing I do, forgetting those things which are behind, and reaching forth unto those things which are before, I press toward the mark for the prize of the high calling of God in Christ Jesus. Let us therefore, as many as be perfect, be thus minded: and if in any thing ye be otherwise minded, God shall reveal even this unto you. Nevertheless, whereto we have already attained, let us walk by the same rule, let us mind the same thing.—Philippians 3.13-16

We all know that the Book of Psalms is a collection—a divine collection—of the expressions of spiritual experiences experienced by the people of God of every age. And among this divine collection of 150 psalms is to be found a very special group of fifteen with the unusual title of "the Songs of Degrees." These are the psalms numbered 120 through 134.

We do not know how these fifteen among the many psalms ever came to be termed "songs of degrees." We only are aware of the fact that this particular group of mostly very short psalms are as a matter of fact called songs of degrees. Now by "degrees" here is meant steps, stages, gradations; or an ascending up, a mounting, a climbing. Indeed, some find that *within* each of these fifteen psalms one can detect a gradual building up or ascending in their very *structure*. One verse will lay down a particular idea and the next verse will build upon that idea and proceed a step further. Others have noticed that *between* these fifteen psalms one entire psalm will advance a little further beyond the preceding one, with a third song going still further, and the song after that a bit further yet, etc., etc., until the summit is reached, until the ascent to the very top is achieved. But whether these degrees or stages are to be found within the individual psalm or are to be seen between and among the fifteen songs as a whole, of one thing we can be certain: as we read these Songs of Degrees we shall discover that pervading them all is the concept of a gradual going up. . .a gradual mounting. . .a gradual ascending. We shall find expressed throughout the idea of progress.

Our spiritual life is just like that, is it not? It is a life of degrees. Our spiritual experiences with the Lord can be described as different degrees, as a series of steps, as varying stages. The pinnacle of our spiritual walk is not something which is achieved all at once. For we will notice from the very day we come to know the Lord that there begins a gradual ascending—there commences a gradual going up until we arrive at our goal; which is, a full union with God. Our life is accordingly characterized by progression. The Christian life is a continual advancing. A continual going forward and going up. Never should there be a standstill. If we remain stationary in one experience or become stranded at one stage, we shall find that our spiritual life suffers; it becomes frustrated. We should instead be stretching out always to the things which lie before us.

My heart has therefore been greatly exercised that we may together learn something from these Songs of Degrees. I believe these fifteen special psalms can verily show us the principles or the steps that govern the ascent of the soul of the Christian. And hence our theme during these meditations together can quite properly be designated as "the ascent of the soul." From the moment he is saved that soul begins to move ahead and to ascend. We shall see him climbing, mounting, proceeding upward to God until that saved soul is united completely with God into one.

We will recall in the history of the Israelites how God, after they had experienced the salvation of passover, commanded them to march out. They left Egypt as the army of the Lord of hosts and marched forward. And we know that they advanced with a definite goal in view. They were not marching around without knowledge of what they were about or where they were going. On the contrary, we understand that when God commanded them to get out of Egypt He had in mind for them the land of Canaan, the Promised Land. So that the Israelites had a goal, a destination, an end in sight. Hence once out of Egypt they marched towards Canaan, the Land of Promise.

Notice, though, that as the people of Israel marched out and onward their journey began to be marked by removing and encamping. They went a certain distance and then they encamped. If you were to read Numbers 33 carefully you would discover a record of all their removings and encampings. Have you ever taken the time to count the entire number of these encampments to determine the total number of stations the Israelites experienced? Were you to do so you would learn that between their separation from Egypt and their arrival at the border of Canaan, exactly 40 encampments were encountered. God's people went from one station to another, from this encampment to that encampment. They were not permitted to stay in one place too long. Sometimes they spent a few days, sometimes a few weeks, even a few months; but God's command ever and always was: Go forward! Go forward until the land of Canaan is reached! So in reading the history of the children of Israel you can easily discern the fact that their life was a progressive one. They journeyed continuously until they entered the Promised Land.

Is not the same thing true with us? Does not our Christian life bear a similar stamp? Recall how Paul, even towards the very last part of his spiritual pilgrimage, related to us the identical thought: "Brethren, I do not consider myself as having already obtained possession of these things; but one thing I do, forgetting what is behind me, and stretching forward to the things which are before me, I press towards the goal of the upward calling of God in Christ Jesus." And, he added, "as many as are perfect should be thus minded." If we are otherwise minded, we should learn to be thus minded. But let us understand that to pursue such a goal we shall have to proceed one step at a time. A person cannot expect to simply vault over the stations in between and arrive at the goal immediately. He must ever be advancing—and doing so one step at a time. That should always be our heart attitude. We should never develop the attitude that we have obtained everything—we have arrived—and that is enough. If we come to have this mentality, we shall instantly discover we are at a standstill. Not only may we find ourselves at a standstill, we may even be tempted to go back. Within us instead must be that spiritual disposition which prompts us to go forward continually. We shall always be pushing forward: we shall always be ascending: we shall always be going up: until we realize that unitive life with God.

No doubt you have come to recognize that spiritual experience is a very personal matter. In passing through one event after another, you realize you are completely alone. Not even the closest most intimate acquaintance seems to be able to understand you, seems to be able to help you or to accompany you. Very often as you encounter situation after situation, you find yourself isolated and alone. And why? Because spiritual experience is personal, in fact, very personal. Nevertheless, you will in addition come to see that spiritual experience is not so personal that there is nothing more to it. Actually, the Christian journey has about it a further dimension: and that dimension is corporate in nature. You will awaken to the fact that you are *not* going through these situations alone. On the one hand you *do* feel you pass through them by yourself; on the other hand, though, you will come to discover that many others are going through these experiences together with you. And this is the reason why in these fifteen psalms you will observe that although it is intensely personal—in the first song, for instance, you read: "in *my* distress I called unto the Lord and He heard me"—yet it is also very corporate: *Israel* is always in view. And this is the paradox of spiritual experience. The Christian encounters both feelings at the same time, and they both exist side by side. So that in one sense the Christian soul goes through these experiences entirely by himself; but in another quite opposite sense he discovers he shares these along with his brothers and sisters in the Lord.

Now in our first consideration together it is necessary that a proper foundation be laid concerning these Songs of Degrees.

We should not delve into any one of them until a general background has been established. Among these fifteen songs it will be noticed that a few are written by David, "the sweet psalmist of Israel." But some of them lack any indication of authorship whatsoever. Whether or not these songs were composed entirely by David, actually, this is not too important. The one paramount point for us to grasp here is: all of them are inspired, all of them are breathed, all come into being, through the Holy Spirit. Every song, therefore, is precious. Each of them teaches us something very essential, which we cannot be in lack of as we journey on in our spiritual ascent.

We do not know for sure how these songs were used in olden days. Some authorities have told us they were sung by the pilgrims as they journeyed towards Jerusalem for their annual festivals. We know from Exodus 23.14-17 and mentioned again in Deuteronomy that according to Law all males of the children of Israel must appear before the presence of the Lord three times a year. Every male citizen of the nation of Israel must travel to Jerusalem to offer before God three times a year: on the occasions of the Feast of Unleavened Bread, the Feast of Harvest, and the Feast of Ingathering at the end of the Jewish year. No matter where they lived, they had to leave their homes and travel towards Jerusalem in order to be present before the Lord. Now as these pilgrims from all over the land journeyed towards Jerusalem, they sometimes met each other on the way and hence became great crowds. And as they traveled along, they would break out into singing. These fifteen songs thus became their singing repertoire as they climbed the hills, descended the valleys, and ascended towards Jerusalem and Mount Zion. This interpretation might just be so. Certainly, when we travel we oftentimes sing. At times we have nothing to do and at other moments we may encounter perils and difficulties; consequently, these will be natural occasions for travelers to break into song. And so they sang these songs on their way up to Jerusalem. This idea is supported by the word in Psalm 122 and verse 4: Jerusalem—"whither the tribes go up, the tribes of the Lord, unto the testimony of Israel to give thanks unto the name of the Lord." The tribes of Israel traveled together towards Jerusalem to worship the Lord.

On the other hand, other authorities believe these psalms must have been sung by the priests at the temple. We will recall that the temple had steps. And in 1 Kings 10.4-5 we are told that "when the Queen of Sheba had seen all Solomon's wisdom, and the house that he had built, and the meat of his table, and the sitting of his servants, and the attendance of his ministers, and their apparel, and his cupbearers, and his ascent by which he went up unto the house of the Lord; there was no more spirit in her." Oh! The Queen of Sheba was immensely stirred, amazed, and attracted by the wisdom of Solomon, by the house of God, by the food on his table, by his servants and their apparel, by his cupbearers and all these things; at the last, though, how she was stirred *deeply* by the way Solomon ascended towards the house of God! The ascent to the house of the Lord, for her, was something deeply impressive. To see that man can approach the holy God was for the Queen of Sheba a most fearful and wonderful experience. It left her absolutely breathless! The very thought that there is a way of approaching God, that there are steps by which man can approach God and worship Him! Now *that* was something which profoundly moved the spirit of the Queen of Sheba.

Just contemplate for a moment: we who were sinners and rebels, we who were outcasts, we who deserved nothing but death, and yet—there *is* a way, there *are* steps, by which we can come into a perfect union with God. That should take our breath away too! Can such a thing be possible? Is there truly such a way? Are there such steps? Oh! If only we can *see* that, I think we would experience the same intense feeling as did the Queen of Sheba.

Consequently some have surmised that these songs were sung on the steps leading up to the house of the Lord. And by reading Ezekiel we will note in the vision of the Lord's house recorded in Chapter 40 that there were seven steps to the outer court followed by eight steps to the inner court; all together, fifteen steps. And most probably—although we do not know for certain —the priest who was serving would sing one psalm on each step as the people would ascend together to worship the Lord.

If we can see it, is it not a most beautiful picture!

Still others, however, have told us that these Songs of Degrees were sung by the remnant of the children of Israel when they returned from the Captivity. Because they had disobeyed God they had been captured and carried away into Babylon; even so, we remember that in the mercy of God they were allowed by their captors to go back to Judah. And as the remnant journeyed out from their seventy years' captivity they sang these songs on the way to Jerusalem. Psalm 126 may convey just such an idea as this.

Surely, however, these fifteen psalms need not be so narrowly applied. For whether they were used in this way or in that way, it really matters little; that was history. But what essentially matters is this: that these songs which tell of the going up or the ascending to the Lord of Zion still remain available to *us*, for us to sing as *we* journey towards that goal of a unitive life with God. Brothers and sisters, as we said in the beginning, these songs are the expressions of spiritual experiences. These psalms are songs of degrees which lead us onward from one step to another, from one stage to another, until we achieve that life of union with God Himself. As we journey towards God in Christ Jesus we will have to pass through each one of these steps; we will have to pass through every one of these experiences; and these songs, which graphically describe those steps and experiences, can be of tremendous help. Sometimes they can encourage us. Sometimes they can instruct us. And sometimes they can strengthen us.

It is therefore my prayer that we may come into an appreciation of these songs in such a way that we too may sing them as we ascend towards our Lord and our God. May we not merely apprehend them mentally but may we first and foremost come into an appreciation of them *experimentally*. If we do the latter we shall indeed arrive at our goal.

I am reminded of Jacob as he fled for his life. At one point Jacob rested his head upon a stone. Darkness had completely enveloped him; and there he dreamed a dream; and in that dream he saw a vision. He beheld a ladder which was set upon earth and reached up to heaven. And as he beheld the vision

Jacob saw the heaven opened, with God on heaven's end of the ladder and he himself on earth's end. Suddenly Jacob saw angels ascending and descending upon the steps of the ladder. Exactly what was this vision? This vision explains God's dealings with that man Jacob. Here is this man, one who *does* have a desire for spiritual things; and yet here is a man who is extremely clever and tricky, one who is so full of deceit. Here is Jacob (which means supplanter)—a selfish grasping man, a man who in all respects is entirely unsuitable for God. And yet we find that by that ladder and through the ministration of the angels God is going to remake this man until he becomes Israel, a *prince* of God, until he comes to the point when he will leave that which is earthly and enter into that which is heavenly.

This, my fellow-believers, is fulfilled today in us in Christ Jesus. If we should be asked, Is there a way to that union with God?, we most assuredly can answer: Yes, there *is* a way and that way is Christ Jesus, Who said of Himself, "I am the way: no man comes to the Father, but by Me." We will recollect that familiar passage in the Gospel of John in which Jesus is found announcing to Nathanael, "Thou shalt see greater things. . . . Hereafter ye shall see heaven open, and the angels of God ascending and descending upon the Son of man" (1.50,51). Is not the meaning now clear? Christ is in truth the ladder. It is through this divine ladder of God—the Son of Man Himself—by which we leave what is earthly and enter into what is heavenly; it is by Christ Himself that we are going to leave what is selfish and of self and enter into what is selfless and of God; it is by this divine way of ascent that we shall be delivered from natural and earthly bondage and released into spiritual and heavenly freedom.

Dearly beloved, how blessed that Christ is the ladder. The way to God is a mounting or an ascending in the Lord Jesus. It is a growing up more and more in Christ. It is experiencing the Lord one degree upon another. Each Christian experience is simply an upward step—like a ladder's rung—in the experience of Christ, Who is our ladder. There is no Christian experience aside from Christ, because the whole ladder is nothing but Christ. Without Him we cannot have spiritual experience. In a word, spiritual experience is experiencing Christ. And we experience Him not all at once; we do so from one step to another and from one stage to another until we realize that unitive life with God. What a spiritual ladder we have in Christ Jesus the Lord!

And the angels ascending and descending? They symbolize spiritual ministry: the ministration of the Spirit of God: the activity of the Holy Spirit through whatever He may use. And the ministration of God's Spirit is to lead us into more experience of Christ. And all spiritual ministry or ministry in the energy of the Holy Spirit must be of that kind, the kind which leads us to mount towards God in Christ Jesus until we are united with God into one.

Now in studying the lives and the writings of various individuals who know this way—who know something of spiritual experience—one finds all of them in agreement that there are different steps or stages in the saint's life with the Lord. They can all trace the beginning and ending of each stage or period and describe each in detail. But these saints then present us with differing *series* of stages or degrees. Mrs. Jessie Penn-Lewis, for example, tells us in her writing that our spiritual life may be divided into four stages. The first stage is new birth. Obviously, of course, we have to be born again with new life before we can proceed anywhere. A person must have life from above before he can experience Christ any further. Hence she has stated that the first degree is new birth. The second is revival. At the time of new birth a child of God is utterly on fire for the Lord. During this period he feels as though he has reached the top; yet such a happy state does not last too long: sometimes one or two months, sometimes one or two years. But then the child of God discovers he is in need of revival. He senses within himself a slightly cold and distant attitude towards God. He therefore needs a revival—he needs a cleansing—he needs a stirring. Consequently Mrs. Penn-Lewis declares the second stage must be one of revival. And next follows the way of the cross as the third stage. The Christian soul comes to learn the way of Calvary. Here it is not a revival in the sense of stirring or in the sense of an emotional uplift; it will be instead a deeper working of the cross in his life. And finally she marks out the fourth step or stage as spiritual warfare. It being Mrs. Penn-Lewis, we will not be surprised that she pronounces the last period to be one of spiritual warfare. The saved soul will enter into spiritual combat as found in Ephesians 6. These then are the four degrees or stages by which Mrs. Penn-Lewis has described our spiritual ascending.

Madame Guyon, on the other hand, in her writing of the inner life or way has told us that our spiritual ascent can be identified by three successive steps. First, God draws us. God uses joy and enjoyment to lead us out, to lead us forward and make us grow. How the joy and the enjoyment of the Lord stir us to go forward! This is the first step. Second, God uses stripping and depriving to make us grow further. No longer is it joy or enjoyment; on the contrary, it is a stripping and a depriving: stripping us of our beauty, stripping us of our ornaments, depriving us of this, depriving us of that, and by this means He leads us to advance further. And in the third step, God uses pure love to make us go forward even more. It is love, the pure love of God, which so burns within us that we cannot but rush forward.

That is how Madame Guyon has portrayed it for us. As yet another instance, we can cite our brother C. H. Yu, a Chinese medical doctor. Dr. Yu was for long an elder in the church in Shanghai as well as a worker with brother Watchman Nee; and his special emphasis in ministry stressed particularly our inner life with Christ. And so he too has divided the Christian walk into periods, but in the following way: (1) Grace received, (2) Inner conflict, (3) Yieldedness, and (4) Harmony. Still others would characterize the Christian's walk as follows: (1) In Christ, (2) Abide in Christ, (3) Christ in us, (4) Christ formed in us. Hence as we read their biographies, as we study their writings, and as we consider their lives, we learn how the various children of God will present us with different descriptions. No matter if they differ, however, we can easily detect one general principle which runs through them all; namely, that the Christian life is a progressive one. With as it were one voice they proclaim the Christian experience to be a life which is gradually mounting, progressively ascending, until the soul is fully united with God in Christ.

How fast you will walk, how rapidly you will climb—or how slowly—this, nobody can tell you. Some lives mature very quickly; others grow quite slowly. A soul's growth and maturity depend upon how real, how eager, how willing, how cooperative he is with God. The more utter his consecration, the more complete his yieldedness, the greater his willingness, and the greater his cooperation with God's Spirit, the more quickly that soul will climb. But the less utter and the less yielded and the less willing and the less cooperative he is, the more retarded will be his progress. The principle nonethless remains: it is by degrees, it is by steps, it is by ascents that we move from wherever we are to where we ought to be.

Generally speaking, Christians tend to divide spiritual progress into three periods or stages. Because we feel that new birth should already be present, we do not designate it as one of the stages. Roughly then, we may say that these three stages (to borrow concepts which have been commonly applied by earnest Christians down through the ages) are: purification, enlightenment, and union. And as far as these fifteen psalms are concerned, they too can be divided, it seems to me, into these three periods, with each period possessing five steps. The first five songs fall into that initial period or stage of purification. Here we shall find the Spirit of God will deal with the soul more in the matter of the world—how the soul will need to be delivered from the world, even the *spirit* of the world, that he may be united to God in a fuller way. The second series of five constitute the middle stage we call enlightenment or illumination. There we shall observe how the Spirit of God touches the soul more in the matter of the *expressions and activities* of the flesh. Unless his flesh in its various manifestations is dealt with, his union with God will be hindered, restricted, and limited. Finally, the last five belong to that concluding stage we have designated as union. The Spirit of God will deal with the soul during this period more in the matter of the *life* of the flesh—in a word, the natural *self*—that he may be fully united with God in Christ. As we read and consider together these fifteen songs we will see how the Spirit of God shall lead us forward one step after another and from one stage to another.

To conclude our introduction, I think it may be helpful if I simply indicate a key word in each of these psalms as an aid to our private study and meditation:

Purification	Enlightenment	Union
120—deliver	125—trust	130—wait
121—keep	126—turn	131—weaned
122—peace	127—build	132—habitation
123—gracious	128—fruitful	133—unity
124—escaped	129—afflicted	134—bless

Our heavenly Father, how we praise and thank You that You have provided us a ladder by which we can ascend to You. Oh how we thank You that Christ IS the Way. How we praise You that by the ministration of the Holy Spirit we can experience Christ from one step to another and from one stage to another. How we praise and thank You for the prize of the upward calling of God in Christ by Whom we can be united with You into one. Now Father, do draw us, do stir us, do move us onward, that we may be neither indifferent nor content, but that we may have the mind of Paul, that perfect mind; that we may pursue onward, forgetting that which is behind and STRETCHING OUT *towards that which is before us. Do lead us on. In the Name of our Lord Jesus. Amen.*

The Stage
of
PURIFICATION

The Awakening of Desire

PSALM 120*
A Song of Degrees.

1 *In my distress I cried unto the Lord, and he heard me.*
2 *Deliver my soul, O Lord, from lying lips, and from a deceitful tongue.*
3 *What shall be given unto thee? or what shall be done unto thee, thou deceitful tongue?*
4 *Sharp arrows of the mighty, with glowing coals of the broom tree.*
5 *Woe is me, that I sojourn in Meshech, that I dwell in the tents of Kedar!*
6 *My soul hath long dwelt with them that hateth peace.*
7 *I am for peace: but when I speak, they are for war.*

Psalm 120 is the very first of the Songs of Degrees. No one knows for certain who the author of it was. Most likely it was written by David; but even if David should not be its author, at least it was written after the spirit of David. Neither are we told the particular occasion which prompted the writing of this psalm. Probably, though, it was set down by David on the occasion of his bringing up the ark of God to Mount Zion. The Scriptures reveal that David's heart was very much out towards

---

*The text of each of the fifteen Songs of Degrees quoted at the beginning of each chapter is, except for a few words, the rendering to be found in the Authorized Version of the Bible (AV). The few words of exception are from the Revised Standard Version of 1952 (RSV).

the ark of the Lord. During the days of Saul it had been neglected entirely and had never been consulted. We know that the ark represented the glory and presence of the Lord. And so David, immediately upon ascending his throne, and recalling the ark, desired to remove it from Kirjath-jearim to the Mount of Zion. 1 Chronicles 13 records the first removal of the ark from Kirjath-jearim (vv.3, 5, 6). We remember how David and all Israel, when they went down to this Judean town and brought up the ark, played mightily before it with singing and with all kinds of musical instruments (v.8); but because of an unpleasant incident the ark was carried aside to the house of Obed-edom (vv.9-13). After a short period David's heart was again aroused. He still yearned to bring up the ark to Mount Zion and carry it into the tent which he had prepared for it. According to 1 Chronicles 15 he once more gathered Israel and they together went to the home of Obed-edom and brought up the ark with singing, playing and the sound of musical instruments (v. 28).

Now it is most interesting that the very word used to describe this removal of the ark is the term "bring up," it is the word "ascend" or "degree"—the very same word. Most likely, therefore, Psalm 120 was composed by David during this occasion concerning the ark, or so at least tradition holds it to be that way. And in writing this psalm at that particular time his thoughts must have raced back to many years before, to the period when he had to flee for his life from before the face of Saul. As he fled from Saul he escaped to the city of Nob where the priests were. Here he received the holy loaves and retrieved the sword of Goliath. But he found an Edomite there: Doeg, a servant of Saul. And at once David inwardly sensed that the Edomite would tell Saul and that something awful was likely to happen. (See 1 Sam. 22.22) And sure enough Doeg, in telling Saul of David, *slandered* David before the jealous King. And because of this Saul ordered Doeg to fall upon all the priests of Nob and to slay them, which order he obeyed. Eighty-five priests, along with many men, women, children, and animals of Nob, were slain by that Edomite's wicked sword. Hence when David brought up the ark to Zion and began to set this

30

psalm down his thoughts took him back to those horrible days when, fleeing for his life, he met up with that wicked man Doeg. How those lying lips, how that deceitful tongue *slandered* him, and resulted in such great damage. It is consequently not surprising to observe in this initial song of degrees such reference to "lying lips" and "deceitful tongue."

This is most likely the background for the song of degrees before us now. But whether it is the exact background or not is actually of little consequence. What is of greater moment for us is the spiritual lesson which can be learned from this psalm. For the lesson will be the same no matter what the precise background. And what is the spiritual lesson which we can discern from this initial song of degrees? It is necessary for us to bear in mind what we have said before, that all the psalms constitute expressions of the experiences of Christians with the Lord, and the fifteen Songs of Degrees are no exception to this fact. Because of this, Psalm 120 cannot be said to reflect the experience of an *un*believer. It is not the crying of a non-believer for deliverance from sin or from the wages of sin. True, once upon a time we *were* unbelievers, we *were* yet sinners, we *were* dead in sins and transgressions; and when the Spirit of God awakened our conscience, how we were troubled by its censure, how we felt its pricking; and how we thereafter cried to the Lord for the forgiveness of our sins and for the deliverance from the penalty of sin. And we today know that as we cried the Lord answered us and we were saved. Our sins were forgiven because of the precious blood of the Lord Jesus Christ. So that this forms the experience and the expression of one who was an unbeliever and is subsequently converted to be a child of God. But the psalm which is presently before us is not related to such an experience. This psalm is on the contrary the experience and expression of a soul who has already met the Lord, who has already been converted, who is one who *knows* the Lord already; and once having come to know the Lord that soul *is beginning his ascent to God.*

The beginning point of a Christian experience, then, is the expression of *a cry*—a longing, a desire. . .upward. In Psalm 120 this soul* is in trouble. He confides, "In my distress I cried unto the Lord and he heard me. Deliver my soul*, O Lord." Here is a soul who is *longing* for something: he is longing for deliverance. He has dwelt in Meshech and among the tents of Kedar long enough and yearns to change his dwelling place. He cries out for a change. He no longer wants to live in Meshech or among the tents of Kedar because the longer he lives there the more he finds himself in trouble and distress: he is surrounded by lying lips and deceitful tongues: he is for peace but they are for war. And hence he yearns for a change, a change of dwelling place. And that is the starting point of Christian experience.

What about you and me? Now that we have become Christians how are we going to ascend to that life of union with God? It must begin with a desire. If we have no desire and no longing, if we have no hope, then there can be no progress. Only when the Lord has stirred within us such a desire for a change and such a desire for more of Him can we ever make any progress towards the Lord.

Call to mind the Song of Solomon, *the* song of songs. How does that song begin? We are aware that the Song of Solomon is an expression of the experience of a virgin who is to be united to her lover. And how does this whole experience begin? It begins with a prayer—"Let him kiss me with the kisses of his mouth" (1.2). That virgin of course had had some relationship with her lover already, but because she sensed that there was a distance between them, she began to yearn for a closer, more intimate, more direct relationship with her lover—Oh, let him kiss me with the kisses of his mouth! And it was this intense yearning which propelled her on the way towards a closer union with her lover. Brethren, there must be such a desire within *us*. An aspiration to know him more. A yearning to have a deeper more intimate relationship with our Lord. For this is

---

*Even as the Scriptures, so the author here speaks of man as both (1) *being* a soul (as in the first instance above), and (2) *having* a soul (as in the second instance above). As a total person man is frequently referred to in the Bible as a soul (see for example 1 Peter 3.20 and Gen. 46.27). On the other hand, there are also many instances in which the term soul is used to refer to but one of the several parts of man's tripartite nature (see for example 1 Thess. 5.23 and 1 Sam. 18.1), the other parts being his spirit and his body.

the starting point of Christian experience.

But let us ponder another example, seemingly opposite. Here is a son. He has left his father's house in possession of his portion of the family property. But soon he degenerates into a prodigal son: he wastes everything away: he is reduced to the state of slavery. This wastrel is sent into the fields to feed the swine, yet he himself has nothing to eat. And upon approaching death, he suddenly awakens within and comes to himself: he begins to envisage the abundance of his father's house and to realize by tremendous contrast his own pitiful condition. Needing no further urging, he says to himself, "I will arise. I will go back to my father's house." What, dear friends, do we see in this? What can we perceive here? Is it not a desire, a longing, a hope? There is that prodigal son. Reduced to starvation and to near death, he turns his eyes and his heart towards his father's house. Kindled within his breast is a longing and a hope. But of course we must acknowledge that that desire is not very noble; in fact it is quite mean and base. Because as his thoughts are re-directed towards his father's house, that wasted soul is not longing at all after his father. Nay, he is craving after his father's food, abundance, creature comforts, *things*. It is a very mean and low desire, yes; but nonetheless it *is* a desire. It is a hungering and thirsting after something which belongs to his father. And even if that thirsting desire is mean, low, ignoble and base, it nevertheless impels him on his way back towards union with his father. In our Christian experience, then, the very first element which must be found within us is a thirsting or a longing after God our heavenly Father.

The nation of Israel, we will remember, was taken captive to Babylon. Yet during their captivity they were permitted to return to Jerusalem to rebuild the house of God. But how did it happen? What precipitated it? It began in this way: the Spirit of God *stirred up* the heart of Zerubbabel, of Joshua, of Nehemiah, of Ezra, and of many other people. And as their hearts began to be aroused with a desire and with a longing to rebuild the house of the Lord, they were inwardly moved to go back to the Promised Land and to Jerusalem. But without such a stirring up within their hearts not one of the Jews in captivity would ever have returned. They would have simply remained where they were.

Naturally speaking, human beings possess a great capacity for adaptability. It is a healthy thing that we can adapt ourselves. When it is too hot our body can gradually adapt itself to the heat so that we do not feel it very much. When it is fairly cold we are highly sensitive to it at first, but after a little while our bodies become adjusted to the coldness and thus we do not feel it too greatly. Adaptability unquestionably is an extremely good thing, but it is likewise a very *dangerous* thing. It is good but it at the same time is bad. Because as we adjust ourselves to our environment and to our circumstance, we lose *sensitivity*. We get used to things; and we get used to them to such an extent that we are no longer sensitive. We grow dull. We are lulled to sleep. We become content, restful; we would much rather stay in Babylon and build our house there than be stimulated to return to Jerusalem and rebuild the house of God. Consequently, that is the danger. All of us harbor within ourselves just such a danger of settling down peacefully and comfortably and of salving our consciences by confessing, "True, my situation is not the best, but it is sufficiently good enough that I can live with it anyway." If we develop such a spirit as this, then that marks the end of our spiritual progress. We will never ascend to a greater union with God if we do not remain sensitive to our present circumstance.

There must be a holy dissatisfaction with things as they are and there has got to be that holy desire which stretches out in our spirit towards something *more* of God. This aspiration which the psalmist so intensely gave expression to in Psalm 73 must become our aspiration—"Whom have I in heaven but thee? And there is none upon earth that I desire beside thee." This must be the longing within us if we too would make progress in the Christian life.

But, you may ask, How can such a yearning be aroused within us? How *can* we have such a desire for God? The best and most positive way to this is, by the love which is within us. God has planted the love of Christ within; and this love so constrains us that we desire more of Christ. The more we love, the more we

34

desire. If the pure love of God is in our heart then we shall be motivated and agitated inside to stretch ourselves forward toward God. Once again that virgin in the Song of Solomon comes to mind. What she has is this pure love. There is a holy affection *burning* in her heart; and because such affection is aflame within her she longs for her lover. Mary Magdalene too was driven by such a love as she went in search of the body of Christ on the morning of His resurrection. Such a love of Christ resided within her breast that she refused to go home. She absolutely refused to give up. She sought and searched until she in fact found her Lord. Oh, may we, like these two, come ever and always to the Fountain of Love Himself with our vessel empty that we may be filled. Let our cry forever be, "More love to Thee, O Lord, more love to Thee!"

In some cases—not too many; in some souls—only a few, such a pure love of God *is* resident within them. For no other reason than that there is such love towards Christ within them does their appetite for God increase. They long for God, they thirst for God, they hunger after God. Is this your case? Is this true of you? If God has planted within your heart such a love for Christ, then you are blessed of the Lord indeed; because that love will create a hunger and a thirst within you after God Himself. And this will start you on the road of union, that perfect union, with God.

Sad to say, however, due to the weaknesses of our flesh, not many of us are so pure. Most of God's people seem to lack such a pure love within them. Most of us seem to follow the pattern of the prodigal son: not too noble, but oh so very practical. To put it frankly, we need to be *in trouble* before *we* desire after the Lord. If everything is smooth, if all is good, if everything is comfortable, if all is prosperous, we easily forget God. Actually, at one time we all remembered the Lord, we all desired after Him—for I believe that every Christian has indeed once had such desire at the very outset of his spiritual experience with God. And were we to follow such desire we would find that God would satisfy it, because He is the Satisfier of all our holy aspirations. Unfortunately, however, too many of us, though possessed at the beginning with a strong desire after God, somehow gradually lose it. We settle down at ease and enjoy ourselves. And so we have very little, if any, desire left for God. But the moment we get into trouble, the moment we become surrounded by problems, when we are faced with death or are in some dire need, *then* we begin to discover we need more of Him. We commence once again to long for Him: "In my *distress* I *cried* unto the Lord, and He heard me." Now this is the very reason God allows us to be in trouble. There is a *positive* meaning behind it. God permits us to be in difficulties and allows us to have problems of different kinds in order that there may be stirred up once more within us a longing after Him. By having us pass through hardships and permitting us to fall into difficulties, God recreates that desire within us for Himself. And if we by His grace learn this lesson it is extremely worthwhile.

What is the trouble which confronts this soul here? What has he discovered? We must acknowledge that the soul in Psalm 120 is in some real trouble. Why is he in trouble? What is his particular predicament? Listen to what he said: I have dwelt long enough in Meshech, among the tents of Kedar; I am for peace, but when I speak they are for war. He says he has dwelt *long* in Meshech and in Kedar. Where is Meshech? and where is Kedar? Genesis 10 informs us that Meshech was the descendant of Japheth. And Meshech and his descendants eventually came to dwell in the region between the Caspian and Black Seas. In other words, they lived to the north of Palestine, the Land of Promise. And Kedar? Again in Genesis, not in Chapter 10 but in Chapter 25, we learn that Kedar was a descendant of Ishmael. The families of Kedar thus settled in the Arabian deserts. Hence they are to the south of the Promised Land. Can we now visualize the picture which this poetic soul has drawn? He declares, I have lived long in Meshech—that is, north of Palestine; and I have lived long among the tents of Kedar — which is to say, south of the Promised Land. But where *should* he be dwelling? Should not a soul who belongs to God be dwelling in the Promised Land? Strangely enough, though, instead of dwelling there, he finds he has pitched his tent to the north and to the south of it; in short, he is living *outside* the Promised Land. And because of this he gets into trouble. The psalmist is not neces-

36

sarily saying here that he dwells physically in Meshech or physically in Kedar. That would be impossible—to write that you are abiding in two places at the same moment, in one area to the north and in one area to the south. We must not forget that this is a poem. A psalm is a poetic form of writing; and poets, we know, sometimes indulge in poetic license. The psalmist is trying to convey a sentiment or feeling deep down within him. And so he writes in symbolic language, using the imagery of Meshech and Kedar to help communicate that sentiment. So that even though he may have physically made his home in the Promised Land—and most likely he is even presently dwelling there—spiritually he finds himself wandering away from the Promised Land. In his heart he finds himself settling down in places other than the Land which God has given him. That soul should be abiding in the Land of Promise. But instead of abiding there he discovers to his great sorrow that he is dwelling in a place other than where he should be. And what place is that? *The world.*

Dear friends, is that not our experience? As a child of God, as one who is saved, who has been purchased at enormous cost, where should I live? Jesus has made it only too clear—"Abide in Me and I in you." As a Christian we should abide in Christ. Christ Himself is our Promised Land. He is our habitation. He is our home. He is our supply. He is everything to us. So that as Christians, we should dwell in Christ. But, instead of abiding in Him, we suddenly make the terrible discovery that we are not abiding in Him. We are abiding somewhere else and that somewhere else. . .is. . .the world. Whether it is in the north or whether it is in the south, this is of no consequence; it is nonetheless the world.

As those who belong to Christ we ought to remain in Christ. In our daily pathway of life we ought to continue in Him. Very often, however, and not too long after we are saved, we wake up to the fact that we have moved to other places. We have removed ourselves to Meshech, we have settled in Kedar. Our experience is not unlike the experience of Lot. How that man Lot moved away from Abraham, the father of faith, and edged himself closer and closer to the Cities of the Plain until he found

37

himself and his family verily abiding in the city of Sodom. Was he happy there? He was *un*happy there. For consider what Peter has to say of Lot: "Righteous Lot (was) greatly distressed by the licentiousness of the wicked (for by what that righteous man saw and heard as he lived among them, he was vexed in his righteous soul day after day with their lawless deeds)" (2 Peter 2.7-8 RSV). Lot was deeply troubled and distressed daily by what he saw and heard as he dwelt among that wicked people. He was beyond question a most unhappy man; yet how sad, he did not cry out to the Lord for deliverance. Lot was troubled, yes; he was distressed, yes; but there he remained, quite settled down in Sodom. God had warned him; he had even been captured; and Abraham had had to deliver him. Yet in spite of all this, Lot had not learned his lesson. He went right back to Sodom and remained there until he nearly lost his life. (And could it be that Lot was unduly influenced by his wife, who we know loved the world so much that she could not refrain from looking back and so was turned into a pillar of salt?)

We ought to abide in Christ and not in the world. We ought to make Christ our supply: Christ our defense: Christ our wealth: Christ our food: Christ our home. We ought to remain in Him, but how so easily we allow ourselves to linger on in the world. We try to befriend the world, we try to love the world, we try to be one with the world. Can you be happy? You cannot. The life of Christ within you becomes grieved, and, as the life of Christ within you is grieved you become grieved too! You can*not* be happy! But do you turn to the Lord and cry for deliverance? Ah, there lies the difference. Do you call out to the Lord to be released? Do you desire to be delivered from the world as it is? Or do you remain in the world and say, "It is not too good, that is true; nevertheless I can make some gain here."?

What is it which this seeking soul feels most acutely about the world? The world, you know, can manifest itself to us in thousands, nay *millions,* of forms. But among all these various manifestations, what is it that that soul feels most acutely concerning the world which he is in? The trait or characteristic of the world which troubles this particular soul lies in this: lying lips and deceitful tongue: he feels *this* most sharply. It is to lying lips and deceitful tongues that he is most sensitive.

I am reminded of the prophet Isaiah. He went one time to the temple, and there he beheld the glory of the Lord. But upon seeing the Lord's glory that great prophet of Jehovah instantly cried out: "Woe is me, for I am undone!" Why? "Because I am a man of unclean lips, and I dwell in the midst of a people of unclean lips" (6.5). The impression Isaiah had of the world was, unclean lips—and it was not only around him but was even within him too.

Unless the spirit of God is awakening us we shall not notice what is around us. Lying lips and deceitful tongues may completely surround us, yet we will not even be aware of them. And the reason? Because we are precisely the same. As the Spirit of God commences to speak to us, however, as He begins to awaken something within, as the Spirit of truth and righteousness begins to strike our conscience concerning our lips and our tongue, we at once are struck by the realization that all around us are lying lips and deceitful tongues. Hence, to be delivered from the world *around* us we must be delivered from the world *within* us. To be saved from the world around us we first must be saved from the world within us. The world within is as worldly as the world without. The reason we commence to notice the world's features all about us is because the Spirit of God has begun to awaken us and to make us sensitive; and when God's Spirit creates within us a sensitivity towards these outward symptoms of the world, He is in reality dealing with the world within us. He wants to deliver us from those unclean lips within *us* first.

Why is it though, that what strikes this soul is the lip and the tongue and not something else? Why of all things should it be lying lips and deceitful tongue? Perhaps by recollecting something our Lord Jesus said, we will understand. Jesus asserted that it is out of the abundance of the heart that the mouth or the lips speak (Matt. 12.34). What manifests our heart most clearly? Is it not our lips? How do I know, for example, what is in your heart? Only God knows our heart. And should you keep your mouth clamped shut, nobody else will know either. But once you open your mouth, automatically everybody knows what is in your heart.

Our speech betrays our heart. Whatever is within the man is exposed by whatever is spoken by the man. If there is treachery, falsehood, deceit, wickedness, malice, hatred, jealousy, or uncleanness in our heart, it will eventually emerge in our words. The Apostle James devoted almost the entire third chapter of his Epistle to this very matter of the tongue. Listen to some of the statements he makes there: The tongue is a world of iniquity: The tongue is a fire of hell: The tongue is a very small member of the body, yet how the tongue is a defiler of the whole body: If anyone can control his tongue he is a perfect man because he is able to bridle his whole body also: Man can tame anything else, but the tongue can no man tame! Paul too, in detailing in Romans the sin of this world, focused as did James on this matter of the tongue. This is what he said about it in Chapter 3: Our throat is an open sepulchre: Our tongues have used deceit: The poison of asps is under our lips: And our mouth is full of cursing and bitterness! Brethren, the world is especially characterized by this one thing: by lying lips and deceitful tongue. To that distressed and troubled soul the world is most noticeable in the form of lying lips and a deceitful tongue—no truth in speech, but much deceit in the tongue.

We should be reminded once again, however, that to notice the world around us we *must* see the world within us. Are we conscious of the wickedness of our own lips and tongues? Do we recognize the tongue as a world of unrighteousness? Have we suffered from the lips and tongues of other men? If we have seen and experienced all this, then we, like that soul in Psalm 120, shall indeed notice the world around us. And if we have begun to notice the world around us, then this is an unmistakable sign that the Lord has begun to deal with us within.

How fearful is the word of man! It kills without shedding a drop of blood. How subtle are the lips of man! What strife, what backbiting, what gossipping, what spreading of rumors, what twisting of news, what double tongues (speaking one thing to one person and another thing to another person). How deceiving the tongue can be! Our words may be sweet, but the genuine feelings which they cover are bitter. How distorting the tongue can be! Words are twisted to suit one's selfish purpose; distorted pictures are drawn to convey untrue impressions. Only those who have suffered at the word of man know how humbling it can be. It cuts; and it makes deep, almost incurable, wounds. How fearful is *this* world of unrighteousness, the world of the words of man.

Do we see *this* world inside us? Are we longing to be delivered from *this* world within? In the beginning of our Christian experience the Spirit of God will awaken us and lead us to see that we are not where we ought to be. We are not abiding in Christ. We are abiding in the world, therefore we are not able to control our lips. And what is the damage which continues to be wrought? Incurable wounds are inflicted because we do not speak carefully. We utter half-truth and untruth, we slander and murmur, we speak more than we should, we pass words and criticisms, we gossip and spread rumors, we give people different impressions, we drop words to arouse suspicion—in fact, what can our lips *not* do?!? Unless we are delivered from all this, we are not delivered from the world.

He who would be godly is he who has his lips guarded. How we need to watch our mouths that we may not sin against the Lord. Do we recognize the world as embodied in lying lips and deceitful tongues? Oh that we may learn how far better is it to be silent before man but eloquent before God. Yet how we are eloquent before man and are deathly silent before Him. How we try to speak to make peace, how we try to speak so as to offer explanations and so hope to create in the other party an understanding of ourselves, but the results we achieve are precisely the opposite: we are misunderstood even further, and we provide additional opportunity for our enemies to make war upon us because they always attempt to incite us to speak more and more in order to gain advantage over us (see v.7 of this song). Our Lord Himself was tempted in this very fashion.

We should take serious note of verses 3 and 4. There the psalmist writes: "What shall be given unto thee? or what shall be done unto thee, thou deceitful tongue? Sharp arrows of the mighty, with glowing coals of the broom tree." He asks what can be given, recompensed, or rewarded to lying lips and deceitful tongues? And David answers with two very, very interesting figures: "the arrows of the mighty one" and "the glowing coals of the broom tree." We can readily appreciate the difference between an arrow and a sword. The latter when taken from its sheath can easily be returned. But with an arrow, there is no retreat once it has been flung forth. Once it is gone, it is gone forever. You cannot retrieve it. Now our word is like the arrow. Once the word escapes our lips, it goes straight for the target. It cannot be retrieved. We cannot take it back. And that is why we must be so careful with our word. If man's word were like a sword, he could draw it back quickly before striking. But this is impossible with an arrow. For an arrow of a mighty man flies swiftly and strikes deeply! Hence in dealing with our lying lips and deceitful tongue, the Word of God is not only like a two-edged sword, but is also similar to the arrow of the mighty one. The Word of God will counteract the word of man. God's Word can go swiftly and penetrate deeply. Only as the Word of God cuts deeply into our conscience do we begin to realize the ugliness, the awfulness, and the terror of our lips. The Word of God will find us out; it will ferret out the lie and the deceit of our lips and our tongue.

The second figure employed is "the glowing coals of the broom tree." In the desert are to be found trees called broom trees or juniper trees. Travelers through the desert will cut down the branches of these trees and burn them in order to keep themselves warm during the night. For these broom tree branches can be easily ignited and can make a great fire; and furthermore, its fire dies out very slowly. Is not this an accurate description of our word? Our word, like the broom tree branch, is kindled very easily, creates considerable fire, burns everlastingly and retains its heat protractedly. And even as lies and deceitful words spread rapidly and last a long while in their evil effect, even so is the judgment of God equally swift and permanent. Give, and it shall be given, says the Scriptures, even returning to you in heaps—"Give, and it shall be given unto you; good measure, pressed down, and shaken together, and running over, shall men give into your bosom" (Luke 6.38). The recompense or punishment will therefore be the same. We shall suffer for what we have ill-spoken. For did not our Lord declare that for "every idle word that men shall speak, they shall give account thereof in the day of judgment" (Matt. 12.36)?

Dear brothers and sisters, like the seeking soul in this psalm, we must experience an awakening, an awakening to the world inside us as well as to the world outside us. We, like him, must have a desire and a longing to be delivered from the world. And one particularly noticeable feature of this world, as we have seen, is lying lips and deceitful tongues. That seeking soul has deeply suffered inwardly from this world of unrighteousness and longs to be freed from it. He longs to be delivered from such a world that he may dwell in peace in the house of God. And so like him, we too must desire to escape, that we may abide in Christ. The world—no matter how it manifests itself—is not our dwelling place. The world in fact should find no place in us at all. May the Lord therefore deliver us completely from this world, because only such deliverance can set us in the right direction. It will lead us to that abiding in Christ.

Hence the very first step to God is to have a desire—a desire to be delivered from the world that we may abide in Christ, our Promised Land. That is the lesson of this initial song of degrees. May its lesson be learned and learned without delay.

Our Father, we do desire that there may be created within us a holy desire and a holy longing after Yourself. We pray we may be shown where we dwell. We have dwelt in Meshech and among the tents of Kedar long enough. Oh that we may return to Jerusalem, to the City of our God; that we may not abide in this world and suffer for it, but that we may be awakened to know the world as it really is and return to Christ. May we all abide in Christ. There is life, there is peace, there is abundance, in the Father's house. We pray in Your Name and for Your glory. Amen.

Going and Keeping

1 *I will lift up mine eyes unto the hills, from whence cometh my help.*

2 *My help cometh from the Lord, which made heaven and earth.*

3 *He will not suffer thy foot to be moved: he that keepeth thee will not slumber.*

4 *Behold, he that keepeth Israel shall neither slumber nor sleep.*

5 *The Lord is thy keeper: the Lord is thy shade upon thy right hand.*

6 *The sun shall not smite thee by day, nor the moon by night.*

7 *The Lord shall keep thee from all evil: he shall keep thy soul.*

8 *The Lord shall keep thy going out and thy coming in from this time forth, and even for evermore.*

We have come to see that the beginning of our Christian experiences lies in a desire and a holy yearning after God. Somehow the Lord stirs up within us a holy dissatisfaction with our present condition and brings us to a realization that we need to know Him more and to desire Him more. And when this desire is present within us, it starts us on the ascent of the soul. Whether this desire originates out of a pure love which God has implanted in us or whether this desire is re-created as we are in trouble is really of little concern. What truly matters is this: only a hunger and a thirst for God can ever set us forth to *begin* our ascent towards being united with God in Christ to the fullest measure. And this ascent our pilgrim soul in these songs before us has begun to make. Let us now follow the course of his ascent one step further by considering the next of these Songs of Degrees. For there is no doubt that this second song of degrees stands a rung higher than the preceding one.

In Psalm 120 that soul was looking around him. And he made an important discovery. He perceived that he was dwelling in Meshech, he was living among the tents of Kedar. He observed his surroundings and discovered all those lying lips and deceiving tongues. He glanced everywhere about him and found himself in deep distress and trouble. This will always be the case. If you look around, you soon will get into trouble. If you look around yourself you will find you are surrounded by lying lips and deceitful tongues. For as a matter of fact, what can you ever find around you *but* the world and what the world is? Lying lips and deceitful tongues, trouble, problems and distress. But thank God, if you know how to cry to the Lord, unquestionably there is hope.

In turning to Psalm 121, though, we very soon learn that the soul is no longer looking *around* him. Where does he now look? He looks *up*: "I will lift up mine eyes unto the hills, from whence cometh my help. My help cometh from the Lord, which made heaven and earth." Instead of looking around, he is at this moment looking up. Surely a degree higher, certainly one step further. And in looking up, he finds help. Brothers and sisters, this should invariably be our attitude. We should always be looking up. If we look up to the Lord we then find the help we need, we then are delivered from our trouble, from our problem, and from our distress.

We do not know when nor under what circumstances this psalm was written. According to tradition it is presumed to have been an evening song sung by pilgrims on their way to Jerusalem. And the intrinsic sentiment expressed by the psalm itself would seem to confirm the traditional view. We recall that all the Israelite males had to make their way three times a year to Jerusalem to worship and to serve before the Lord. And as these pilgrims would journey towards Mount Zion and the nights would overtake them, they would naturally encamp and set up

45

their tents in the open air. With the night, though, came every sort of danger and every kind of peril. And consequently many travelers would gather together and commence to sing this even-song—they as one man would sing of the *keeping* power of the Lord.

Most probably this was true. Nevertheless, whether this was or was not the occasion for the song we cannot be absolutely certain. We are certain of one thing, though: that this is a song we each must sing. I do not know, my friends, if you have ever sung this song—if you have ever been brought to that degree or stage or circumstance wherein you *had* to voice this song of divine help—if you have ever been compelled to sing this song in your own experience. We find at the beginning of the Christian walk, that is, in the experience of the preceding psalm, that the Christian soul is distressed to find himself dwelling in Meshech and among the tents of Kedar, places north and south of the Promised Land. In other words, he is deeply disturbed to discover that, spiritually speaking, he has been abiding in the world and not dwelling in Christ. And so he cries to the Lord. At that very moment the love of Christ has begun to attract him and to draw him, with the result that his feet commence to move. Instead of continuing to settle down in the world, he is now gradually moving himself away from the world and moving himself towards the Lord.

We must call to mind once more the virgin in the Song of Solomon. At the outset her very first cry is, Let him kiss me with the kisses of his mouth! She has a desire for a much more intimate relationship with her Lord. And upon uttering this cry, she instantly implores: "Draw me, and we will run after thee." If we have a desire for the Lord we shall discover that the love of Christ at once begins to draw us. The love of Christ is the strongest drawing power. It draws us away from the world both within and without us. It draws us towards Himself. Paul emphasizes in 2 Corinthians that "the love of Christ constraineth us; because we thus judge, that if one died for all, then were all dead: and that he died for all, that they which live should not henceforth live unto themselves, *but unto him* which died for them, and rose again" (5.14-15). Have you ever felt the constraining power of the love of Christ upon you? Have you ever cried out for that drawing power? Have you ever prayed: "Draw me, draw me! I am in the world, I am entangled in its grip; but draw me with Your love; and if only You draw me with Your love, I will run after You. And not only myself, but my whole family; not only myself, but we will run after You."? The love of Christ constrains us, and with this magnetic force upon us, we shall run.

The drawing is from the Lord, that is quite true; but please note that the running is up to us. He draws us with His love, but *we* must run after Him. It is not enough simply to feel His constraint; we must respond by pursuing after Him. Do we run after the Lord? When the love of Christ constrains us, do we run? Even so, we know we cannot run unless we fulfill certain conditions. Sometimes we *do* experience the drawing power of the love of God upon us. Yet we do not respond because we cannot run. Why is this? Hebrews 12 may shed some light upon the matter. In the second and third verses the writer indicates that if anyone desires to run he has to lay aside the sin which easily entangles and in addition every hindering weight. When we have laid aside the sin that so easily entangles us and every weight which would hold us back, we can then run with endurance the race which lies before us, looking steadfastly to Him Who is the Pioneer and Perfecter of our faith. And so why is it that even when the drawing love of God at times *is* upon you and *is* drawing you, you nevertheless cannot run, you nevertheless cannot move your feet? It is simply because, first of all, you are entangled by sin. *All* the sins of our life must be laid aside. This is the first condition which must be fulfilled before we can run the race. Is there any sin in your life which you are unwilling to give up? Every single sin must be dealt with, must be confessed; we must ask His forgiveness, we must claim the cleansing of His precious blood. This is something each of us must do. For if we continue to cling to sin, we cannot run: if we continue to cherish sin in our heart, then, even though we should pray to the Lord for forgiveness and cleansing He will not hear our prayer. For does not the Bible clearly warn that "if I had cherished iniquity in my heart, the Lord would not have listened"? (Ps. 66.18 RSV) Consequently, the first step in moving towards God is a moving away from sin.

But beyond the matter of sins in general, we find that "sin" in this passage from Hebrews 12 denotes an even greater degree of specificity. For the wording there is quite peculiar: "Let us lay aside . . . *the* (singular) sin which doth so easily beset us." Most probably the sin especially in mind here consititutes something other than simply our individual sins but is a particular one which is the common lot of Christians as a whole. It is a sin which entangles, besets, and clings closely to all of us. And what is that sin? It is the sin of *unbelief*. It is the sin of disbelief —of not trusting God—of having no confidence in the promises of God. The entire book of Hebrews treats of this very problem of a lack of faith: Without faith we cannot please God: Without faith we cannot go very far in our journeying towards heaven: Without faith we cannot climb very high in our ascent to God (11.6). Above all other sins is to be found this basic one of unbelief. We simply do not *believe* Him. We *have* believed the Lord and received Him as our Saviour, yes—most emphatically yes; but beyond this point our faith so often disappears. How can we run the race if we do not believe His promise? The Israelites attempted to journey towards Canaan, but a heart of unbelief persisted within them continually. And the outcome was that their carcasses fell in the wilderness.

Do you as a Christian really believe in Christ? Can you trust yourself absolutely and entirely into His hand? *Dare* you trust Him? *Dare* you trust in His promises? Or is there a streak of doubt and unbelief within you which insists upon arguing, "If I give up the world what will I have left? How can I go on if I give up the world"? Can you not believe that the Lord has something far better for you? Can you not believe He is able to deliver you from all your sin? Can you not put your trust in Him? If we truly desire to run the race we must lay aside the sin of unbelief and cast ourselves upon the Lord. And trust Him.

To lay aside sin, and especially the sin of unbelief, constitutes the first requirement which must be fulfilled if we would run after God in response to His love. But secondly, we must lay aside every weight which would heavily weigh us down. *Weight* may not necessarily be *sin*. Weight may be something legitimate, lawful, even respectable. Suppose I clothe myself with, among other things, a shirt, a tie, a coat, a heavy pair of shoes. This is respectable, this is quite legitimate, this is perfectly appropriate —if I am not running a race. But if I am running a race, then all these articles are quite unnecessary. Not only unnecessary, but they all become a burden to me! They weigh me down. They hinder me from running well. I have to strip myself to the uttermost, to the least necessaries, to the barest essentials. *Then*, I am free to run the race.

With some people it may be sin, with so many others it is heavy weights. Oh, the cares of this life; the ease, the comfort, the luxury of it all. The many good things in this life. All which goes to make up the so-called affluent way of life. These elements may not be bad; they may in fact be very good and very respectful. But my dear brothers and sisters, if we desire them to such an extent that we *must* have them, if we desire them to such a degree that we cannot exist without them, to such a degree that they become a weight and a load upon us, then they hinder us from running fast; nay, they may hinder us from running at all! Our souls are not able to rise and ascend.

Recently we have all become keenly aware of the eventful developments surrounding travel into outer space. We know that upon our planet we experience that tenacious force known as gravitation. There is a force deep within the center of the earth which exerts its power upon us and draws us down to that center; but if man can manufacture a power mighty enough to overcome this gravitational force—a thrust mighty enough to countervail the power of gravitation—so as to propel him beyond the bounds of earth's pull and into that region known as outer space, then he can be inducted into that totally new experience of weightlessness.

Spiritually, you know, it is equally true. There is a power or a force which is always exerting itself upon us, trying to pull us down and to make us earthbound, worldly. Yet there is another pull. The love of Christ. The love of Christ possesses such tremendous power that it can thrust us up and through and beyond the reach of that worldly pull and thus set us free in those outer heavenly regions where we become weightless. We are freed from worldly weights and loads and cares.

Was this not the burden of Paul's exhortation in his first letter to the Christians at Corinth? Carefully observe what he has to say: "Time has grown very short; from now on, let those who have wives live as though they had none, and those who mourn as though they were not mourning, and those who rejoice as though they were not rejoicing, and those who buy as though they had no goods, and those who deal with the world as though they had no dealings with it. For the form of this world is passing away. I want you to be free from anxieties" (7.29-32a RSV). What ever can Paul be meaning by all this? What ever is he trying to say? It simply points to this: You may have a wife, you may have a husband, you may have a family, you may have goods, you may have occasion to weep or occasion to rejoice, and you may have transactions with the world and its mundane affairs—are these not what life is preeminently composed of, are these not what life is all about?—but though you have all these things, even though you experience them all, yet they exert no grip upon you, they do not pull you down by their weight and hold you within an earthbound worldly level of existence; you instead are as one who appears not even to have these things nor to traffic in them in the slightest. In other words, you are without care, you are without entanglement, these matters do not press and overwhelm you and tie you to this earth. In short, you have become weightless.

The Lord allows us to have, to use and to do many things in this world. But when they become a weight to us and load us down, then something is radically wrong. We may possess these things, but they have to be weightless. We may make use of these things, but they must not produce anxieties. We may indulge in these things but they simply cannot be the means of holding us down. To sum it up, we have to arrive at the place where the weight and downward pull of this world begins to exert no power over us. And only the love of Christ can bring us to this place.

Now once the seeking soul has laid aside the sin which clings so closely to him and every weight which holds him down, then

50

he can run. He can thereafter run the heavenly race. His feet are moving, and moving fast. Nonetheless, shortly after that soul begins to pursue the Lord, he makes a very important discovery, which is, *that he is in need of help.* We should not forget that in Psalm 121 the soul has by this time begun to make his ascent. He has left the tents of Kedar and the dwelling place of Meshech and is presently journeying toward Jerusalem. But somewhere along his pilgrim journey he begins to experience an increasing awareness of his own inadequacy. The further he moves towards God the more he becomes conscious of the need of help. The road, he now notices, is growing rough and thorny. It is becoming a narrow and constricted way. On every hand his path is being beset by temptations, trials, and perils of all kinds. He realizes that it has become impossible for him to pass through alone. He is in need of help, and that help, he now knows and readily confesses, must come from God.

Let me ask you a very simple question. In your Christian experience do you ever feel the need for divine help? Or do you feel you can get along entirely by yourself? If you assume that you can get along by yourself, let me candidly tell you it is but a sure sign that you are *not* running after the Lord. Only those who are not moving on towards the Lord feel no need of divine help. On the other hand, a sense of one's helplessness is one good sign that he is ascending towards God. If you are pursuing the Lord, you will inevitably come to recognize that you need divine help. Hence again we can turn to this pilgrim epistle of Hebrews, and there we can identify the very same thought as it is expressed in such verses as 4.16: "Let us . . . come boldly unto the throne of grace, that we may obtain mercy, and find grace to help in time of need." Hebrews is a book of travel, and in traveling on our journey to God the writer says we need help. And where does our help come from? The soul in Psalm 121 knows. He affirms, "I will lift up mine eyes unto the hills, from whence cometh my help." Dearly beloved, our help does not come from what is around us. Our help comes from what is *above* us.

Someone has put the second part of this verse into the form of a question—"Whence shall my help come?" Does my help come from the hills? From the mountains and hills which are very high and solid, extremely formidable, which seem to be able to assist me? No, no, no. Look not to natural resources. Even the mountains and hills cannot support me. No, I look further than to the mountains and the hills, however formidable they may appear, and gaze upward and beyond to the One who *creates* the mountains and the hills: "My help cometh from the Lord, which made heaven and earth." In other words, my aid comes from God and God alone. Neither the might of princes nor the swiftness of horses can help us. Our help comes only from the Lord, the Creator and Fashioner of the heavens and the earth. That is where our help comes from, and His help never fails.

Now as this traveling soul journeys towards Jerusalem the trail may require him at times to climb the steeps and at times to descend the valleys. On his pilgrimage he finds the way is narrow, prickly, uneven. He experiences many temptations, hardships, and testings. And so he is confronted by Danger Number One: as he climbs the elevations he finds he can easily slip. And if he should slip, he will fall. And if he falls, he may suffer serious injury or even suffer death. Danger Number Two: when night descends, that pilgrim soul and those whom he meets on the way have to pitch their tents in the open air, exposing themselves to the peril of wild beasts and to the danger of robbers and thieves. Who will keep them and guard them? Danger Number Three: during the day the sun may scorch them. They may become sunburned and even experience sunstroke. And during the nighttime the moon can hurt them too. Or so some have interpreted it that way in accordance with the commonly accepted notion of that day which held that if a person were to lie down beneath the moon with his eyes towards it, and even were his eyes very much closed in sleep, the moon's pale light could blind him or could even make his mind delirious. Here then is the danger of the day and the presumed danger of the night. And further, Danger Number Four, perhaps the most serious of all: as a pilgrim makes his way towards his goal and is confronted by numerous trials and difficulties, he may become so discouraged that he may give up the journey; he may want to return.

We see that a pilgrim's path is not too smooth. If anyone

genuinely desires the Lord and wants to go on with Him, if any-one really yearns for Jerusalem—yearns to be united with God in the fullest degree, then he must accept the fact that the way will not be easy. Do not entertain the mistaken notion that our journeying towards God is smooth-sailing. Not at all. You will dis-cover that the road, naturally speaking, is uninviting. The more you hunger after God, the more you will encounter hardships and difficulties all about you. The more you aspire after holiness, the more intense will be your temptations. The more eager you are in your desire for God, the busier will be the enemy in his attempt to ensnare you, to threaten you, and to harm you. For when anyone is delivered so as to run after the Lord, auto-matically the enemy of our souls becomes doubly active. He will waylay us and tempt us to walk astray. It is therefore not a very easy way. The path to God winds always by way of the cross. If anyone desires to come after Me, insisted the Lord Jesus, he will have to deny himself, take up his cross daily, and follow Me.

Because the way is not easy, because it is full of dangers, pitfalls, temptations, and trials, there arises in the heart of that young pilgrim soul one foremost question. I am afraid I may fall, he gravely muses. I am afraid I may slip somewhere. No matter how careful and watchful I am, I still may slip, I still may fall. Who then can keep my feet from falling, who can make my feet unmovable? Who can make me steadfast and firm? Brothers and sisters, is this also your question? Is this also your fear? You want the Lord, and you are running after Him; yet perils abound around you and fears lurk within you: Can I stand? Can I be steadfast? Can I be firm and immovable in the Lord? Or can I slip? Will I fall? Who can keep me steadfast and firm? It is a very real question. If we are left to ourselves we *will* slip, we *will* fall, however careful we are. But thank God, there is One Who is able to keep us from falling. The pilgrim soul in Psalm 121 found the answer, for he confidently avows: "The Lord which made heaven and earth . . . will not suffer thy foot to be moved: he . . . keepeth thee . . . he keepeth Israel . . . The Lord is thy keeper . . . The Lord shall keep thee from all evil: he shall keep thy soul. The Lord shall keep thy going out and thy coming in . . . for evermore." The Lord Himself shall keep us.

Let us remind ourselves too of what Jude has to say: "to him who is able to *keep* you from falling and to *present* you without blemish before the presence of his glory with rejoicing, to the only God, our Savior through Jesus Christ our Lord, be (the) glory." The One Whom we trust is able to keep us without stumbling and to exultantly set us blameless before Him. Moreover, we can be encouraged by what the psalmist declares in Psalms 56 and 116: "Thou hast delivered my soul from death: wilt not thou deliver my feet from falling, that I may walk before God in the light of the living?" And again: "Return unto thy rest, O My soul; for the Lord hath dealt bountifully with thee. For thou hast delivered my soul from death, mine eyes from tears, and my feet from falling. I will walk before the Lord in the land of the living."

In our continual ascent towards God, we soon learn that *we* are insufficient to keep ourselves from falling, but *God* is able. The Lord is able to keep our eyes from tears and our feet from falling. He is competent to make us walk in the light of the living and in the land of the living. But how exactly does the Lord keep our feet from falling? He does it either by steadying our feet like the hind's feet (Ps. 18.33) or by enlarging our steps (Ps. 31.8) or by planting us on the rock (Ps. 40.2) or by giving light to our path (Ps. 119.105) or by restraining our feet (119.101) or by plucking us out of the net (Ps. 25.15) or by lifting us out of the miry clay (Ps. 40.2).

God is able to do all this for us. Yet there is an important element here which cannot be minimized; which is, that we must trust ourselves into His keeping. If we want to walk this path and run this race we will have to present our bodies a living sacrifice. We will have to hand ourselves over to Him and say, "Lord, I am Yours. I am in Your hand. Keep me, keep me. I know Whom I have believed, and I am persuaded, fully persuaded, that He is able to keep what I deposit to Him until that Day." A renewal of our consecration is most necessary. It is the secret of the soul's ascent.

Not only, though, will He keep us from falling; He will also guard us: "He that keepeth Israel neither slumbers nor sleeps." How reassuring to know that the Lord is our keeper. When night comes we go to sleep; but there is One over us Who neither slumbers nor sleeps. For He is ever watchful, and He watches over us: "He is thy keeper and he is thy shade upon thy right hand." One day, a woman in the East went to consult her King and asked him to recompense her for her loss of property. The King inquired of her as to how she had lost her property. "I fell asleep in the night," she explained, "and meanwhile the thief crept in and stole it." Whereupon the King said, "If that is the case, it clearly is your own fault. Why then should I recompense you when you are to blame?" To which the woman replied, "O King, I fell asleep because I believed that you were awake." And do you know, that woman got what she wanted! We, my dear friends, fall asleep; but the One Who keeps Israel neither slumbers nor sleeps. Is not this good enough? Can we not entrust ourselves to such a One as this? Here is One Who shades us from the merciless sun at high noon and from the "bewitching moon" at midnight.

But is this to imply that we shall not have temptations and trials? To ask it is to answer it. For the keeping power of our God signifies that though we must walk through the valley of the shadow of death, we still shall fear no evil. The sun will shine upon us, yes; but it will only make us suntanned and not give us sunstroke! The moon will shed its pale light upon us, yes; but it will not disturb us adversely; it will instead give us the light to guide our step. As that virgin in the Song of Songs has said: "I am black but comely, because the sun has looked upon me." God has not promised sky always blue, but He *has* promised strength for the day. Why? How? Because the Lord is with us. He that keepeth Israel neither slumbers nor sleeps. Fear not, therefore, little flock. Follow the Shepherd without hesitation. Be like Abraham, who being called by faith obeyed God to go out into a place which he was later to receive for an inheritance. And he went out, not knowing where he was even going but only knowing Whom he was following. Quite different today, though, for we *do* know where *we* are going as well as we know the One Who is leading us.

Oh, dearly beloved, let me repeat, that as we journey toward Jerusalem in our spiritual pilgrimage to God the way will not be easy. We will be surrounded by perils and risks and temptations of every kind; so that the most important consideration for each one of us during this stage becomes, How can I be kept? Even so, we need not fear, for the Lord *is* our Keeper and our Shade upon our right hand. Let us simply trust ourselves into His hand for our going out and our coming in and He *will* keep us from henceforth till evermore. There shall no evil be upon our soul. To Him be all the glory.

Our Heavenly Father, how we praise and thank You for that drawing love of Yours. How You do draw us with Your love. Draw us, then, away from this world; draw us, then, unto Yourself. O Father, how we praise and thank You, there is not only that DRAWING *power but there is equally that* KEEPING *power. We thank You for Your encouragement. Though the way be rough and thorny, we need not fear, for You are with us. You keep us because You neither slumber nor sleep. We can trust ourselves completely into Your hands. For You are well able to keep our eyes from tears and our feet from falling. You are well able to bring us to Jerusalem and to set us before Yourself, blameless, in love. We thank You. In the Name of our Lord Jesus. Amen.*

Companionship

PSALM 122
A Song of Degrees of David.

1 *I was glad when they said unto me, Let us go into the house of the Lord.*

2 *Our feet shall stand within thy gates, O Jerusalem.*

3 *Jerusalem is builded as a city that is compact together:*

4 *Whither the tribes go up, the tribes of the Lord, unto the testimony of Israel, to give thanks unto the name of the Lord.*

5 *For there are set thrones for judgment, the thrones of the house of David.*

6 *Pray for the peace of Jerusalem: they shall prosper that love thee.*

7 *Peace be within thy walls, and prosperity within thy palaces.*

8 *For my brethren and companions' sakes, I will now say, Peace be within thee.*

9 *Because of the house of the Lord our God I will seek thy good.*

Anyone who reads this song of degrees will agree, I believe, that it surely is a rung higher in the soul's spiritual climb towards God. In Psalm 120 the soul was dwelling in the land of Meshech and among the tents of Kedar, a poetic way of saying that spiritually he was not living in the Promised Land but was in places *other* than the Promised Land. The Christian soul should always be abiding in Christ as his Promised Land, but he finds instead he is abiding in another place—the world. And because that soul dwells elsewhere than in Christ, he is deeply troubled within. Psalm 121, however, indicates a shift away from the world of Meshech and Kedar and a movement back towards the Land of Promise: the soul has commenced his journey towards Jerusalem: he has begun his ascent to Mount Zion. Hence the second song constitutes a further degree upward than the first. And as we come to the third song of degrees we shall discover still another step taken; for the pilgrim who had earlier left his original dwelling place and had begun to move towards Jerusalem shall be found *approaching* the city in Psalm 122. The *gates* of Jerusalem are now in view, so that the pilgrim soul is almost in Jerusalem. Clearly, then, this third of the fifteen songs is one gradation higher.

This is a psalm written by David. Any study of the life of David must eventually disclose the fact that his life was deeply entwined with the city of Jerusalem. This city occupies a singular place in the heart of God. It stands in a very special relationship to the purpose of God. The first time Jerusalem appears in the Bible is on the occasion when Abraham defeated the four kings. And as he was returning from his victory Abraham was met in the way by Melchizedek, King of Salem, who blessed Abraham with the blessing of God (see Gen. 14.18-20). This city of Abraham's day known as Salem (meaning "peace") is traditionally held to be the very city of Jeru-salem of a later day. During that earlier period Salem (or Jerusalem) was situated in the midst of the cities of the Gentile nations. In spiritual terms, therefore, it represented the testimony of God in the midst of the heathen world. For we will remember that during this period the whole land of Canaan was inhabited by seven tribes who were not in the least God-fearing. On the contrary, these seven were extremely sinful and wicked nations. Yet there was to be found among the wickedness of that world one city, Jerusalem, with Melchizedek (whose name means "king of righteousness") reigning there: a testimony on earth for God. Here, then, is the first mention of Jerusalem in the Scriptures.

Much later, when David was anointed King by all Israel at Hebron, the very first action he took was to capture Jerusalem from the hands of the Jebusites (2 Sam. 5.6-9). And David made Jerusalem his capital. Now in this city was to be found two most prominent things: On Mount Moriah was situated the temple or the house of God; on Mount Zion was built the palace or the house of David. Jerusalem was therefore a place where God was known, appreciated, worshiped and served. It was also the site where the power and the authority of God was recognized, exercised and manifested. Hence in our study of the Scriptures, let us continually bear in mind that Jerusalem has always stood as a representation of the testimony of God on earth; it is where God is honored and respected, worshiped and served. That is Jerusalem. It is a city which occupies a unique place in the heart and purpose of God—it also occupies a peculiar, soft and tender spot in the hearts of all those who truly love the Lord—and the heart of David is no exception. All this we shall come to recognize as we continue to consider together these Songs of Degrees.

We do not know the occasion for the writing of this song. Probably—though we cannot be certain—it was written by David when he was *returning* to Jerusalem, the place which the heart of David cherished so much. It was to there that David had moved the ark of God, it was there that David had made his capital, and it was there that David lived. But we may have forgotten that King David at one time had had to flee from the city which he loved so well. In fleeing, David leaves the ark of God behind, declaring that if it should please Him God would subsequently allow him to return to Jerusalem and to worship Him there (see 2 Sam. 15.25). Now it is only after Absalom has been killed and the rebellion put down that David is to be found moving with his people back towards Jerusalem; and so very likely David may have composed this psalm in celebration of his return at this particular moment to Jerusalem. Oh how David's heart, reflected in this psalm, is out towards Jerusalem. How he longs for the city of peace; how he takes delight in the city of God; and how he is gladdened in heart because of the others with him whose hearts are also devoted to Jerusalem. Quite possibly this is the background of the song. It is not of great consequence, though, whether this was actually the occasion or not. What truly concerns us is, that this is a song which is sung by pilgrims whenever their feet approach the gates of Jerusalem.

Consider for a moment the beginning notes of this psalm: "I was glad . . ." I was glad!—It is a song of gladness, a hymn of rejoicing. Dearly beloved, we all know our Christian pilgrimage has its Marahs and its Elims (see Ex. 15.23-27). There will be moments of sorrow and there will be moments of gladness and rejoicing. Our pilgrimage will take us at times into valleys surrounded by precipices and enveloped in darkness, and at other times onto mountain tops with very open horizons and unobstructed views. On one occasion we may find our way is hilly and treacherous, difficult, slippery, narrow, thorny and rough; but on another occasion we may find our path to be a fertile plain whose landscape is dotted with flowers, gardens, and trees under a heaven whose sky is cloudless blue and whose air is filled with the movement and song of birds. Is not our Christian life marked out like that? Is not our pilgrim journey akin to this pattern? We are confronted on the one hand with disappointment, trial, sorrow, malice, and bitterness—we cannot drink "the waters of Marah." On the other hand, we come to Elim with its 12 sweet springs and 70 shady palm trees—and there we can encamp by its restful waters. It is true, then, that in the ascent of a soul towards God, he shall encounter valleys and mountain-tops, hills and plains, Marahs and Elims. And in this very connection, we can easily see that the preceding psalm is a song of sorrow "sung at Marah"; even so, in his sorrow that pilgrim discovered that God is the Keeper of his soul; he experiences the reality of the Lord. But in this song, sung at Elim, the note has changed to one of gladness and rejoicing; and in rejoicing he discovers the blessedness of the fellowship of the saints.

If in our pursuit after God there extends before us only a continuous valley, an unbroken path of trials, an interminably rough and thorny way, we may lose heart and not be able to finish the course. In His wisdom and in His goodness, therefore, God sometimes affords us seasons of refreshing: after our period of difficulties God gives us a time of smoothness: following a season of great conflicts He grants us a time of resting. God in His infinite mercy and grace has ordained that there shall be heights as well as depths, oases in the midst of deserts. This is the goodness of the Lord. Consequently, be encouraged, dear people, because although we do experience difficulty, it is not that way without respite; for in the providence of God He prepares for us those needful times of gladness, rest and joy. Hence David opens his song with just such a note: "I was glad"!

Why is he glad? What has made him happy? Why is he full of rejoicing? Because he discovers that there are others whose hearts are towards the house of God too. "I was glad when *they* said unto me, Let *us* go into the house of the Lord." As we are pressing on to God and as we meet with all sorts of hardships and testings—those many crosses on the way—nothing rejoices us more than when we discover we are not alone in our pursuit. Many others of likemindedness are traveling this way also. Do we not recall how Elijah, in his hour of great testing and conflict, murmured to God and cried out: "Lord, I am left, I alone! And they seek my life, to take it away. It is too much for me! How can I carry on, seeing that I am all alone?" Let us recall as well, though, how the Lord comforted him by affirming that He had 7,000 *other* souls who had not bent their knees to Baal! (See 1 Kings 19.14,18) Even the great Apostle Paul fell into distress and depression of heart when, as he was in Troas, he found that Titus had not come to him. So distraught in spirit did he become that he could not remain to do the work of the Lord there. He bade farewell and went away to Macedonia! (2 Cor. 2.12,13) If we turn to 2 Corinthians 7, however, we learn that when he met up again with Titus, his soul was greatly strengthened, comforted, stirred up, and gladdened by the fellowship of that younger man (vv. 5-7).

Nothing strengthens and rejoices our soul more than when we realize we are not alone in this way, when we discern that there are others who are of the same mind, when we find that there are others who have a desire for the house of God too. Oh joyful thought, that there are others who will say to us, "Let us go into the house of the Lord." And here David's heart sings out, "I was glad." Dear friends, as we continue on in our ascent to God we begin to experience a peculiar blessing, which is the singular blessing of fellowship. We find we are not alone in our pursuit of God. We see that there are brothers and that there are sisters who possess the same longing and exhibit the same desire. So that when we meet them and have fellowship with them we are strengthened in our souls. And this makes us glad.

Now the pilgrims who are making their way to Jerusalem come from every direction; they travel from all over the land of Israel. But as they *approach* Jerusalem and draw near to the gates, they fall into lines in order to enter through the gates. And thus they automatically have fellowship. And out of such fellowship emerge two experiences. One is that "our feet shall stand within thy gates, O Jerusalem." Fellowship with the saints brings our feet *within* the gates of Jerusalem. While we search and seek and pursue after God we must admit that at times it is very hard—sometimes we do not find God—sometimes we do not know where He is—sometimes we discover it is very difficult to experience Christ. But when you see your brothers and sisters with you and around you, it then becomes quite easy to find your feet within the gates of Jerusalem. It is difficult for us to follow Christ individually; but relatively easy is it for us to pursue the Lord with all the saints.

Again must we turn to the Song of Solomon, that song of songs. We will recollect that at its very inception the virgin expresses a desire for a closer fellowship with her lover: "Let him kiss me with the kisses of his mouth." And because she has such a desire she later on finds herself in the banqueting house enjoying the feast of love. But in the process, she calls out once: "O thou whom my soul lovest, where dost thou feed thy flock? Where dost thou let them rest at noon? Why should I be as a veiled one beside the flocks of thy companions?" She is trying desperately to find her lover, but she cannot locate him! She therefore cries aloud, Where are you? Where are you? I want to find you! But where are you? And remember how her lover replies to her: "Oh, if you want to find me, follow thou the footsteps of the flock. If you follow those footsteps you will find me." (1.7,8) Where can we find the shepherd? Wherever we detect the flock; because a good shepherd will never leave his flock. Where the *flock* is, *there* is the shepherd. Let us not follow a wayward sheep. If we follow any wandering sheep we will wander away too. But if we follow the footsteps of the flock which trails the Shepherd whithersoever He goes, then we most assuredly shall find the Shepherd.

Is it not sometimes the case in our Christian life that despite our effort and zeal to know Christ, to find Him and to experience Him, He is nonetheless difficult to be found? We do not know where He is! But the Lord will direct our attention to the footsteps of the flock—"Fear not, little flock; for it is your Father's good pleasure to give you the kingdom" (Luke 12.32). What is the flock? The flock today is none other than the church. If you cannot locate Christ, then look at the footsteps of the church, the true church, those who follow the Lamb wheresoever He goes. Gather with those and pray with those who seek the Lord out of a pure heart. And the blessing of such fellowship with other members of the body of Christ will be to guide and to lead us to the gate. How formidable at times for us to find our way, yet if we are found among the flock we shall soon be at the gate. In our spiritual experience it is most true that we make greatest progress when we are found among the Lord's own people. This is the jostle of fellowship as well as the joy of fellowship; that is, we experience spiritual advancement through being in close touch with the saints. Consequently, if we identify ourselves with the church, if we follow the footsteps of the flock, we shall surely discover our feet within the gates of Jerusalem and shall find our Shepherd there. This is the first result of our fellowship with the saints.

Fellowship among the saints will bring in a second experience; namely, a vision of Jerusalem. In our seeing, *negatively,* what the world is—as in Psalm 120—we long to be delivered from it. We go through sufferings as we part with the world. We become strangers and pilgrims. We are lonely. But now we are brought into a seeing which is *positive* in nature: we see the city of Jerusalem and the blessedness of its fellowship. We are delivered out of the kingdom of darkness into the kingdom of the Son of God's love. For as we migrate as pilgrims away from the world and towards God our goal, we simultaneously find ourselves migrating towards one another. We lose one kind of life—that of the world—only to gain another. It is another, that is, corporate life, the life of the church. Because we love Him Who is unseen, we shall come to love one another who are seen.

So as these pilgrims approach the gates of Jerusalem, they converse with one another and have fellowship together; their hearts are encouraged, are gladdened, become full; and then they lift up their eyes to behold the city of Jerusalem splendidly laid out before them. Oh! How it is built as a city which is compacted together! Brothers and sisters, as we have fellowship one with another our eyes are gradually opened to see a heavenly vision, and that is the vision of Jerusalem.

Fellowship always brings in vision and revelation. Is it not a fact when sometimes reading your Bible alone that you simply cannot understand? But when gathered with your brothers and sisters to study the Bible together, suddenly your eyes are opened and you begin to know what the Bible says. Is it not a fact when praying by yourself that sometimes you just cannot pray through? Yet in praying with the brethren, you experience an entrance to the throne of God. Is it not a fact when in solitude that no matter how earnestly you seek and sincerely you meditate, certain spiritual things nonetheless sometimes remain hidden from you, nonetheless sometimes evade you? As you fellowship with the church, however, the scales upon your eyes are removed at last to perceive the purpose of God in Christ Jesus. This is the case with all of us repeatedly.

What exactly is it that these pilgrim souls see as they gaze out upon Jerusalem? Jerusalem, we know, means the abode or the habitation or the city of peace. Jerusalem is a dwelling place, a city. And a city is not something which comes naturally; on the contrary, it has to be *built*. That word "built" I like very much, for it invariably takes my thought back to the book of Genesis. In Genesis 2 God, after He had created Adam, declared it was not good that man should be alone. God therefore put Adam to sleep. And out of Adam's side God removed a rib. But what does the Scripture next say? It explains that God *built* the rib into a woman (v.22 ASV margin). God fashioned the rib of Adam the man into Eve the woman. Genesis records that a woman is built. And here we find that a city is built. Jerusalem does not arise naturally. Every city—including the city of God—has to be built. But *how* is *God's* city to be built? We must return to Genesis 2 once again. How was Eve built? With what material was she fashioned? The woman was built with the rib of Adam. So how is Jerusalem to be built? By the working of the same principle: Jerusalem is built with the love of Christ.

It is the love of Christ, Christ within us, that becomes the material for the *building* of Jerusalem, the church of God. We everyone of us have come to know Jesus Christ as our Savior, and as a consequence, Christ is within us; He is within you and He is within me. And that is the rib. Hence God fashions the church (Eve) with that rib of Adam (Christ). God builds the church with the love of Christ which is within you and within me. But if this is the case, what an extremely exacting demand there is upon us! Because whatever is not of Christ within us cannot serve as the material with which to construct Jerusalem. Anything which is of ourselves, anything which is natural, earthly, fleshly or carnal within us has to be set aside. All such rubbish has to be cleared away. Hence the absolute necessity for the work of the cross. The principle which I therefore wish to leave with you here is that Jerusalem can only be built with the rib of Christ which is within us; it cannot be erected with material which is natural but must be built with materials which represent Christ within each one of us.

Jerusalem is built into a city. We know what a city is. A city is a corporate entity. It is composed of *many* parts and of *different* parts; yet it becomes one unit: a unity of plurality: a unity of variety. Is not the church, the body of Christ, comparable to that? "We being many," says the Lord in His Word, "are one body in Christ" (Rom. 12.5). Brethren, we are all different. Not only in our features but even in our experiences of Christ and in our spiritual gifts we are unalike. All of us are different, a situation similar to a human body having many members which are unalike one from the other; nevertheless, each member without exception is endowed with something of the life of that body. And thus too is it with the body of Christ. Though we are many parts, yet are we the one body of Christ because we each have had the life of Christ imparted to us. Accordingly, we together form a corporate testimony as the church, the body of Christ.

Please take note of still another feature about this city of Jerusalem. The psalmist describes the city as being not only built but also compacted together. It is not something un-planned. Some towns and cities have no planning behind their settlement and growth at all; they arise in a most haphazard fashion. A few families move into a certain area—say, by the bank of a stream or a river. Each will select a plot of ground and there erect a house. And while these first families are be-coming settled in the area, other families arrive to establish their homes here too, selecting lots which suit their tastes and whims as with those at the first. With the result that you soon find streets and roads winding here and there, some too narrow, some unnecessarily wide, and some which terminate as dead ends. Is the town compacted together? Is there design and coordination for efficiency and protection in such a city? Not at all. It is a very loose and discoordinated mass.

Such is not the case, though, with Jerusalem. She is a city which is compacted together, that is, a city which is laid out according to plan: house after house, row upon row, street after street: all elements are well-built, compacted, and gathered together: it almost resembles something *organic,* something *living.* As a city like this, Jerusalem is easily governable and can be well protected. Dear saints, the church is like that. In our pursuit of God, we discover we are not alone but that God has given us many brothers and sisters. And our relationship with each other, far from being loose, is such that we resemble a body fitly framed and connected together like a compact entity. Whether we meet or do not meet together, we are so inter-related in spirit that we become like to a compact city. For it is not that on Sundays we assemble together but that on week-days we are scattered. No, not looseness but compactness. And anything which is compact is efficient. Because we are joined together into one compact whole, it is very efficient.

Take note, if you will, what Psalm 48 has to say: "Walk about Zion, and go round about her: (number) the towers thereof. Mark ye well her bulwarks, consider her palaces; that ye may tell it to the generation following. For this God is our God for ever and ever" (vv.12-14). Jerusalem possesses towers, bulwarks, palaces: and all are compacted together according to Psalm 122. Does this not bring vividly to mind the description of the church in Ephesians 4? How Paul exhorts us all to "grow up in every way into him who is the head, into Christ, from whom the whole body, joined and knit together ('fitly joined together and compacted'—AV) by every joint with which it is supplied, when each part is working properly, makes bodily growth and upbuilds itself in love" (vv.15-16 RSV). Let us be clear that the church is not a loose, disconnected affair. The church is an organic whole in which the member saints are so inter-related that they minister one to another according to the gift God has given to each one in order that they may *grow* together and increase towards the building up in love. And this is precisely the character of Jerusalem.

Do you have that vision? Do you see that vision? What is the vision of Jerusalem which is here described in Psalm 122? All the tribes of Israel, says the psalmist, gather themselves together to Jerusalem and there testify as to *the oneness of Israel* (see v.4). We must not overlook the fact that these Israelitish pilgrims came from many diverse places: some lived in the mountains, some dwelt in the valleys, some inhabited the plains, and some made their homes by the seashore. Moreover, they were engaged in a variety of employments. Some were farmers, some were shepherds, some were soldiers, some were artisans, and some were occupied in something else. Their occupations were quite different one from the other. Everything about these Jewish pilgrims—their origins, background, jobs, education, even their mental outlook and point of view—were all varied and quite distinct. Now with such a variety as this, how do the Israelites ever find their unity? Where is the oneness of Israel to be found? They find their unity *in Jerusalem*. As they journey towards the city of God they realize they are indeed one people. They are not a scattered race; they are as a matter of fact one people. Hence Jerusalem is the place where they find and express their sense of unity. It serves as a testimony to the oneness of the Israelites.

Oh my fellow-saints, we are *not* as so many grains of sand on a seashore, scattered and void of organic relatedness. As we continue to follow the Lord and as we grow in spiritual life, we not only experience great comfort and encouragement in *having* many brothers and sisters, but we additionally learn one other very important lesson; which is, that we are *organically related to* all those brothers and sisters of ours. How we need one another! It is quite true that we cannot live without God, but neither can we live without our brothers and our sisters. We need each other not only in encouraging one another to love the Lord but also in perfecting our service to the Lord. We cannot be isolated. Has not God made known from the very inception of things that it is not good for man to be alone? We need to be together. We *have* to be together! We are parts of a city which is compacted together; we are members of an organic whole which is the body of Christ, the church of the living God. And we find our unity and that oneness in the body of Christ. The unity is already there; all which God exhorts us to do is "to keep the unity of the Spirit in the bond of peace" (Eph. 4.3). And this we verily must do. We will turn away from everything which tends to divide God's people. We wish instead to show our oneness in the testimony of the one church. We will not be at odds with each other. Rather shall we be united in peace. Instead of allowing ourselves to be divided, let us see and accept the reality that we are in fact—all of us—one in Christ Jesus. We must believe in, and commit ourselves to, the seven onenesses God has given us; namely, the one body, the one Spirit, the one hope, the one Lord, the one faith, the one baptism, and the one God and Father of us all, Who is above all, and through all, and in us all (Eph. 4.4-6). If we observe these unities we shall flow, as did the Israelite tribes of old, into Jerusalem, and there we shall maintain the testimony of the unity of the saints.

Jerusalem, as we indicated at the beginning, is distinguished by two very prominent features. On Mount Moriah is found the temple; on Mount Zion is found the palace: on Mount Moriah, the house of God; on Mount Zion, the house of David. On the first is the Holiest of all, and the ark, where God is worshiped and served; on the second is the throne of David, where judgment is dispensed: on the first serve the priests, on the second rule the kings. Hence, one is the *priestly* feature; the other, the *kingly* feature. Jerusalem possesses both. And so does the church.

The church is the place where God is known and appreciated, and out of their appreciation of God there issues forth from the saints a corresponding worship and service—the priestly function of the church. Brothers and sisters, do we know God? Do we appreciate Christ? And out of that appreciation, do we worship Him? Do we sing praises to His name? Do we serve Him in diverse ways? Every Christian believer is a priest in Jerusalem. Fellow-believers, we know God through Christ. We experience the grace of God. Do we appreciate it? Do we want to express our gratitude? How do we express such appreciation? We express it by our worshiping Him, by our singing praises to His Name. This is the very reason why it is so essential for us to gather on every Lord's day for the Lord's table. We come together to remember Him; we assemble together to express our appreciation towards Him; we gather together to worship and to praise Him. Let us therefore assemble ourselves for the time of worship. It troubles us and saddens us when we see so many of God's people failing to assemble at the Lord's table. And of those who do assemble, many do not express their appreciation. They hold back their worship, their praises, their thanksgiving. But let us remember that that *is* Jerusalem. In Jerusalem, God is known, is appreciated, worshiped, and served. So by all means do let us come and worship together, express our gratitude to God, exercise our priestly functions, and sing praises to His Name.

In Jerusalem is to be found also the house of David where the authority and government of Christ is known. Unless we know the authority of Christ in our lives we can exercise no authority. How can we represent God, how can we judge, how can we see things in the right light, unless we ourselves are *first* put under the government of Christ? As we learn His authority we are given spiritual authority to judge (not to criticize) and to discern in order to help.

With such a vision of the church as this which we have glimpsed in this song of degrees, what can we do? There is but one thing we can do, which is what that soul in Psalm 122 does—he commences to pray: "Pray for the peace of Jerusalem: they shall prosper that love thee. Peace be within thy walls, and prosperity within thy palaces. For my brethren and companions' sakes, I will now say, Peace be within thee. Because of the house of the Lord our God I will seek thy good." If we have tasted and experienced the goodness of fellowship, if we have been given the vision of the church, then there is one thing we must do and we will do, which is, that we will pray for the *peace* of Jerusalem: pray for the peace of "the abode of peace," "the house of peace," "the city of peace." If Jerusalem *is* the habitation of peace, then let peace in fact reign in Jerusalem. In the church let us not be at odds with one another. Let us instead be at peace with one another. Let us seek the good of Jerusalem. And let our vision become our vocation. This should be our prayer. May the Lord bless us through this precious song of degrees.

Our heavenly Father, how we praise and thank You that as Your love draws us towards Yourself, and even as there are perils and testings and difficulties on the way, we find we are not alone. We find that You have drawn others with the same mind, that You have others who desire the house of God, who do desire after Jerusalem. Oh how grateful we are that we may find comfort, encouragement, and strength; that we may build up one another and minister to one another in Christ Jesus. How we praise and thank You that in Jerusalem You are known and worshiped; in Jerusalem, Your authority is experienced and exercised. Father, we do pray for the peace of Jerusalem; we do pray for the prosperity of Jerusalem; we do seek the good of Jerusalem. May it be so. We pray in the Name of our Lord Jesus. Amen.

Under Discipline

PSALM 123

A Song of Degrees.

1 Unto thee lift I up mine eyes, O thou that dwellest in the heavens.

2 Behold, as the eyes of servants look unto the hand of their masters, and as the eyes of a maiden unto the hand of her mistress; so our eyes wait upon the Lord our God, until he (be gracious unto)* us.

3 (Be gracious unto)* us, O Lord, (be gracious unto)* us: for we are exceedingly filled with contempt.

4 Our soul is exceedingly filled with the scorning of those that are at ease, and with the contempt of the proud.

*The rendering of J. N. Darby, *The Holy Scriptures, A New Translation.*

The seeking soul has by this time covered a considerable distance in his ascent to that place of perfect union with God. For in this fourth song of degrees our pilgrim soul has at last made his entrance into the house of the Lord. He is a step closer to his goal. Two psalms before, as he was traveling towards Jerusalem, he could only lift up his eyes towards the hills, but now we see him lifting eyes up to God Who dwells in the heavens. Formerly he could only think on God as the One Who made the heavens and the earth, but here we see him addressing God Himself—"O thou that dwellest in the heavens." Previously the soul was some distance from Jerusalem; currently he is *in* Jerusalem itself. In the earlier song the soul was at the gates; at this moment he is verily within God's house. Without question, therefore, the pilgrim soul has by now ascended quite a few

71

steps. Having left far behind him those foreign lands, he today has entered into the house of God. No longer with the world, he is with God Himself.

But does this mean this soul has today reached the peak of Christian experiences? He *is* in the house of God, that is true; he *can* lift up his eyes towards God Himself, yes; nevertheless, we have to acknowledge that he is still some distance from God. In reading this psalm I am somehow left with the impression that the situation of this soul is not unlike the situation of that man whom our Lord Jesus described as recorded in Luke. A man came into the temple to pray one day, and there far away in the outer court he stood and prayed that simple yet sincere prayer: "Oh God, be merciful to me. . .a sinner." The pilgrim soul whom we are observing in these fifteen songs is of course a saved soul; he is admittedly not a sinner. Yet despite the fact he is a believer and is in the house of the Lord, his position is nonetheless as if he were still in the court—even the *outer* court —of the temple: though he can lift his eyes upward and visualize the ark within the Holy of Holies, though he can stand and contemplate the glory of God, yet, somehow, he looks from afar. His is a distant gaze. So that that is his condition at this moment. For the psalmist immediately follows up with: "Behold, as the eyes of servants look unto the hand of their masters, and as the eyes of a maiden unto the hand of her mistress, so our eyes wait upon (are directed to) the Lord our God until he be gracious unto us."

The figure here employed has its origin in Oriental culture. We know that even today in the Near East and elsewhere in the Orient people continue to maintain servants and slaves. And it is still the custom or habit of Oriental masters and mistresses not to tell their slaves and maids what they ought to do—especially in the presence of guests. They consider it in bad taste to have to verbally command their servants in their duties. Hence, when guests are present in a master's home he will indicate his wishes to his slaves not with words but by certain gestures, perhaps a waving of the hand or a movement of the finger. And as is the custom, the servant or servants stand at the lower end of the banquet hall or whatever. Do we get the picture? Here is a large room in which the master is entertaining his guests. The slaves are stationed at the far end of the room with body erect, hands folded, and eyes attentively directed towards the master. There they stand, watching. They are on the alert, they are very keen, and they look in but one direction. What are they on the look out for? The servants are watching for even the slightest movement of the master's hand. Now his guests may not notice any movement. But his servants do; and when the master moves maybe just a single finger, one way or the other, instantly they recognize the wish of the master and hasten to carry it out. Yet what is even more interesting is that oftentimes a master need not even indicate his wish: the slave has already anticipated his master's will and executed it without further delay.

How does a slave come to have such an intuitive sense of the desire of his master? Most likely it is because of quite a lengthy period of association and of training; with the result that there develops between them such a mutual understanding that the slave can even sometimes anticipate the movement and wish of his master. The master and his servant thus come to understand each other very well. We know of course that in ancient times the master was an absolute monarch in his house. He had complete authority. No one dared rebel, resist, or talk back; nobody dared risk it! In his home the master was absolute ruler and that was that. So that the servant or the slave in response rendered without question absolute obedience to him. Whatever the master willed, the slave carried it out—obediently, humbly, willingly. To our modern notions this appears to be quite cruel and heartless. Despite appearances, however, we can often find instances of an extremely mutual closeness between master and slave. Sometimes the mutual affection is of such high degree that it surprises us. The master will protect the slave at the cost of even his own life; and so too will it be of the slave towards his master. The master is wholly responsible for his slave, for better or for worse. And there is such a closeness of relationship that the simplest movement of the master's hand will be noticed by the slave and be executed without fail.

Turning once again, then, to that soul who is ascending step by step to God, we see that he has arrived at a place where he today finds himself in the house of God. And in the house of God he awakens to the fact that he is a slave, a servant, a maid to his Lord. Brothers and sisters, have you come to such a realization in your life? Has this become your experience? You are saved, you love the Lord, you are seeking after Him, and you want to know Him more. Have you, then, discovered that you are now in the house of God? Have you discerned your place in the church—that you are no longer in the world but are in the church and that there is a place for you in the house of God? And have you at last recognized that the relationship between you and God is the relationship of a slave to his master—a willing slave to a loving master? The Lord Jesus is not only your Savior; He is your Master as well. He is the Master and the Lord of your life; and you become a willing slave to Him. Have you arrived at this stage? If you love the Lord and seek the Lord, you *will* come to this stage. You will learn that though you are a son, nonetheless, while a son is young and immature his position is not unlike that of a slave. We have an explanation of this in the Letter to the Galatians. We *are* the heirs and sons of God, quite true; and yet when we are young and immature we are like servants and bondmen before our God (see 4.1). We need to be trained, to be disciplined, to be helped, to be matured. Are we therefore humbly waiting upon the Lord? Are we willing to stand and to wait upon Him, with our arms folded submissively and our eyes directed attentively to Him—that we may discern and obey His movement and will? Or are we still intent upon going this way and that way, doing this thing and that thing, according to our own desire? What stage are we really at in our Christian walk?

We should understand that symbolically speaking "the hand of the master" may signify several things. It may first of all indicate *supply*, a master supplies the need of his servants and maids. The servants and the maids never need worry about their supply. When they are in want of any kind, that lack is met bountifully by the hand of their master. I need not remind you that this thought has been expressed many times over throughout the Psalms. For instance, in the 104th Psalm we read: "Thou openest thine hand, they are filled with good." Another example is in Psalm 145: "The eyes of all wait upon thee; and thou givest them meat in due season; thou openest thine hand, and satisfiest the desire of every living thing." The hand of the Lord means supply.

With this in mind, we would do well to pause and ponder a few moments on this question, How are *we* supplied in *our* needs, *Where* do we go to get the supply to meet all kinds of want? When you are in need—whether it be one which pertains to your daily physical life or whether it be a spiritual need such as comfort, strength or wisdom—now I ask you, where do you obtain your supply? If you are your own master, if you govern your own life, then obviously *you* will have to be the one to take care of all your needs. Whenever a lack arises you cannot look to anybody else, but you yourself will have to try to find a way to meet that lack. But if you are a *bondman* of Christ, if you have surrendered your life completely to the Lord, who is responsible then to supply your wants? Must you continue to look this way and that? Must you continue to depend upon your own strength to see you through? Not any more! For you can henceforth look to the hand of your Master and there find the supply for your every need. The source has changed because the master has changed.

The Christian life is a dependent life: it is dependent upon the Lord. Do you rely upon the Lord for each of your needs? Or are you going this way and that, pondering this solution and that solution, and even losing your sleep in trying to find an answer to the lack? Let me tell you that that is *not* the life of a bondslave of Christ. A bondservant of the Lord can always look to the hand of the Lord. And when the Lord opens His hand the desires of the heart are completely satisfied. The life of a Christian is a dependent life. He depends upon the hand of the Lord for supply.

Yet supply is but one meaning of the hand of the master. It may also convey the idea of *support* or *succour*. Take for instance Psalm 63.8: "Thy right hand *upholdeth* me." Oh, how often we need support! We feel we are weak, that we cannot go on. We are surrounded on every hand by temptations, difficulties, and enemies; and so we need support. But where can we go for support? Ah, we can look to the hand of the Lord, for His right hand upholds us wherever we may go. Can we ever forget those assuring words of David? "If I take the wings of the morning, and dwell in the uttermost parts of the sea; even there . . . thy right hand shall hold me" (Ps. 139.9-10). No matter where we are, dear people, no matter in what situation we may be, you and I must look to the hand of the Lord for our support, for our succour.

If we turn to consider our present song of degrees we will clearly observe that this pilgrim soul has arrived at such a point in his spiritual ascent that he can now wait upon the hand of the Lord for his every need. He is in a sense purified from the defilement of the world, for he no longer looks to it for supply or for support but has learned of the bountifulness and the strength of the arm of the Lord. He has become a lowly sheep dependent upon the arm of the Shepherd-Lord. He looks not to the strength of princes nor to the swiftness of horses, but towards the Lord for his deliverance: "They remembered not his hand, . . . the day when he delivered them from the enemy" (Ps. 78.42). That soul is like Peter who confessed to the Lord: "To whom shall we go? *thou* hast the words of eternal life."

The hand of the master may indicate still another important aspect of our relationship to the Lord. A soul learns to be *guided* by the hand of the Lord. "Even there shall thy hand lead me" (Ps. 139.10). Not by His look or eyes yet, but by His hand is he led; that is, guided and led by the ordering of His providence, by his noticing the changing circumstances of his walk in order that he may know the mind of the Lord. The soul consequently walks according to the pointing of God's finger. No more is he walking according to his own mind; this he had been doing for some time. He is paying attention instead to God's hand and is willing to be guided by the Lord. Admittedly, he has not arrived at that more intimate guidance through the eyes. At the present moment he has to see the movement of the hands before he knows God's mind. He only knows God now by His acts. But someday he shall know God by His heart. Nevertheless, this soul today is no longer a wild ass going his own way. He instead is waiting for God's guidance through the ordering of His providential hand. And this indeed is a big step in the right direction.

Having said all this, though, have we exhausted every meaning of that phrase, the hand of the master? I do not believe so, for there is at least one more idea—and a highly significant one at that—which suggests itself to me by such a phrase. And in this song of degrees presently before us, the sentiment expressed there is more along the line of this idea than it is in terms of supply or support or guidance. And that idea is *discipline*. We need to look to the hand of the Lord for discipline. We must have the attitude which distinguishes the servant or the maid who stands and watches attentively the hand of the master or mistress "until he be *gracious* unto (them)." It is particularly during the time when we are young—not that when we are old we do not require it anymore, but especially when we are young—that we are in need of discipline. Young people dislike it. They desire to have a free hand; they want to do whatever they wish. The notion of a young person is: he likes to be loose. But because of this, it is the very time for correction and chastening. Does anybody ever really enjoy discipline? Yet, if we are not chastened by the Lord then are we bastards and not sons—so says the Bible. But those who are led by the Spirit are the sons of God, and as sons they will be chastened. A true servant or maid of the Lord must be one who undergoes constant discipline. He is truly a disciple of the Lord. Consequently, if anyone genuinely loves the Lord and wishes to go on with Him he will in fact be chastened by the Lord. And why? Because there is so much in us which needs to be beaten out, crushed, purified—the wickedness, the flesh in us. We do indeed need discipline. And so the hand of the Lord will be lowered and placed upon us to chasten and to discipline us, to chase the foolishness, the wickedness and the fleshly life from us.

You may perhaps wonder on occasion why it is that during the time when you do not quite love the Lord it seems as though you can live a life of relative ease. Yes, you are saved; yes, you know the Lord; yet you do not earnestly and passionately follow after Him; and so it seems that God does not bother you too much. It would appear you are able to get by with doing many things and to follow whatever notions may come to your mind; it seems to be all right. But the more you draw near in love to the Lord, seek earnestly after Him and sense a closer walk with Him, the more His hand becomes evident upon you and the more you discover you are under His discipline. The contrast is most telling. When a child of God is *away* from Him, the Lord is quite soft and easy; but just let that child of God *draw near* to the Lord, and His hand will immediately begin to chasten such a one—the Lord seems to be hard on him.

Why is it? you may ask. It is because He loves you. Whom the Lord loves, He chastens (Heb. 12.6). The Lord wants to train you. He wants to complete you, to perfect you. He wants to conform you to the image of Christ. And it is only natural that during any period of discipline there is bound to be sorrow and sadness. But if you will simply remember that the Lord chastens only those *whom He loves,* then you can willingly adopt the attitude of the servant in this psalm. When you are under the disciplining hand of the Lord, *do not fight back.* When you sense the chastening rod of God, *do not run away.* On the contrary, when under the Lord's corrective hand, learn to wait upon Him and to look at His hand attentively *until He be gracious to you.*

Let us be like that soul in the psalm we are presently considering, who has gradually been awakened to see his position as a slave. He has developed the right disposition of waiting on the hand of the Lord until the Lord be gracious to him. For this soul now realizes that there is grace in His severity. This servant-soul today wants the Lord to be strict with him. He does not want the Lord to give him up. While under discipline no one ever feels happy; yet the true servant of the Lord sees the necessity for it. He has learned to humble himself beneath the mighty hand of the Lord (1 Peter 5.6). And how gracious is the dealing of that mighty hand with him. His very rod is the sign of His love. The soul here is shut up with God. He has voluntarily shut himself in to God, for he looks at no one else *but* at God. His eye has become single, seeing no one but Jesus only. He does not look for grace to come from any other source than from God Himself. He will from this moment onward wait with expectation until he learns his lesson and the Lord lifts His hand accordingly from him.

Unlike this soul, however, countless Christians forfeit very valuable lessons for their lives when under the hand of the Lord because their response is negative: they murmur, they fight back, they rebel, they struggle, they pry themselves loose, they flee, they escape. Oh my dear brethren, if you find yourself under the chastening hand of the Lord, your attitude should be, Look at that hand of His until He be gracious towards you; for His hand is a hand of love. Was it not Madame Guyon who once remarked: "I will *kiss* the rod of His chastening"? When God is dealing with us, let us kiss that hand which disciplines us, because the hand which disciplines us is a hand that was *pierced* for us.

In verses 3 and 4 the soul turns to prayer. In verses 1 and 2 it is a declaration of heart attitude. Since his attitude is such as we have described, he next prays that God will be gracious to him. God is his trust, his only refuge, his help, and his comfort. He asks for grace. Nothing pleases God more than when we are petitioning Him for His grace. How foolish we are in thinking we can do anything by ourselves, that we can obey His laws, fulfill His commands, serve His purpose. We assume we are doing Him good if we try hard. Actually, it gives pain to His loving heart for He knows there is no good in our flesh. We who are in the flesh can never please Him nor will we obey Him. What we must do is to direct our eyes towards the hand of the Lord and accept with humbleness of heart the correction and training which He knows is needful for us. And let us then wait upon Him until the work is done and His hand lifted—until *grace* is imparted to us. And our Lord, Who ever waits to perform it, shall dispense such grace to us.

What *is* grace? Let us review that tremendous event in Paul's life, told by the Apostle himself in 2 Corinthians 12. Paul recounts there of how on one occasion he had received great revelations, of how he had seen ecstatic visions, and of how he had heard things too glorious to be spoken of; and because of that, the Lord permitted Paul to be buffeted by the enemy that he might not exalt himself. There was given to him a thorn for his flesh; and this thorn in the flesh caused him discomfort, made him weak, and humbled him. Now because of this, Paul earnestly prayed to the Lord for deliverance. The Apostle petitioned *three* times: "Let this thorn be taken away from me!" How he wanted to be *free*, to be liberated from that troublesome thorn. Yet we know what the Lord told Paul: "My grace is sufficient for you." There was Paul, wanting to be freed *from* the thorn; but on His side, God gave Paul grace *for* the thorn. Brothers and sisters, can we not see ourselves in this episode as well as Paul? For when we are under discipline of some kind, is not our prayer likewise always, Oh let the hand of the Lord be lifted from me! We too want to be delivered from the thorn, from the trouble, from the problem, from the hardship. Why? Because we want to be free that we may feel strong. But dearly beloved, the most precious thing is not the removing of the thorn: the most precious element here is to learn grace, to learn the lesson of grace. "My grace is sufficient for you."

What is grace? Grace is something given to us freely. Grace is not something we deserve: it is favor *un*deserved. Grace comes from Christ. Grace *is* Christ. The grace of God is Christ Himself. When you are being pressed, when you are in trouble, when you are under the disciplining hand of the Lord, oh may you make that happy discovery, that by looking to the Lord with meekness and with humbleness you come into a marvelous realm: the grace of God—Christ Himself—becomes *real* to you: He is imparted to you by that very hand of discipline. And so you grow in Christ. On the other hand, though, you may be one of those who seek to escape suffering by fleeing from the disciplining touch of God. You may in fact be successful in avoiding any suffering whatsoever. Yet such a course can only mean loss for you, because you forfeit the opportunity of learning grace. I ask you, Which is more important—grace, even Christ Himself, or ease and comfort of life? Can there be any comparison?

Hence we see from this fourth song of degrees that as the soul enters the house of God he learns that in His house there is discipline. In no other place can we experience discipline more than in God's house. If a boy flees from home, he may think he has fled from the discipline of the house. But we all know the outcome. Yet a child who remains in the home, a well-ordered home, will be disciplined; but he is disciplined towards his good; it is for his maturity. Let us all therefore realize that as we come to see our place in the church as the family of God, we must be chastened by the hand of the Lord. The Lord Jesus is the faithful Son over God's house (Heb. 3.6). We shall surely be disciplined in one way or the other. Even so, we should not look at the things or problems which befall us nor at our brothers and sisters who may just happen to be the instrument of our trouble but instead recognize this to be the hand of the Lord and direct our eyes thereto—let us look in that direction and there we shall in truth find grace. "Our eyes look unto the hand of the Lord our God until he be gracious unto us!" This is the way to grow in Christ. This is the way we may be delivered from our foolishness, from our carnality, from the natural life which is in us. This is, simply stated, the way of the cross; and yet it is the only way of our knowing Christ.

As that soul experiences the chastening of the Lord, though, he is moved to pray from the depths this prayer: "Be gracious unto us, O Lord, be gracious unto us: for we are exceedingly filled with contempt. Our soul is exceedingly filled with the scorning of those that are at ease, and with the contempt of the proud." Here is the heart cry of a soul who is undergoing a completely new trial. It is a trial common to all those who seriously seek the Lord. For when they are under the discipline of the Lord, one of the things which hurts them most acutely is their discovery that others seem to be enjoying a decidedly easier path. The hurt goes very deep. Here you are, a soul who loves God, but because of this you are under discipline. It seems that the Lord is extremely strict with you. It seems as though the Lord is at you all the time, as though He is needling you without letup—He does not let you go freely. You sense, to your discomfort, that you are living a life of discipline. But when you look at brothers and sisters around you, what do you see? They appear to be enjoying themselves greatly; they appear to be able to talk of many matters, to do many things, and to go to many places—unimpeded. And nothing happens to them!

With others, not even their mouths are disciplined. Their speech and the tone of their speech is uttered without restriction and nothing happens. But let *you* commence to speak and right away there is a restraining hand upon you. Let you say something or or even say the *same thing* as the others, and immediately something happens. For it seems that God comes in to shut your mouth at once. You cannot talk freely. You cannot enjoy yourself. Or take the matter of one's disposition. Even if you should be careful and not so much as utter a syllable, yet somehow the Lord comes in even here and deals with you in your attitude and your manner—He reproves you for being proud or reproaches you for being jealous. You simply are not at liberty! Other brethren can go on quite easily in thought, word, and act. But you! You are under unceasing restraint, you are undergoing training of the Lord all the time. It is indeed puzzling, it is indeed paradoxical: that those who do not love God at all or those who only love Him lukewarmly are at ease and even in prosperity, while those who run earnestly after God encounter difficulties and trials everywhere. The more one loves the Lord, the more, it seems, he gets himself into trouble. He is chastened constantly while the rest go free.

But this is not the worst part of the hurt which the soul who seriously seeks God experiences. Far more deeply wounding is when our brothers and sisters who are at ease *look at us with contempt*. "Our soul is exceedingly filled with the scorning of those that are at ease and with the contempt of the proud." They scoff at us contemptuously and say: "Look at that brother!" or, "Look at that sister!" Our thought is naturally drawn back to that dark day when our Lord Jesus hung on the cross. How people mocked Him and derisively shouted up to Him: "If God is pleased with You, why does He not deliver You? Why do You not come down?" How that must have pierced the heart of Christ! Yet so too must it pierce and break the heart of the saint today, because the same thing will happen to the one who loves the Lord; for the world will laugh at him and mock at him as it did Christ. Yet, not only will the mocking of the *world* be his experience; even those in the *church*, those Christians who are worldly, will assume a like attitude towards him. For even among brothers and sisters can be found these two distinct classes: one is under discipline and the other, seemingly at ease. And those who are at ease look down upon those who are not at ease and free. "Ha ha!" they say, "What's the use of being like that? Why so earnest? Why so serious? Why so foolish? Do not be a fanatic, but be prudent and moderate like us. Then you can enjoy the best of both worlds as we do and everything hereafter will be all right." Oh, the contempt of those who are at ease and the scorn of the proud! Their conscience bothers them not in the least, their thoughts trouble them not one whit, while the Lord deals with them hardly at all.

We in a sense can stand the contempt of the world, because its people do not know the Lord in the slightest. But when we become objects of scorn and derision among the brethren in the church, it is almost too much to bear. Oh, the ultimate in contempt and mocking comes not from the world but from brothers and sisters. And how we are nearly overwhelmed by its wounding and hurt! Like that soul in our song for today, we are filled exceedingly with their contempt. In Hebrew that phrase "exceedingly filled" means "to be saturated"—"to be drenched"—"to have the appetite fully satisfied": as much contempt, therefore, had been heaped upon that soul as could be; he could experience no more. The soul in this psalm, who loves the Lord so much and is under His hand of discipline so constantly, has become so filled with the contempt and so saturated with the scorn of others that in desperation he had to cry out to the Lord for deliverance: "Be gracious to me, O Lord, be gracious to me. If you are not gracious towards me, I may fall—I may go *their* way!" But thank God, His grace *is* sufficient for us.

Oh my dear friends, do not admire those who are at ease, who seem to be so carefree. Do not listen to their mocking, do not heed the scorning of the proud. Sure enough they may be at ease, sure enough they may be proud. But do they know the grace of God which is in Christ Jesus? They have missed out on a most precious lesson: they have forfeited the chance to learn what is grace. They may consider themselves the gainer by their pride and their ease of life. But are they growing in Christ, that is, growing in grace? Just who is the loser after all?

You today may be in difficulty, you today may be humbled, you today may even be humiliated; but thanks be to God, though you lose your self you gain more of Christ—you experience the grace of God which is sufficient for your every need. And not only you but all those others whose hearts are out towards the Lord. For if we will turn to this psalm one final time we can learn one more worthwhile lesson from it. Note, if you will, that in verse 1 the pronoun is singular and personal, but that in the succeeding verses it has become plural and collective. That pilgrim soul is not alone in knowing these trials. A kindred spirit prevails in the heart of all the godly, in the heart of all who love Zion and seek the prosperity of Jerusalem. It is their common lot.

Hence, my fellow pilgrims, let us not be surprised to learn that as we make our ascent together to God all this that we have been speaking about will be a part of our experience. Even so, let us thank the Lord that we have *this* song to sing as we experience *this* way of the Lord—the love of God in chastening, in disciplining, and in child-training.

Our Father, how we praise and thank You that Your love is real—real not only in the sense of supplying our every need, in supporting us in the time of trouble, in leading us when we are in doubt, but we praise and thank You also that Your love is so real that You even discipline us, You even chasten us—because You love us. O Father, we pray that our eyes may be opened to see that in Your house this is inevitable, this is necessary, and that this is something we should love and covet and not despise nor try to avoid. O Lord, we do pray that we may be those who are UNDER Your hand and not those who are OUT from under Your hand. Do not let us go our way, do not let us go out free. Lord, we want to be in Your house, we want to be Your bondslaves; we are willing to be chastened for our foolishness and for our flesh, we are willing to be trained that we may be partakers of Your holiness. We pray, O Lord, that when we are under discipline there might be within us the spirit of humility and of meekness, that we may look attentively upon Your hand until You complete Your work and lift Your hand. We pray we may learn grace through discipline. Oh be gracious to us. We ask that we may not be tempted, by those who are at ease and by those who are proud, to walk their way. Be merciful to us, Lord, and be gracious towards us. We ask in the Name of our Lord Jesus. Amen.

Reminiscence

1 *If it had not been the Lord who was on our side, now may Israel say;*

2 *If it had not been the Lord who was on our side, when men rose up against us;*

3 *Then they had swallowed us up alive, when their wrath was kindled against us;*

4 *Then the waters had overwhelmed us, the torrent had gone over our soul:*

5 *Then the proud waters had gone over our soul.*

6 *Blessed be the Lord, who hath not given us as a prey to their teeth.*

7 *Our soul is escaped as a bird out of the snare of the fowlers: the snare is broken, and we are escaped.*

8 *Our help is in the name of the Lord, who made heaven and earth.*

Our meditations together have now brought us to the fifth of the Songs of Degrees. It is a psalm of David. The precise occasion for its composition is uncertain; yet all can well agree that David had lots of experiences which would have easily enabled him to write such a personal song. David, though, wrote it not only to express before the Lord his own feeling, but we do believe he set it down to convey as well the sentiment of *all* Israel—of all those who are the Lord's—of all those who are seeking the Lord and who are ascending to Him. So whatever may have been the occasion which served as the inspiration for this psalm, we know that in our Christian lives there are numerous opportunities for us to experience the realness of this psalm and for us to sing this song.

As we by this time know there are fifteen Songs of Degrees, and it is my impression that this fifth one gathers up and sums up the four preceding ones. Hence may we say that these five psalms constitute one section, the first of three. And this initial section represents the initial stage of our spiritual life—the stage of purification. As we move forward and make our way step by step and degree by degree upwards towards a full union with God, we, like the pilgrim soul in these songs, discover how God is our Helper, how God is our Leader, Protector, and Guide; we discern how God disciplines us and chastens us for our good; and we also begin to know happy fellowship and companionship with brothers and sisters because we find there are others of likemindedness who are making this ascent as well. Now as we go through these various experiences there will come a point in our path when we too can look back and say with that pilgrim soul: *The Lord has been for us, the Lord has been on our side; and it is good.*

If we read this song in that light, then we can readily see how Psalm 124 gathers up all the past experiences which have occurred during this initial stage of purification. At the present moment the soul is inside the temple, he is in the house of God. That was not the case, though, in the very first song of degrees. Way back then the soul was in an alien place; he was not abiding in Christ. And because he was not abiding in Christ he found himself in distress. He therefore cried to the Lord for deliverance and the Lord in response began to move him. And so we saw in the second song that the soul began to move towards God; but in his journeying towards Him he encountered many temptations, hardships, difficulties, and hindrances; he consequently had to discover God as his Helper and as his Keeper. This we observed in the 121st Psalm. By the time of Psalm 122 we learn that in his traveling onward our pilgrim soul has made his way to the very gates of Jerusalem and experiences happy fellowship there with the saints of God. Because of this new position and relationship he can command a better vision of what Jerusalem is, that is, of what the church is. Finally, by

Psalm 123 the soul has made his way into the court of God. Although he is still at a distance, that is, he is but in the outer court and not yet in the Holiest of all, even so, he can lift up his gaze to the throne of God and as His servant wait upon the Lord and recognize that the Lord is merciful and gracious towards him.

Hence, as we come to this fifth meditation on the Songs of Degrees we do find that this seeking soul *is* in the temple, he is indeed in the house of the Lord, he is indeed in fellowship with God. And as this soul is having fellowship with God, his mind goes back. He mentally retraces the steps of his advancement from the worldly and carnal realm to the heavenly and spiritual sphere. He has gone through a great deal to get to that sphere and therefore has much for which to be thankful. He recalls the past mercies of God. He recalls the past deliverances of God. And as he recalls, he commences to worship and to praise God: "If it had not been the Lord who was on our side." He proclaims with all Israel, that is to say, with all the children of God, that it is the Lord who has brought him through; because he knows that this is the one and only explanation for his having ever gotten to where he is now. This, then, is the sentiment of this psalm: "If it had not been the Lord who was on our side, now may Israel say, If it had not been the Lord who was on our side."

Here the soul is heard to exclaim, *If* it had not been the Lord who was for us!—If it had not been *the Lord* who was for us! Sometimes when we see that word "if" we think, well, it is conditional, that there is some doubt to it: it may be so or it may not be so: as if, in this case, the Lord *could* be against us. But the if in this passage does not carry in it such a thought; it does not mean the soul is in doubt at all. The if here, on the contrary, is employed in the sense of making the statement more emphatic by putting it in suppositional form: "If it had *not* been the Lord who was on our side." In other words, the Lord *is* for us — therefore, we have escaped, we are delivered; the Lord *is* for us—therefore, we are here. Hallelujah! the Lord is for us. Dear brothers and sisters, as we journey on to God and as we pass through many experiences one thing becomes most dear, which is, we learn the lesson *that God is on our side.* And if *God* is for

88

us, who can be against us? We are reminded of that triumphant declaration of Paul's in Romans:

> If God be for us, who can be against us? He that spared not his own Son, but delivered him up for us all, how shall he not with him also freely give us all things? Who shall lay anything to the charge of God's elect? It is God that justifieth. Who is he that condemneth? It is Christ that died, yea rather, that is risen again, who is even at the right hand of God, who also maketh intercession for us. Who shall separate us from the love of Christ? shall tribulation, or distress, or persecution, or famine, or nakedness, or peril, or sword? . . . Nay, in all these things we are more than conquerors through him that loved us. For I am persuaded, that neither death, nor life, nor angels, nor principalities, nor powers, nor things present, nor things to come, nor height, nor depth, nor any other creature, shall be able to separate us from the love of God, which is in Christ Jesus our Lord. (8.31-39)

Brothers and sisters, we learn one fact—that God *is* for us. O blessed thought! that the Lord, the covenanting Lord, is for us. He is with us and is for us.

Frequently, however, we do not feel it that way. We may sometimes feel God is not for us but against us. We are inclined to believe God sides with somebody else or with something else —that God is *not* on our side—that He is very hard upon us. Yet even though it may appear to be that God is not on our side, we must nevertheless stand on the fact that He is still for us. It may not seem to us to be so, but there is a very good explanation for it. Do you know the reason why? It is because God wants to bring us to *His* side that He *may* be for us. Often *we* are not on *His* side; therefore it is that we do not feel He *is* on our side; and in point of fact He cannot be on our side. But that does not mean God is not for us. In all these arranged or permitted difficulties, He is trying to bring us to His side that He may reveal Himself as One Who is absolutely for us. The Lord is for us; and not only is He for us, He is with us, and is within us. Because God has so loved us and has given His only begotten

Son to us, let there be no doubt and let there be no fear: the Lord *is* for us. Can it ever possibly be that He is against us? He is working towards our eternal good. He is attempting always to bring us to His side. He *is* for us. He is for us to eternity. That is our God. And thus, in retrospect, we understand He is the Lord Who is for us. Hind knowledge is more perfect than fore knowledge.

Why is it so imperative that God be *for* us? Simply because there is something or someone *against* us. The psalmist declares: "If it had not been the Lord who was on our side when men rose up against us." It is vitally important that God is for us; otherwise, we would become undone whenever men rise up against us. The Lord Jesus warned us when He prayed to the Father: "I have given them thy word; and the world hath *hated* them, because they are *not* of the world" (John 17.14). The world always rises up to persecute those who dare to leave it.

Brethren, since we have accepted the Word of God, since we have followed Christ, since we have sought Him Whom it hates, therefore, the world hates us. Why? Because we do not belong to the world. We know that the world is a cosmos, a system; it is not a disintegrated, loosely connected entity like sand on the seashore. The world is a very tightly organized network. It is a coherent order organized under the dominion of the god of this world. No phase or feature of it stands as an isolated unit. The whole world is organized, compacted and fitted together under the dominion of the enemy of mankind who is the god of this world—Satan himself. Whether it be political, or economic, or social, or artistic, or even religious in nature—you will find the world to be one vastly organized system. It may exhibit itself in the form of wealth, fame, position, power; or in the form of wrath, fury, persecution, poverty; or in the form of beauty, enticement, attraction, detraction. The world is as a chameleon which changes its color to merge with the natural environment. Hence we are continually being exposed to a thousand and one different manifestations of the world as a coherent mass. But though it may express itself in these various forms and ways, nonetheless in actuality the world is but one constituted order.

Now if you *belong* to the world and its value system, you can go on smoothly. If you are one of the world you will not be bothered, for the world goes along with you and you go along with it. But just you try to be separated from the world, just you try to break away from its entangling network and instantly you will discover that the world will *hate* you: because now you no longer belong. Oh! let us see that the Lord has delivered us *from* this world and has transferred us into a new world, another realm, the kingdom of Christ, a new kingdom. Because we do not belong to this old order, therefore the world hates us; it rises up in wrath, in fury, in persecution, trying to swallow us, trying to overwhelm us, trying to entrap us in its snare.

It is not unlike those astronauts who attempt to escape from our planet into space. It is not an easy matter, you know, for an astronaut to escape the earth and climb into space. For there is that force of gravitation which will continually try to pull him back to the center of the earth. Hence, for him to break away from the earth he needs a powerful countervailing thrust. As the astronaut attempts to pull away from the gravitational force, he finds that the entire force of this earth seems to be upon his body. His body suffers in order to be rid of this power; but once he escapes the earth, he becomes *weightless*—he is at last free! Brothers and sisters, spiritually, this is also the case. The world, spiritually speaking, has its gravitational force too: it is forever trying to pull us to the center of its system: it is forever trying to yank us back in. If you attempt to get away it will try to pull you back—and not merely back to the periphery of things but right back to the *center* of this world! It will attempt to get you so involved, so occupied with the things of this world, that you are caught in its very grip and held in its very sway. The world possesses tremendous power. Do you want to break away? Do you want to escape from this world? Oh, you soon see that within yourself there is the flesh, and the flesh *responds* to the world's downward pull—just as iron is attracted to, or responds to, a magnet. The world exerts its power upon us Christians, and the flesh within us responds to that power. So that if a Christian ever wants to sever himself from the world, the flesh must suffer a great deal for it.

Do not think that to be separated from this world is a smooth and easy matter. It is not! As is the case with the astronauts so will it be with you and me. To break away from the earth the astronaut must suffer bodily because all the earth's force will be concentrated upon his body. By the same token, the more you desire to be separated from this world the more you will experience the power and the force of this world as an all-embracing system being exerted upon you. But do we need fear? Observe the astronaut; he does not possess that necessary overcoming thrust in himself; he merely places himself in the space vessel so as to be thrust upward by a powerful rocket. We likewise do not possess in ourselves the power to overcome the world. But thank God, He has placed a power—a rocket of unlimited power—within us; and that unlimited force is *the love of Christ.* Oh! the love of Christ that God has put within us is so tremendous that it enables us to break away from all ties and forces of this world-system. We do thank the Lord that His love is all-powerful.

My dear friends, do you sense the Lord's love? If His love constrains you, you will find that nothing can hold you back. When His love is constraining you, when His love is moving you, you will discover that all these earthly, worldly attractions and ties will be cut to pieces. The Lord thrusts you up to heaven and to that realm of weightlessness. You are free! Nothing of this world can now hold you down, nothing of this earth can again draw you back into its orbit. You are above it! You are weightless! You are free in Christ! Hence the meaning of that Scripture which says that the law of the spirit of life sets us free from the law of sin and death; who then can condemn us who are in Christ Jesus? (See Romans 8.2,1) Brethren, have you tasted of the love of Christ—that love which thrusts you upward and sets you free, that love which severs all worldly ties and overcomes all worldly forces? The Lord is for us. Who then can be against us? Oh do not forget this fact, that the Lord is for you. It is an eternal fact. A fact which is not altered by how you may or may not feel today. He *is* for you. His love *is* in you. Consequently, only turn to Him, seek Him, and let there be released that infinite power of love which is within you.

"If it had not been the Lord who was on our side, when men

rose up against us: then they had swallowed us up alive, when their wrath was kindled against us." In this and succeeding verses the psalmist is attempting to communicate to us what the world is like. Often we are deceived by the world. We do not know what it really is. The psalmist therefore tries, by the use of figures of speech, to unfold to us the true nature of men and the world and how they, if provoked, will deal with the children of God: he likens the world to three things in this very short psalm. First, he likens the world to a wild animal, a carnivorous beast which will swallow its prey alive. Does this come as a shock to you? The world is compared to a beast: When men rose up in anger against us, they would *swallow us up* like wild beasts! One day long ago the great king Nebuchadnezzar had a dream. He dreamed of a world power, the world kingdom. And in his dream he beheld a huge statue, an image: a man with a golden head, silver shoulders, brass belly, iron legs, and iron clay feet. It was a glorious, magnificent, impressive figure. To Nebuchadnezzar the world was exactly like that: full of splendor and of majesty and of glory and as bright as that glorious image of his. *But,* the Lord gave a similar vision of this world to His servant Daniel. Now what did *Daniel* see? Daniel beheld the same object, the world empire; yet what he saw was not a glorious human statue; what he saw was a composition of beasts! Wild beasts!!

Do you not remember that, according to the book of Revelation, towards the end of this age the final stage and form of this world—the last empire—will be headed up by a beast? The beast there is of course symbolic; it is a man, yes, but in the sight of God it is no different from a wild beast. Have you ever incurred the anger of men? It is just as unreasonable and just as untamed as a beast. The world may be attractive, the world may project an excellent facade, the world may appear refined, civilized and cultured; but brothers and sisters, once you incur the wrath of man *then* you shall know what the world is. If you go along with it all the time the world may seem to be very civilized and quite refined; but once its wrath is kindled, once you attempt to break away from its tradition, customs, ways and thought, what then do you find? The *real* nature of this world is revealed, and it is the nature of a wild beast! The wrath of man is like a savage, uncontrollable animal. It is so covetous that it has hardly the patience to chew you, it instead wants to *swallow* you! It is as greedy and insatiable as hell, and as cruel as hades! In figure it is not unlike that incident in the Old Testament of the earth being opened and swallowing up all which belonged to Korah, Dathan, and Abiram (Num. 16.32). Let us recognize the world for what it is: it is like a wild irrational beast: it is trying to devour you, to swallow you, to kill you—spiritually. Is it not true? Is it not true? But thank God, the Lord is on our side. And if the Lord is for us, the world can*not* swallow us. No matter how it may try, it cannot swallow us up.

Second. The world is likened to a flood: "Then the waters had overwhelmed us, the torrent had gone over our soul: Then the proud waters had gone over our soul." I do not know whether you have ever witnessed a flood. But if you have ever gone through a flood experience, you know what it is. I recall once that when traveling through interior China I visited a certain area in the South. And on the first day of my stay everything appeared to be perfectly normal. I was located in a place on one side of a river which flowed by there. The river I noticed was wide but not too wide; but by the time I awoke the next morning I could not cross the river; it had become a raging torrent. A flood had come up out of nowhere and the bridges had all collapsed. It had come upon us quite abruptly; so abruptly, in fact, that people there have told me that those at the time who might be walking on the bridge could easily be swept away with it without warning. It is as quick as that! No warning! When a river floods its banks it arises suddenly without any warning and quickly subdues, submerges and carries away everything before it. It is proud and arrogant. It is sudden and subtle. It is overwhelming and almost totally irresistible. It is hard for us to stand against a flood. And the world is precisely like that.

Have you, dear friends, experienced the world as a flood? It comes upon you with no warning. You may think you are safe; you may imagine all is normal; but the very next moment you find you are submerged. The world is like that. Thank God, though, when the adversary shall come in like a flood, the Spirit of God shall raise up a banner against him (Is. 59.19). How we thank the Lord that when the world comes upon us as suddenly as a flooding stream He is our banner, His love is our banner. He will raise up a standard against the flood and the world can*not* carry us away. The Lord—and only the Lord—can withstand the flood. He asserts that He has overcome the world (John 16.33).

And third. He likens the world to a fowler's net: "Our soul is escaped as a bird out of the snare of the fowlers: the snare is broken, and we are escaped." A fowler is one who attempts to catch birds by whatever device he may employ. He has several means of capturing them. Sometimes he makes use of a net; and well under the net he places some food. As soon as the birds swoop down upon the food, the snare or net is quickly closed and the birds are caught beyond any chance of escape. Or the fowler can be even more clever by planting in the snare as a decoy several fowl—tied of course—to attract the innocent birds to come under the net and thus be caught without their knowing and again with no way of escape. A bird which is snatched in this way cannot extricate itself. It is beyond the bird's ability.

How the world, in like fashion, tempts us with some little dainties in order to ensnare our soul. And so we are caught. But, the Lord is for us. He breaks the net and sets us free! We are escaped, we are set at liberty. And why? Because the Lord has done it. How many times we are as these little birds, so foolish and so ignorant and so enticed by a tiny morsel or a little dainty of this world. How unconsciously we slide under the net; and how we are snared by this world many times over. But we do thank the Lord that in His grace and mercy He breaks the net. The spell of this world is cut asunder. We are as free as the birds. We will fly straight towards the sky, back to the throne of grace. What a mighty deliverance is ours!! And how did we come out? Surely not by our own wisdom and cleverness. We are escaped today, not because we are any wiser than our brothers and sisters, but because the Lord has broken the net for us.

We see in this song of degrees, then, how David looks back upon his past life. It is a life which has been very full and quite varied. He has passed through countless experiences. On occasion the world has come upon him as a mighty flood which tried to sweep him off his feet. On occasion the world has cast itself about him as a fowler's net, seeking to ensnare him. How David has truly passed through many experiences. Here is a man of God who loves the Lord and desires Him and aspires after Him; and because of that, how the world hates David and tries to pull him down, tries to entrap him, to quench him, to subdue him, to submerge him, to swallow him, yes to destroy him—spiritually. And on many occasions it has seemed that he *has* been overwhelmed, that he *has* fallen. Yet the Lord is for him. The Lord is on his side. Consequently he can stand in the house of God and there proclaim: "My help is in the name of the Lord, the maker of heaven and earth." Is it not likewise true with us today?

It is manifest, therefore, that this fifth song of degrees stands as the summation of all the past experiences during this first stage of our Christian walk. In this initial stage of our ascent to God, our greatest difficulty is the world—the world within us as well as the world around us: How can we be rescued from Egypt? How can Egypt be put out of our heart? How can we be delivered from this wretched man, both within and without us—this that is a dead weight, a cumbersome, unholy union? How can we be set free from this world that we may abide in Christ, that we may dwell in a new world and live in another kingdom? Now that is *the* problem during this incipient phase of one's Christian experience. But thanks be to God, if only we have a heart towards the Lord, then remember, He is for us. We cannot do it ourselves, but He can do it by His cross. His glory will so attract us that all the things of this world appear dim to us. His cross will so work in our life that the world is crucified, so far as we are concerned, on the cross; and we are crucified, so far as the world is concerned, on the same cross. The beginning stage of the working of Calvary is to deliver us from the sin and death of this world. And the Lord is our Deliverer. And even when we are sometimes caught, the Lord will break the net and set us free.

What a triumphant note is this: "If God be for us, who *can* be against us?"

Our Heavenly Father, we do want to lift up our hearts and bless Your holy Name. How we praise and thank You that You are for us, and who then can be against us? The world may seem to be all-powerful, and yet You are the Almighty One. How we praise and thank You that You have broken the power of this world, the power of the god of this world. You have set us free, and we are free indeed. So Father, we do pray that we may look up to You and find our help in You, the Maker of heaven and earth. Turn us to Yourself. We pray in the Name of our Lord Jesus. Amen.

The Stage
of
ENLIGHTENMENT

Inner Conflict and Victory

PSALM 125
A Song of Degrees.

1 They that trust in the Lord are as Mount Zion, which cannot be removed, but abideth for ever.

2 As the mountains are round about Jerusalem, so the Lord is round about his people from henceforth even for ever.

3 For the scepter of the wicked shall not rest upon the lot of the righteous; lest the righteous put forth their hands unto iniquity.

4 Do good, O Lord, unto those that be good, and to them that are upright in their hearts.

5 As for such as turn aside unto their crooked ways, the Lord shall lead them forth with the workers of iniquity: but peace shall be upon Israel.

We have been observing together the journey of a pilgrim soul as he step by step makes his ascent towards full union with God. In the first five songs of degrees we have seen how the soul began a shift away from the world and a gradual movement towards and into the house of God. And upon arriving at this station in his journey he could look back in praise to the Lord for all the deliverances he had experienced by the grace of God. In other words, these initial songs taken collectively distinctly mark out for us the very first phase of any Christian's ascent to God, which is the phase of purification. We all, upon our initially trusting in the Lord, are in need of being purified—we need to be delivered from the sin and death of this world. But beginning with this new song before us and running through Psalm 129, we shall discern a second phase, the next stage in our pursuit after God. And this is the stage of enlightenment or illumination.

God's people must understand, however, that in things spiritual they cannot draw a line by believing that here is the end of one experience and there begins a second experience which in turn will end at a certain point only to be succeeded by still a third kind of experience. It is not like this at all. In spiritual matters such a fine line of demarcation cannot be drawn. For the nature of Christian life is such that our experiences will be repeated, will be emphasized, will be deepened and broadened; they shall ofttimes overlap. We cannot differentiate so sharply and contend that, Well now, this experience terminates here and another and different one commences from this moment on.

Yes, it is perfectly true that during the first period of our Christian walk we generally encounter the purification of our life; we experience the Lord as One Who delivers us from the sin and death of this world and thereupon enter into that phase of abiding in Christ. But can this mean that during such a period we have no enlightenment, we experience no revelation, we see no light? Of course not. It simply signifies that during the incipient stage what is *more* before us is purification. It is primarily purification which distinguishes this period. And by the same token, when a person enters upon the second phase of his Christian life, he will discover that that phase is chiefly characterized by illumination. But as before, it does not at all imply that in this second period purification is never again necessary. On the contrary, we need to be purified all the time. Our purification needs ever to be deepened and broadened —not merely our experiencing a purification from the world but a purification as well from the expressions and activities of our natural self life.

Please let us remember, therefore, that purification still continues to occur during succeeding stages; it touches areas which have never before been touched. Even so, let us equally be clear that during this second period what is most prominent and what marks this period out particularly is the element of enlightenment or illumination. The seeking soul sees and understands a great deal. Light is given, vision granted; the spirit of wisdom and revelation is accorded him, the eyes of his heart are opened: he is made acquainted with spiritual things, he begins to have discernment into spiritual principles which are eternal and real and applicable. It is a time of revelation, a time of sight and insight, a time of emancipation, a time of great joy. This will be the situation when a soul enters upon the second phase of his spiritual ascent.

On the one hand the Christian sees more and more things spiritual during this period of enlightenment—he understands these matters in a better way. On the other hand the cross works deeper into his life during this phase. It is no longer simply a matter of dealing with the world around him, or even with the world within him; the dealings of the Lord with him are not so much circumstantial and peripheral; they become instead more essential and central. In other words, the cross touches more than what surrounds us: it touches something which is more closely related to our *selves,* that is to say, the activities of our natural life. We shall find that this is a time of clash and combat; but not of an *outward* sort. Formerly our struggle was confined to external matters: we felt we were at odds with the world and the world was at odds with us. Now, however, the contest turns increasingly *inward.* We soon detect the outlines of a battle raging within, because the Lord has shone upon us and has enlightened us. It is God on the one side and our old life on the other. We begin to perceive that within ourselves there is that which is of the Spirit and that which is of the flesh. The flesh lusts against the Spirit and the Spirit lusts against the flesh. It is a period of intense warfare, plunging us at times into deep valleys, even into the depths of the waters of great sorrow, keen disappointment, untold frustration.

We shall consequently come to see, brothers and sisters, that this second phase of our pilgrim journey is one in which we sometimes are atop the mountain peak beholding a magnificent view of the land but are at other moments in the valley below, seemingly shut in and overwhelmed by darkness and shadows. It is a period of joy mingled with sorrow, emancipation mingled with bondage. It is a period in which we sometimes sing and sometimes sigh. It is, in short, a period of inner conflict.

Even so, dearly beloved, this is also a period wherein you can learn *the lesson of faith.* Formerly you lived by feeling; you required something tangible to help you along. If there was nothing you could feel, if there was nothing you could sense and hold on to, then you could hardly move. Today, though, the Lord is delivering you from the world of feeling and the world of the senses. The Lord is leading you into the realm of faith—that element which, in its own way, distinctively characterizes this period too. You now begin to live by faith and no longer by sight. You now come to know the death and the resurrection power of the Lord Jesus. Not only do you learn to abide in Christ but you also learn His abiding within. And as a result He becomes resurrection life within you.

Hence this phase in our Christian experience can be said to be one of progress, a time of moving on, a stage during which we make great strides forward and when doubtless spectacular things often occur. Nevertheless, let us realize that this is *not* the end yet, the goal will not yet have been reached. Perhaps an illustration may prove helpful here. A Christian entering upon this second phase can be likened to a torrent which rushes forward impetuously, forming on the way many falls and rapids. It is undeniably a beautiful and dramatic sight to see. And how inspiring, too, to behold a soul such as this! Like the rapids and the falls, he moves on swiftly, spectacularly, gathering more strength with the momentum. There appears to be tremendous power and energy. But please note that that torrential stream has not yet reached its destination: the greater ocean which lies at its mouth. For when water reaches and flows into the ocean, suddenly all becomes calm and still. The scene which is then presented to the eye is a far less dramatic one. Everything is restful, all has become quiet, because the stream—as great and as forceful as it was before—has now united with something far more vast and deep. It has now merged with the boundless sea. Can we not see the similarity between this natural phenomenon and a person's spiritual advance? It is an illustration of the Christian soul's *full* union with God. Like that spectacular and rapidly moving torrent which has yet to reach the mouth of the stream, the soul, though advancing with great strides, has not arrived at his end either. By means of this second phase of which we have been speaking, the Lord will lead the Christian on until he is *merged* into God's life just as water makes its entry into the ocean. God deals with us and takes us on until we are *united* with Him in such a way that there arises a full peace and rest— until we are lost in God Who is vast, deep, and boundless. Hence, as by the Lord's enabling we enter into the next phase of Christian experiences, let us ever be mindful that, good as this period may be, it is nonetheless but a transitional one. It is towards something even yet further.

Now Psalm 125 marks the inauguration of such a period of experiences. We cannot be certain as to the occasion or circumstances which prompted its composition. Some say it was written following the Exile when the remnant returned to Jerusalem from Babylonish captivity and found themselves under the dominion of heathen rule or possibly under the rule of their own brethren who did not fear the Lord. In either case, the psalm expresses an experience which occurred *in* the Promised Land, not *away* from it. And so they expressed their feeling accordingly. Others have held that it was composed by David probably during the time when he was being persecuted by Saul in the land; or, when he fled out from under the short period of his son Absalom's rule. Here again, the trouble was internal and not external. It was a conflict between the godly and the wicked in the same land. But whatever may be the background for the writing of this psalm, it is important that we discern the spiritual experience it describes and learn the spiritual lesson it contains. For it has been the prayer of my heart continually that we may enter into the spiritual experiences and learn the spiritual lessons of these Songs of Degrees because they always lead us onward to God.

At the very beginning of this psalm the reader can detect a *new* dedication, a *new* consecration. This will always be the case for that one who has tasted and experienced the Lord's mighty deliverances from the world—not only rescue from the world as a beast with its persecution and anger and wrath, but also rescue from the world as a fowler's net with its subtlety and its temptation. It is only natural that the heart of a soul who has been

105

delivered by God from the world will be touched by the love of Christ. And if one's heart is touched by Christ's love, what will that one do? The natural consequence will be to present himself a living sacrifice to God. Whenever our heart is touched by the love and mercy of God, the natural response will surely be that we will want to rededicate ourselves afresh and more thoroughly to the Lord. We will want to *entrust* ourselves to Him out of a grateful heart. As a matter of fact, the key word in this psalm is "trust" or "confide." Hence what we find the soul doing here at the very outset is entrusting himself to the Lord: "They that *trust* in the Lord."

Brothers and sisters, in spiritual life one thing always stands out as being very fundamental, and that is consecration. Do not think consecration is merely for a few, for those for example who desire to preach the gospel. These of course need to be consecrated, of this there is no doubt. But *you too* need to be consecrated. "Brethren, I beseech you by the compassions of God to present your bodies a living sacrifice." Everyone who is redeemed, everyone who is touched by the love of Christ, must commit his life to God for *His* service: not merely for preaching the gospel but for God himself and whatever He desires. This is consecration.

But are we to infer from this that we need consecrate ourselves only once? Not so. Consecration is something which needs to be repeated; it needs to be deepened and broadened. In the beginning of your Christian life, just after you have been saved, you are so touched by the love of Christ that you pray, O Lord, I dedicate and commit myself to You entirely; use me in whatever manner You would like. That is consecration, to be sure. But at that moment you really do not know how much is involved in it. Thank God, He takes us at our word and commences to work accordingly, until He brings us further on. God opens our eyes, He arranges for us to experience His mercy and grace, and consequentially we begin to recognize our need to consecrate more to Him because we are spiritually more intelligent now and know how much more is involved. And our response is that we want to consecrate accordingly. Hence consecration is an act which must be deepened and heightened and repeated.

This is something which is made quite clear by reading the Old Testament type. Recall, if you will, how the burnt offering of old needed to be presented every day, at both morning and evening. But even this was not enough. At the time of a new moon and during the time of special set feasts additional burnt offerings were sacrificed and in greater number. Consecration is therefore something which needs to be increased all the time.

Thus we find at the very outset that this period begins with a new confiding, a new dedication, a new abandonment of self to the Lord. Here in Psalm 125 is to be found a soul who, because of the past mercies of God, is moved to dedicate himself afresh to the Lord. He has found the Lord so trustworthy that he is most willing to entrust himself into His hand. And do you know what is the effect? As that soul entrusts himself to the Lord a whole new world is opened up before him; he is given a vision—a vision of Mount Zion and of Jerusalem. The mercies and compassions of God will invariably lead to such a step of consecration and confiding (see Rom. 12.1). And once such a step is taken, it opens up an entirely new realm, just as Romans 12.1, standing as the consequences of the preceding chapters which tell of God's mercies, immediately becomes the cause for what followed: a seeing of the corporate life of the body of Christ and its various services. Our confiding in the Lord must therefore ever be increasing. We dare to trust the Lord because He has proven to us His faithfulness. And as the soul commits himself to the Lord he is marvelously enlightened as to the wisdom of his having taken such a step.

Brothers and sisters, is it easy to confide? Is it easy to take things out of our own hand and to commit them and ourselves to the Lord? Naturally speaking we are all hesitant in confiding; we do not quite trust others. We have more confidence in ourselves than in those around us, we even repose more confidence in ourselves than in the Lord. We feel if we hold our lives in our own hands they are safer that way than to deliver them over to God. It sounds strange and unreasonable, but how true it is nonetheless. Do you confide yourself to God? Are you willing to hand your soul over to God and leave it with Him?

Paul declared that he knew Him in Whom he had believed

and was assured that the Lord was fully able to keep for that Day the deposit he had *entrusted* to Him (2 Tim. 1.12). Is this true of you? Or are you still holding your life and the things concerning your life in your own hands? Do you think it is safer that way? Or are you persuaded that it would be more secure to deliver yourself and everything which concerns you into the hand of God and leave them there? Actually, unless our heart is touched by the love of Christ, we will be afraid to trust in the Lord. We are fearful something may happen. Oh how foolish to keep our soul in our hands, trying to save our life and seek our own profit! How much wiser to commit our souls to Him Who is able to save to the end.

"They that trust in the Lord are as Mount Zion, which cannot be removed, but abideth for ever." The soul is here rededicating himself to the Lord, and as he hands himself over and trusts in Him completely, his eyes are opened and he is shown two things. First—"They that trust in the Lord are as Mount Zion." Second— "As the mountains are round about Jerusalem, so the Lord is round about his people from henceforth even for ever." Zion represents stability. Jerusalem represents security. They who confide in the Lord are as Mount Zion which cannot be moved but abides forever: eternal stability. Mountains surround Jerusalem and the Lord surrounds His people from henceforth till evermore: eternal security.

Humanly speaking, mountain and hill give us the impression that they cannot be moved. Nations may change, governments do change, people may change their places of abode, even custom and habit are subject to change, but when one gazes upward towards the mountains they give the impression of having always been there and of their being there ever afterwards. A mountain is immovable, it abides forever; it creates the effect, therefore, of stability, of steadfastness. And in such stability there is strength. Hence the person who trusts in the Lord is as Mount Zion; he, like the Mount of God, is immovable, steadfast and stable.

Why is it that we are not *stable* in our Christian life? One moment we are so zealous and so enthusiastic, we so love the Lord, we are so willing to sacrifice everything for Him; but at the next moment we are like a flat tire—punctured, flattened out, useless, inoperative, and void of any power. Why? *stability* is not in us. Whence comes one's stability? Whence is derived that eternal steadfastness? It is achieved as we confide in the Lord. If you will but entrust yourself to the Lord, you will find He will make you stable. Stability comes from the Lord.

But how is it that it is Mount Zion which is singled out here? For please note that Jerusalem is built on a total of five hills with Mount Zion constituting but one of them. It is because on Zion is to be found David's palace and Solomon's palace. Zion is the place where royalty dwells; Zion is the site where the throne of David is set. Mount Zion thus symbolizes the authority of God.

Brethren, if you confide yourself to the Lord, you shall be infused with a divine stability, a strength which comes from accepting the Lord as your King, as your Authority. The Lord comes and dwells in you; and so you become as Mount Zion. The throne of God is established within your heart. The authority of God is recognized and honored. And whenever the authority of God is established in anyone's heart, he as it were becomes as stable as the Mount of God—nothing can move him. There descends upon that person a regal air, a special nobility, because the throne of David is in Zion.

But please notice here that the pronoun is cast in the plural: *They* that trust in the Lord are as Mount Zion. That confiding soul is not alone, for he cannot possibly attain to such stability by himself. Others of likemindedness there are who *together* form Mount Zion. Zion represents "the cream" of Jerusalem: the overcomers in the church. They are the pillars of the church, constantly abiding in the Lord and therefore immovable.

Jerusalem is not only built upon mountains: it is true as well that "mountains are round about her." According to the topography of Jerusalem, this is quite factual. Except for the southeastern side, the city is literally ringed by a triangle of mountains. Hilly Jerusalem herself is walled in on three sides by still higher hills and mountains. So that from a distance a person cannot even see Jerusalem! One must climb the surrounding triangle of mountain ranges in order to view the city. Yet even at her southeastern corner—where from the city the viewer can gaze towards Jordan and beyond and behold the mountains of Moab on the eastern side of the River—the appearance is given that here too Jerusalem is bounded by a barrier, a barrier formed at a distance by Moab's mountains. Hence, "as the mountains are round about Jerusalem" and protect her, the city being hidden among the mountains, even so is "the Lord round about his people from henceforth even for ever." How vivid is the imagery employed by the psalmist: the physical is transferred to the spiritual.

The protection the mountains afford Jerusalem is a figure to describe the eternal security of the church as provided by God Himself. How God surrounds His own people and protects them from harm and evil from without. Like Jerusalem within the circle of mountains, we are hidden in God Himself: "Your life is hid with Christ in God" (Col. 3.3). And that is security, everlasting security. Is it not the case in our experiences that as we confide in the Lord, as we commit our lives into His hand, we find eternal stability and eternal security? We become both immovable and impregnable! We are established in Christ Jesus.

But does this mean because we are as Mount Zion and because we are as Jerusalem surrounded by the mountains of God that therefore we have no trouble? In such condition there may not, to be sure, be too much difficulty from without; but we will encounter difficulty from within. If there is less trouble from without, that is to say, if the world is powerless to unsettle us because of our having been crucified to it, there will nevertheless be trouble within—that is, from within the city: "The scepter of the wicked shall not rest upon the lot of the righteous; lest the righteous put forth their hands unto iniquity." Trouble is present within; and it is *within* the land, within the city of Jerusalem, that the scepter of wickedness is to be found! Two kinds of people are dwelling there: one is wicked and the other is righteous: the wicked and the righteous dwell side by side in the same land. And sad to say, the wicked seem to have power: the *scepter* of the wicked, it says. Is this not an accurate picture of our spiritual experience? On the one hand we experience the protection of the Lord; on the other hand we sense that there seems to be dwelling within our soul two kinds of persons: there is that which is of the flesh—the wicked, and there is that which is of the Spirit—the righteous. We discover that from time to time a conflict rages between the wicked and the righteous within our own selves, a kind of struggle which Paul described in these terms: "the flesh lusteth against the Spirit, and the Spirit against the flesh: and these are contrary the one to the other" (Gal. 5.17).

The flesh is wicked; not because it cannot think commendable thoughts, not because it cannot make exemplary efforts, not because it does not have noble aspirations, and not because it cannot put up a good front; quite the reverse, the flesh can perform *all* these works. But the flesh is wicked! Why? Because it is essentially opposed to God. The flesh "is not *subject* to the law of God, neither indeed can be. So then they that are in the flesh cannot please God" (Rom. 8.7,8). From God's viewpoint the flesh is no good. The flesh may try to do something quite good; it sometimes attempts, for instance, to be very religious: we can even worship in the flesh; and yet it is wicked in the sight of God just the same, because it is not subjected to God. And what is more, neither can it *be* subjected to God. Brethren, the flesh within us is powerful: the *scepter* of the wicked. The flesh has ruled us for so long that it is extremely reluctant to yield its authority, it refuses to give up its dominion. Who of us has not felt the power of the flesh? All who desire to love and to trust the Lord discover the inordinate power of the flesh in their lives.

During the early period of the Reformation a noted reforming theologian by the name of Philip Melancthon uttered one day this sentiment: "O, this old Adam is too powerful for young Melancthon! The old Adam which is within is too much for this young Melancthon. By myself I cannot fight against my flesh. It is impossible. O, who can deliver me from this wretched man?" Brothers and sisters, do you feel the strength—the powerful scepter—of the wicked? Do you feel the might of the flesh within you? If you do not, you are probably still in the initial stage of your Christian growth. But if you are moving on with the Lord you will discover the flesh within you is even more formidable than the world which is around you. Romans 7 delineates this power fully.

Yet not only is the flesh powerful, it likewise is crooked. It does not tread the straight path of holiness. It is subtle and it leads to self-gratification. The flesh can create an *appearance* of piety, but in the final analysis it is for self. It may seem to strive for the good, and yet it always ends up in sin.

But does all this consequently mean there can be no more steadfastness and security to the seeking and confiding soul? Must we infer from this that the protection of the Lord cannot or will not resolve this conflict? Is the stability of the Lord unable to reach to this sphere? It may seem that way. Nevertheless, thank God, though the contest be great, the outcome is sure. For the psalmist declares that "the scepter of the wicked shall not *rest* upon the lot of the righteous; lest the righteous put forth their hands unto iniquity." The scepter of the wicked may *come upon* the lot of the righteous, but it cannot *rest* there. It can only remain for the short time during which the Lord allows the conflict to rage. And he allows the conflict for a time, only that we may learn the wickedness of the flesh and so no longer trust, depend upon and confide in the flesh.

The Lord will never permit the power of the flesh to remain too long on the lot of the righteous. For when in the contest we are being pressed by the flesh we will experience the Lord coming in and delivering us. Who indeed can liberate us save Christ Jesus our Lord! The Lord *shall* deliver us. He will open our eyes to see that the scepter of the wicked has been broken on His cross. He will open our eyes and give us faith to believe in the all-sufficiency of the cross that we may live in the power of His resurrection and not in the energy of our flesh. And then we shall witness how the power of the flesh will soon be exhausted. Our spirit within shall gain ascendancy over the flesh as the law of the Spirit of life sets us free from the law of sin and death. For as we are led by the Spirit in our spirit, the flesh experiences mortification. The deeds of the body are put to death.

To be sure, the flesh will struggle on for a time, but in the end it will meet its demise. To be sure, we do discover the flesh within us, we do indeed feel its power for a time—we discern its crookedness, its craftiness, but also its destiny. And because we trust and confide in the Lord and in everything which He has done for us by His cross, we shall be set free from its power. The Lord Who knows our frame and is sensitive to just how much we can bear comes in at the proper moment with His deliverance. Though the conflict is severe, He will not permit us to suffer permanently nor beyond what we can endure (1 Cor. 10.13). For the Lord is well aware that were He to allow the scepter of the wicked to *rest* upon the righteous then the righteous too would turn to iniquity.

How perfect are His ways! Here in truth is the steadfastness and the protection of the saints. It is in Him that we find our stability and security because *He is* our stability and security. It is His protection, His care, and His measuring and restraining hand. And as we trust in Him we are made as Zion and as Jerusalem; or rather, "He is made unto us" stability and security (1 Cor. 1.30).

Dear brothers and sisters, it is during the second phase of our Christian growth that we are alerted increasingly to the inner struggle between our spirit and our flesh. The soul receives light from heaven to recognize the fact that the flesh has been rejected by the holy God. He also comes to see God's deliverance out of the conflict through the cross of the Lord. Let us therefore not lose heart and never let us fail to trust in the Lord at such a time, since deliverance *will* come, and come soon.

Finally, because his hope and confidence rests in the Lord and in His deliverance, the psalmist concludes his song with a prayer: "Do good, O Lord, unto those that be good, and to them that are upright in their hearts; (but) as for such as turn aside unto their crooked ways, the Lord shall lead them forth with the workers of iniquity: but peace shall be upon Israel." Such is his prayer. In going through such inner conflict, it will be entirely natural for a child of God to breathe this kind of prayer. And may it truly be the prayer of all our hearts: "O Lord, strengthen our inner man by the power of Your mighty Spirit, that the outward man may be broken; O Lord, break the scepter of the wicked, shatter the power of the flesh; openly expose the wickedness of

113

the flesh. O Lord, may peace be restored to Israel, may the peace of God reign in the heart of every confiding soul."

Our Father, how we praise and thank You: they who trust in You shall find stability and security. How we praise and thank You: those who confide in You may go through times of difficulty but they shall experience the resurrection life of our Lord Jesus over the power of darkness and of the flesh. Lord, we ask You to break the scepter of the wicked in our lives; we ask You to strengthen our inner man by the power of the Holy Spirit; we ask You that the peace of God may reign in our hearts. In the Name of our Lord Jesus. Amen.

The Two Sides of the Cross

PSALM 126
A Song of Degrees.

1 When the Lord turned again the captivity of Zion, we
were like them that dream.

2 Then was our mouth filled with laughter, and our tongue
with shouts of joy: then said they among the nations,
The Lord hath done great things for them.

3 The Lord hath done great things for us; whereof we are
glad.

4 Turn again our captivity, O Lord, as the streams in the
south.

5 They that sow in tears shall reap with shouts of joy!

6 He that goeth forth and weepeth, bearing the seed for
sowing, shall doubtless come again with rejoicing, bringing his sheaves with him.

When reading this seventh song of degrees most people view it
as probably having been set down following the remnant's return
from the captivity of Babylon. For in it we find the phrase, "the
captivity of Zion." This might just be so, because the sentiment
in the psalm is certainly very fitting to that occasion. But I feel
we need not limit this psalm to that particular event. Because in
our spiritual pursuit after God we encounter many captivities
and we experience many turnings and returnings. In our spiritual life we often feel as those who are *captured*. We ofttimes
sense that we are under a certain kind of *bondage* or *limitation*.
But then out of that bondage and limitation the Lord releases us.
The Lord liberates us, and thus we experience turnings and returnings. Hence spiritually speaking this period is marked by a

progressive turning or returning of Zion. During this stage of one's Christian experience the soul is progressively being delivered from the bondage of the flesh. In short, his soul is being set free for God. It is just as our Lord has said, "You shall know the truth and the truth shall set you free. If therefore the Son shall set you free, you shall be free indeed." There is a gradual emancipation of the soul from the hold of the flesh until it reaches that liberty of the sons of God which is in the Spirit.

To come to a real apprehension of the 126th Psalm we will need to understand the relationship between two metaphors which are employed in this psalm. One which we have mentioned already is "the captivity of Zion" and the other is "the sowing and the reaping." The psalm begins with the captivity of Zion or to put it more literally the turning or returning of Zion, and ends with a sowing and a reaping. On the surface these two metaphors appear to have no connection between them at all. The captivity of Zion; the sowing and the reaping; what relationship could they possibly have? By digging beneath the surface of things, though, we shall recognize that there *is* a connection, that they are speaking of one and the same thing.

Our soul can be likened to a seed, a very precious seed. We know that any grain, if it is ever to be increased and to be multiplied, must be sown. Yet for a farmer to scatter his seeds is not, in one sense, a very easy thing to do—especially if it be during a season of drought or of famine—because every seed is extremely valuable to the farmer and to his household. Each grain is considered to be food for his family. A farmer is therefore quite reluctant to scatter his seeds as though he were throwing them away to decay in the field and to disappear and become nothing. In this sense is it not an easy action for the farmer to take. Nevertheless, a farmer knows if he wants his seed to multiply that sowing them is the only way. He must throw away, scatter, and sow his precious seeds. He has to take grains of food away from himself and his family and discard them as it were upon the field and let them die; because this is the only way towards increase. And after the farmer scatters the seeds the life within their hard shells is then given the opportunity to emerge and to multiply. Otherwise—and though there be life indeed within the seed—that life is imprisoned within the hard shell. And if, though it is actually there, the life is imprisoned, it is limited. Only as the seed goes through death can there be multiplied life out of death.

Now this is an illustration of the captivity of Zion. Zion here represents those who love the Lord. It symbolizes the Christ-life which is in us. We know that the King dwells in Zion. We know it is there that God lives. So Zion can here represent the Christ-life which is in us, that life which is full of power, full of authority, full of strength; it is a glorious life, a triumphant life, an all-victorious life. This is the divine power which is within all who love Him. But—this life is imprisoned within us. Brethren, we possess the life of Christ within; yet it is surrounded there. We ourselves, the natural man, our flesh, acts as an outer shell; and within that shell is confined the life of Christ. If we ever want this power to be increased and to multiply, there is but one way for it to be done: the outer shell has to be broken; the outer shell must go through death; and this means that the flesh, this natural life of ours, must be brought to naught. Unless this self of ours has gone through death, the life of Christ—no matter how powerful *it* is—cannot express itself.

This is the problem in Christian lives today. We who have trusted in the Lord have His divine energy within. Yet why is it that the Lord's life is not being multiplied and increased? Why is it after ten, twenty, or even thirty years of belief in the Lord, there does not appear to be much growth, Christ is not increasingly multiplied in us? Why is it that what people can touch and feel and hear of us in our contact with them is not the indwelling Christ but is instead our natural fleshly self life? When our emotion is stirred why is it not the love of Christ which is expressed rather than our selfish love? And why is it not the mind of Christ that is manifested when we think rather than our own mind? Or when in the process of making a decision, why is it not the will of Christ which wills through our will instead of it being our own decision and our own willing? It is because in our everyday Christian experience the power and energy of Christ is *imprisoned* by us. It is because we ourselves—this flesh of ours

—forms a hard shell like a prison wall around the life of Christ within us. It cannot be released.

Recall how our Lord Jesus once exclaimed: "I have a baptism to be baptized with; and how am I straitened till it be accomplished!" (Luke 12.50) Even the Lord Jesus when on this earth felt that His body—think of it, *His* body!—seemed as a prison. He regarded Himself straitened, pressed, squeezed in, limited and confined; and He longed to be released, that His life might break out and flow. And we know that on the cross the Lord Jesus did experience His baptism; on the cross He *Himself* was broken as well as His body; and then His life was released. And we also know how powerful is that life. Call to mind how our Lord carefully explained to His disciples that unless a grain of seed falls into the ground and dies, it will remain alone; but if it dies it multiplies, it increases: even to a hundred-fold (John 12.24). And if this straitened condition was true of Jesus the holy Son of God, how much more must it be true of us who are of wicked unholy flesh. This wicked flesh of ours—whenever it is stirred and however it performs—is always in opposition to God. Hence how much more is the divine life within us imprisoned by *our* body of flesh.

Our soul can not only be likened to a seed; it can also be compared to a farmer. A farmer must carry the seed forth and scatter it. As was earlier indicated, he may be very reluctant, in the face of drought or of famine, to withhold these seeds from himself and his family and to scatter them throughout the field. Therefore does the writer say that he may "sow in tears"—the farmer scatters his seed with tears! Yet this sowing must he do. But when the rains come and the harvest time arrives, how he will then reap with rejoicing!

Brothers and sisters, are we willing to throw ourselves away as though losing our life? No one can force us, and no one can do it for us. Each one of us must—by a voluntary act of will—be willing to let this flesh be reduced to death. For did not the Lord teach us that if anyone wanted to follow Him, then "let *him* deny himself, take up his cross and follow me"? The Lord can persuade, the Lord can enable us to understand, the Lord is even able to arrange our circumstances and to attract us and to move

118

us with His love; but that is the limit of what He can do. He is not able, because He is not willing, to force us to go through death. *We* must undertake it ourselves.

The reason why in our Christian experience we find our flesh remains as usual, that there appears to be little progress, that the life of Christ is continuously encased within, is *not* because the grace of God is insufficient but because the key to it all lies within our own hand alone; it is because we are not disposed to give ourselves to Him and say, "Lord, I am willing to let my flesh go. I am ready to let the cross cut deep into all the activities of my flesh. I am willing to be broken that Christ may be released." Many is the time that our God actually arranges some environment; and through such environment this self of ours could be broken. Innumerable opportunities are afforded us so that our flesh could be dealt with. Yet we rebel against these circumstances. We fight against these environments. We refuse to give ourselves up. We insist instead on having our own will. We insist on doing our own thing. And because of this, these divine opportunities are lost to us.

In this second stage of our Christian life we shall notice on the one hand that God will give us revelation; God will by His word reveal to us the necessity for a brokenness and a going-to-death of our flesh. We are illumined to the need for such drastic dealings. And on the other hand we shall observe that the Spirit of God will arrange countless environments and events; and through these various ways we are given opportunities to have this brokenness worked out in our lives.

Why is it the case that before you know anything about the necessity of your flesh being dealt with, it seems your life is very smooth; there hardly appears to be anything which needs to be cut away. But how strange that upon being enlightened to the need of it you begin to encounter in your daily walk many matters hard to fathom: people, things, events, problems invade your path—in the home, around the office, at your school, on the street, in fact everywhere. It seems as if God has so arranged your life that you are put into many situations in which your self has either to be broken or else hardened. And the reason is that the resurrection life of Christ longs to be released. But the key is: we must be willing.

Notice the first verse: "When the Lord turned again the captivity of Zion, we were like them that dream." It should be pointed out that in the original it can be translated more accurately as follows: "In the Lord's turning to the turning of Zion, we are like them dreaming." Now what scene does such imagery as this cause to arise in our minds? Does it not create in our thought that scene of the rushing out of the father to meet the returning of the prodigal son? That was a meeting at the half-way point, so to speak. And this is exactly the picture which comes to mind by this verse. Here can be seen two turnings: one, the turning of *Zion;* and the other, the turning of *the Lord.* And as they both *turn,* they *meet!* And when they meet, you are as one *dreaming!*

Each one of us must be like that prodigal son. We remember how this son at first turned his back on his father and on his father's house and went to a far country. There he squandered all his goods; he was reduced to poverty; he had nothing to eat. In this very low position of starvation and near death the prodigal came to himself and said: "In my father's house there is abundance; yet here I am starving to death! I know what I will do. I will rise up, I will go back, I will confess my sin, I will ask my father to receive me again." And *he*, the prodigal son, *turned*. Not that it was the father who went to the distant country and took him back. The father waited at home—at the door, to be sure; yet at home nonetheless. He was waiting for the son to turn. But as soon as the son himself turned, what happened next? You find that the father ran to him. The father ran to meet him. Now that is the turning of the *Lord*. Brothers and sisters, there must initially be within us a willingness to turn, a disposition to return from captivity; there must be within us a desire: that we do not want Christ to be imprisoned in us anymore. Such a desire must first be present within us.

Do you have *that* desire? Or do you feel it is all right for Christ to remain sealed off within with no opportunity to express Himself and to be increased in your life? Many Christians are content with just such a situation. Their thought is that as long as they are saved, as long as they are destined for heaven if they die, that this will be sufficient. They are not concerned if Christ be imprisoned within them or not. They want to express themselves and give no opportunity for Christ to express Himself through them. If we are content as this then there can be no fruit, there can be no multiplication or increase. But if we turn in our hearts and refuse to allow Christ to be confined any further in us, if we allow our flesh to be put to death by the working of the cross, if we are willing to have every activity of our soul—whether it be of mind, emotion or will—purified and delivered from the domination of self: if we, in short, have a heart-turning towards the Lord such as this, then as *we* turn *He* turns to us. He meets us half-way. If we draw nigh to God, He will draw nigh to us (James 4.8). God in very fact meets us. And when such a thing happens in our experience we will be as those who dream.

Do you wonder why the psalmist puts it in such a figurative way as that? It is because we all, you know, have our dreams. We have our bad dreams, we have our good dreams too. Our good ones are those which represent something we really want but do not have. And so, it comes in our dream!—it is realized in our dreaming! Dear brothers and sisters, *what* is our dream? What is the dream of the Christian? Let it never be forgotten that as Christians ours is and can be just one dream: the hope of glory: Christ in *us*, the hope of glory. We in other words dream of glory. But how does that glory come? It comes in a most unexpected way. It comes as we offer ourselves to the Lord and say, "Lord, I am willing to be reduced, to be broken, to be dealt with, to go through death." And when anyone is willing for this, the Lord meets him, and such a one will find that His life is fresh and powerful within him. *That* is glory. And it causes that soul to feel as one who is dreaming: It is too good to be true, nevertheless it *is* true.

Have you ever had these experiences in your Christian life? Is it not true that sometimes you feel, Well, If I am dealt with by the Lord, if I give up what I want, if I give up what I would decide to have, if I give up this thing and that thing, I will be reduced to such sadness and misery and loss. Is not this our way of thinking? And yet, so unexpectedly, you will discover that when you are truly willing to give yourself up to the Lord the life of Christ within you becomes so real and powerful, so refreshing, so comfortable and comforting that you are as one who dreams. Has this ever been your experience? This is the way the Lord is set free and increased in us.

When such a thing happens, then is "our mouth filled with laughter and our tongue with shouts of joy." We laugh! Frequently you do not have the right words to describe your feeling; but when you laugh your inner feeling finds its expression. It is too much; you do not know what to say; *but* you simply laugh. And your tongue is filled with rejoicing! You are full of joy because the *Lord* has met you. All the pains and sorrows of captivity are now forgotten for they are more than sufficiently compensated because the life of the Lord has been released. His life of resurrection has become to you refreshment and strength.

No doubt this stage of our experience can be compared to the experience of that virgin in the Song of Solomon which runs from section 2.8 to 3.5. We know that this portion of the Song of Songs represents the second stage of her experience with the Lord. The first stage was marked by love-seeking—love-satisfaction. She had entered into a closer relationship with her Lord, a relationship which had become more intimate and deeper than was the case before. At the present moment, though, the Lord is calling her to remove herself from her own confinement, for He stands behind the wall and peeps through the windows, encouraging her to arise and go elsewhere. She instead lies on her bed and refuses to budge. She wants to find her Lord within her own surroundings; she asks *Him* to *turn and return to her.* He, however, does not return, nor can she find Him within her wall. In the end, love compels her to rise up and go away. And as *she* turns, she finds Him. Oh! the joy of finding Him again! How she holds His feet lest she lose Him once more.

Brothers and sisters, if you are taken out of yourself, if the cross cuts into your flesh, if the cross puts you to death, it invariably releases the Lord within you onto resurrection ground. And when such an event occurs in your life, the latter part of verse 2 will be your experience: "Then said they among the nations, 'The Lord hath done great things for them.'" If these things happen in your life, the world around you will recognize that such a transaction has taken place in your life. The nations will themselves see the work of God in the soul. We need not in the least tell them. They shall know it themselves. They will know it is something which the Lord has done in us and not something which we have done. They cannot help but acknowledge that God has done a great work: for what greater feat can there be than that of the life of Christ being incorporated, constituted, and then manifested in the saints! It is far more wonderful than the work of Creation, as great an act as that truly was. When the remnant returned from captivity the hand of the Lord was so definitely upon them that the enemies had to confess that the Lord had done great things for them. (See Neh. 6.15,16) Even so and in greater degree must the world marvel at the increase, multiplication and release of Christ's life in the saints. They will say, These people have followed Jesus. They see Christ in us. And this is the greatest work of God in the world.

Reflect upon the order here: first, the nations say, and then, we say. Before we open our mouth to utter a word people shall know! How far more effective if our life speaks first before our lips speak forth. Let our life so shine before the nations that they can behold God and His work in us (Matt. 5.16). Then our witnessing by mouth and bearing testimony to the mercy of God will be more effectual. Yes, we will have to open our mouth eventually, for we cannot and we will not hide the grace of God. We will humbly acknowledge, even as the psalmist in verse 3 did, that it is the Lord Who has wrought great things for us whereof we are glad.

This song can roughly be divided into two parts: what we have just mentioned is the first part, from verse 1 to verse 3; the second portion begins with verse 4 and ends with verse 6. In the first section, the psalmist narrates what the Lord has done for him in the turning of his captivity—it is a narrative of something which has already occurred. But the second part is a prayer: "Turn again our captivity, O Lord, as the streams in the south." It is a pleading for a turning of captivity—a prayer for something which is yet to happen. The first section tells us of past deliverance and emancipation. The second section is a prayer looking

forward to future deliverance and emancipation. The first portion is the beginning of the soul being set free from the bondage
of self. The second portion is a prayer for the completion of that
work.

Thus this division may be explained in two ways. One is that
past deliverance will stimulate a desire for further deliverance.
And the other is that the turning at the beginning is still incom-
plete and needs to be perfected. Both are correct, for in our experience we do need to know the working of the cross in an
ever deepening way so that we may be brought ever increasingly
into the flow of the Lord's life. We have to be delivered and
liberated, emancipated and freed—gradually, step by step, until
we are wholly united with God in freedom, until we arrive at the
full liberty of the sons of God. Hence the psalmist continues with
a prayer: "Turn again our captivity, O Lord, as the streams in
the south."

The simile used to describe this turning of captivity is: "as the
streams in the south." The southern part of Palestine is a decidedly dry place. There *are* streams there, yes; but during the
dry season all of them dry up. And since these river beds are
thus laid bare, people can easily walk through them. And since
there is no water, there can be no vegetation. It becomes extremely dry! But then suddenly the rainy season returns. And
the result is that every one of the dry river beds is filled once
again with water. They become full of life, they commence to
flow joyously once again, and vegetation begins to sprout up all
around. Here is another very appropriate figure to represent our
inward condition. Our soul is like the bed of a stream. It was
made for God and for Him to fill. Did not Augustine once say:
"O God, You made us for Yourself, and our hearts can find no
peace until they rest in You"?

Brothers and sisters, this soul of ours is like a river bed: we
are meant for water, we are made for God to fill us: and He Himself is our water, He is the Water of Life to us. Yet very often we
find the condition of our soul to be like those dried up stream
beds in the Palestinian southland. Many a time in our spiritual
experience we feel as though God is not with us—as though we
are barren, as though we have dried up. We feel so aimless and

124

purposeless, we are so dissatisfied with ourselves. Many a time we feel as though our soul has been laid bare, and so we want to hide ourselves; but there is no place to run. We sense there is no life in us. We are in a season of drought. Everything about us is arid and parched. We are ashamed of ourselves and yet there is no hiding. Do we not sometimes feel it to be that way? This is none other than the experience of the cross, for the cross reduces us and lays us bare before God.

How difficult, dear people, how very difficult it is indeed for us, when feeling that way, to give ourselves to God to be dealt with by the cross. When we are filled with life, when we are running over with the sense of the presence of God, when we have just experienced some great blessing, it is relatively easy for us to say, "O Lord, I am willing! I am willing to let go of myself, I am ready to let go of this and of that, I am willing to let Christ have the preeminence in my life." At that moment it is comparatively easier. But during the time of drought when our soul seems like a dried up river bed, it can be likened to that farmer in the time of famine—how reluctant he is to scatter the seed! But this is precisely the hour when we simply must scatter the seed by faith.

During the second stage of our Christian experience we learn this matter of faith. Even though we sometimes feel as parched as the streams in the south, nevertheless, by faith we still offer ourselves to Him and say, "Lord, do whatever You like with me. I do not want to express *myself*. I want *Christ* to be increased. Oh, that I may decrease." If, when in a time of such dryness and flatness, you continue by faith to put yourself in the hand of God and let His cross work in your life, you shall soon experience the latter rain commencing to fall. And then, you shall be filled with living water, full of life and overflowing. Instantly His life flows in and floods you with blessings. He has come back to you in resurrection power, though in reality He has never left you. The streams are full of water once again. And consequently in verse 5 we read that when one sows the seed he may have to sow with tears; but thank God, when he reaps he reaps with shouts of joy. He reaps with rejoicing. The sowing is at the time of drought; the reaping, after a season of rain.

And the last verse: "He that goeth forth and weepeth, bearing the seed for sowing, shall doubtless come again with rejoicing, bringing his sheaves with him." There is an emphasis in the original which unfortunately cannot be fully set down in the translation before us. However, in order to approximate the force of the original, someone has rendered this verse as follows: "He goeth forth, he goeth forth, weeping, bearing seed for scattering; he cometh again, he cometh again, with rejoicing, bearing his sheaves." Brothers and sisters, do you catch the force of that rendering? *He goeth forth! He goeth forth!!* Is *our* soul going forth? Are we too stretching out towards God? Let *us* go forth —with tears, yes; scattering, yes; but let us nonetheless continue, let us be persistent; let us persevere in going forth and in scattering. And shortly thereafter we shall come back, we shall come back again and again with rejoicing, bringing with us numerous sheaves—plentiful fruits in our hands. May this be true in each one of our lives.

Our Father, how we praise and thank You that You do intend to teach us the lesson of faith. You do want us to scatter the seed and let it die, that it may bring forth much fruit. O Father, we do pray that our eyes may be opened to see the necessity of this going through death of the flesh, that we may enter upon the resurrection life of our Lord Jesus. We do pray this day: "Let us decrease, and may Christ increase." We ask in the Name of our Lord Jesus. Amen.

Building and Growing

PSALM 127
A Song of Degrees for Solomon.

1 Unless the Lord build the house, they labour in vain that build it: unless the Lord watches over the city, the watchman stays awake in vain.

2 It is vain for you to rise up early, to sit up late, to eat the bread of sorrows: for so he giveth his beloved sleep.

3 Lo, children are an heritage of the Lord: and the fruit of the womb a reward.

4 As arrows are in the hands of a mighty man; so are children of the youth.

5 Happy is the man that hath his quiver full of them: they shall not be ashamed, when they shall speak with the enemies in the gate.

This psalm stands in the center of the fifteen Songs of Degrees. It is the only one among them attributed to Solomon. Yet whether it is written for or of or by Solomon, we do not know. But the very thought and expression of this song are most certainly his (compare, for example, with Proverbs 10.22 marginal rendering). For the most prominent element in view in it is the thought of building; and this most naturally reminds us at once of King Solomon, because he was the one used by the Lord to build Him a temple in Jerusalem. This, then, is the opinion held by some. Other students of the Scriptures hold to the belief that Psalm 127 may have reference not to Solomon's temple but to the second temple rebuilt by the remnant who returned to Jerusalem from the Babylonian captivity. And that in this psalm they enter into the feeling and sentiment of Solomon who has become their exemplar. Nevertheless, whatever be its background, we readily recognize this song of degrees as representing yet another step of advance in our spiritual experience with the Lord. For the idea of "build" or "building" is considerably evident at this stage in anyone's walk.

Yet we must keep in mind several things in relation to this matter of building. *First,* that there can be no building in the truest sense unless prior to it there is revelation. This song is a part of, and is descriptive of, the second period in our spiritual experience. We have learned that this is a period of revelation and enlightenment. Unless there is revelation there can be no building. How can a person construct a house if he does not first of all possess an architectural plan or blueprint? Even should you be intent upon erecting a very small object and not bother to set the plan down on paper, nonetheless it must at least be in your mind. You must at least visualize some idea in your mind's eye before you can commence to physically create anything.

We remember, do we not, how God gave the *vision* of His house to David first; and later, Solomon was chosen to *build* the temple. The same order was true with Peter. He confessed the Lord as the Son of the living God; and only after this heavenly revelation did our Lord Jesus declare to him: "I will build my church upon this rock." In the experience of Peter there came firstly the revelation of the Lord and afterwards, the fashioning of the church. The same principle applies to Paul. Paul is called to be a master builder: he is used by the Lord to plant His churches everywhere. But before he can build the church of God he must himself see the vision of Christ on his way to Damascus. Hence let us bear in mind that there can be no building unless prior to it there is revelation, vision, a seeing. It is only in the principle of illumination that the spiritual process of "building" or "growing" is made possible. Without a seeing of the Lord, without a perception of the Lord's purpose and His counsel and His plan, there can be no establishment of the church.

Second. You cannot build unless the war is over, unless there is peace. You cannot construct during wartime. You can only do so when there is *peace* in the land. David was not allowed to erect the temple; he desired very much to fashion God a house;

yet he was not permitted to do it. Why? Because he was a man of war. He had shed much blood. He and the nation of Israel were in constant conflict and battles. But out of the battles and out of the victories David gathered much spoil; he gathered lots of materials, garnered many provisions, and made numerous preparations *for* the constructing of the house. And after the land had peace, then came Solomon. Solomon was a son of peace. And he was chosen and commanded to build the temple of God.

Spiritually this is always the case. If there is conflict, either internally or externally, no construction can occur. It is only when the peace of God reigns in our heart and reigns in our midst that the building of the church can take place and continue. On the other hand, though, let us not lose sight of the fact that *there must be war*, and then peace. There is a time for war, and there is a time for peace: a time for tearing down, and a time for building up (see Ecclesiastes 3). We cannot erect God's house and the church cannot be built up unless before everything else there comes a time when the cross can work deeply in our lives, when it can commence to tear down the natural energy, the natural wisdom, the natural strength—whatever belongs to our flesh. The old must be demolished, the rubbish must be removed first, before there can be any actual building up of the church of God in beauty and glory. Hence this psalm speaks of an experience which follows directly upon that of the preceding psalm. Peace has at last come to reign in the heart: the process of building or growing is now in order.

And then *third*. When we think of "build" or "growth" we are apt to conceive of these in very personal terms. Oh, that *I* may grow in grace and in the knowledge of Christ! Oh, that *I* may arrive at spiritual maturity! Oh, that *I* may be built up and made strong! We so often approach this matter of establishment and growth within the framework of ourselves as individuals. But brothers and sisters, this is only partially true. We must of course grow individually, we must be built up personally. Yet according to the Scriptures, when the thought of build or grow is under consideration it is far more than personal; it is additionally corporate in nature and in purpose. We all of us are members one of another. How are we going to grow? Do we merely mature individually, each by himself? No! The whole body with all its members grow together towards a full grown man. They grow relatedly, and they grow proportionally. If it is purely on the individual plane, then suppose my hand wants to grow and it develops so rapidly that it develops out of all proportion to the rest of my body. What is the effect? We will discover that it has become a very ugly object.

Therefore we must remember that the scriptural concept of grow or build is a corporate matter. We must mature in a *related* way. We must be built up together and be fitted together. During this stage of enlightenment the sense of corporateness will be increasing all the time. We must grow together in Christ that we may form the habitation of God, that we may be the body of Christ (Eph. 4.15,16). And if we bear these three thoughts in mind it will help us to understand this song of degrees much better. Let us keep these three matters continually before us as we consider this psalm further.

At the very outset we read these words: "Unless the Lord build the house, they labour in vain that build it." Solomon is going to fashion the house of God. But he has learned one lesson. It is an extremely important and very valuable lesson, one which every soul must learn if he wants to build. And that lesson is: unless the *Lord* build the house, in vain do its workers labor in it. If you desire to build, you must see to it that it is the Lord Himself Who builds. It would appear as though *you* are the one who is going to be building, and yet, it is the Lord Himself Who builds. If you intend to enter upon this construction business but leave the Lord out by trying to labor all by yourself, you shall soon learn the sentence of judgment given by God in the Scripture upon such wisdom and power of the flesh: it is all in vain. Was not the tower of Babel erected by men, but they nevertheless labored in vain. Three times in this psalm do we find invoked this word of emptiness: It is in vain! It is in vain!! It is in vain!!!

If, in constructing something in the world, you put your entire strength and being into it, you may succeed. The way people in the world go about it is spelled out vividly in the second verse— "rise up early, sit up late, eat the bread of sorrows." Should you want to build something you will rise up early and lie down late. Why? In order that you may devote more time to the project. Moreover, you consume the bread of sorrows. Even while you are eating, the thought of building cannot escape you! Even as you lay on your night couch you experience sleepless hours because you are forever thinking of what you have to do in your building. In short, this is a description of the *effort* which one puts into laboring: rise up early, lie down late, eat the bread of sorrows. If you carry on like this, you *will* succeed *in the world*, because you will have invested your entire person in it.

In *spiritual* building, however, it is different. In the building of the church, the house of God, even should you rise up early and lie down late and eat the bread of sorrows, you will not succeed. It is altogether in vain. We have witnessed many servants of God who, really having a heart for the Lord, truly labor hard. They have the best of intentions and exert the greatest of efforts. They sincerely want to help God, they genuinely desire to do something worthy, they eagerly seek to plant the church here and to plant the church there. They try very hard indeed: they rise up early, go to sleep late, eat the bread of sorrows, and exert themselves to the extreme. But what is the outcome of it all? Many of them experience nervous breakdowns or even physical breakdowns, and the house remains unbuilt. And the reason? Because the church which is the house of God is *not* an organizational entity. If the church is simply something organizational or institutional, then even without the Lord you will succeed should you devote all your strength to it and work enormously at it. The church, however, is an *organism*. The house of God is something living—it is something spiritual— it is something heavenly. So that unless the Lord is in the building of it, all is vain, no matter how much time you put in or how much wisdom you employ or how much strength you bring to bear. It is at best a striving after wind!

This does not mean, though, that we are to adopt the attitude of doing nothing: let us be lazy and idle: let us be passive and merely sit and wait because the Lord will do everything: let us simply leave it entirely to Him. Brethren, this is certainly *not* the thought being conveyed here. This Solomon, you know, is the same person who has written the Book of Proverbs. A cursory glance through that book will easily confirm the fact that he has much to say concerning laziness and idleness on the one side and diligence on the other. How Solomon exhorts us to be diligent and not to be lazy! How he implores us to be ever alert and keen, and not to be loitering about! (See, for example, 6.9,10; 31.27) Can the Solomon of Proverbs ever teach us in the 127th Psalm to be idle, to be lazy, to be passive? Can he be instructing us here to do nothing but simply sit down, wait, and go to sleep? Certainly Solomon cannot mean that!

What then does he mean here? How are we going to reconcile these two matters? On the one hand the Scriptures say that *we are* the builders. In 1 Corinthians 3.10 Paul affirms that he is a master-builder—a foreman; he has laid the foundation for another to build on; but let each take care, he cautions, how he builds upon that foundation. In one sense, therefore, we are all builders, we are all laborers. We are not only the building, we are also the builders. So on the one side, yes, we must build. On the other side, however, the Lord is the builder. He said: "*I* will build my church." Unless the Lord builds, it is in vain for the laborers to labor in its construction. Let us not be misled: the Lord *is* the builder. Abraham looked for a city with foundations, the builder of which is God Himself (Heb. 11.10). How then are we going to reconcile these two sides? One side, *we* are the builders; the other side, *God* is the builder. How can one harmonize this apparent contradiction?

We must build; there is no doubt about that; but how? Not by plunging into it wholly by ourselves and attempting to use our own wisdom and strength. Not at all! We *are* to build; but the way to do it is: let God build *through* us. If we allow the Lord to work in our lives, if we allow Him to work out from us, if we simply cooperate with Christ Who is the power and the wisdom and allow Him to work out through us His wisdom and His power, then, dear brethren, we will witness the church being built. What we need to do is to yield ourselves to the Lord. What is required of us is to trust in Him completely, neither trusting in our wisdom nor in our strength. What we must do is to cease from our struggling and striving, and enter into His rest: "For he that is entered into (God's) rest, he also hath ceased from his own works, as God did from his" (Heb. 4.10). Hence the first part of verse 2 in the psalm before us is a picture of the energy of the flesh upon which the cross of Christ must bear down to bring it to naught. We must allow the cross to crush our strength and wisdom, that we may wholly rely upon Him. Only by such a Calvary experience can we ever open ourselves to God and be found waiting upon Him and allowing Him to work His will out through us. We shall then be cooperating with Him, and we shall then be working under Him.

Coming now to the second part of verse 2 we notice a very unusual statement: "He giveth his beloved sleep." Can this signify that while other people rise up early, lie down late and eat the bread of sorrows the beloved ones of God—His children—simply sleep and do nothing? It cannot mean that at all! What then does it signify here? It only indicates this: that the Lord wishes to remind us that in the matter of building it is not how much time we put into it nor how much thought, concern or even sorrow we expend which counts, but that it is a matter of the grace and the mercy of God: He gives His beloved ones sleep. While others hope, yet in vain, to gain exclusively by their own labor, the beloved ones of God receive from the Lord as though they are asleep when it occurs. In other words, they know not how, but somehow the Lord *sovereignly* gives success and accomplishment to them.

Someone once observed that this verse reminded him particularly of Solomon, both in regard to his other name and to the promise of prosperity communicated to him in a dream. You will recollect that Solomon had a second name, Jedidiah (2 Sam. 12.25). The meaning of Jedidiah is: "beloved of the Lord." And what does it say in our verse here? He gives His *beloved* sleep. Moreover, it says that the Lord grants His beloved *sleep*. Remember what happened once when Solomon went to Gibeon and offered sacrifices to the Lord? During the night after Solomon fell asleep the Lord appeared to him in a vision and said, "Solomon, what do you want? You may ask anything and I will give it to you." In reply Solomon said, "Lord, You have been very good to me. You have taken my father David, and now

133

You have set me upon his throne; but I am only a little child. I do not know how to come in and go out among Your people, a great people." "Lord," Solomon continued, "I desire but one thing: that You will grant me an understanding heart, a hearing heart; that You will give me discernment so that I may judge Your people according to Your will." The Lord was very pleased with Solomon's request and accordingly said to him: "You do not plead that your enemies may be put down; you do not request riches or wealth; you do not petition Me for long life; you only ask for understanding, a hearing heart, in order that you may understand My will and that you may judge My people." How the Lord was pleased with Solomon! And consequently the Lord declared to him: "I have heard you: I will give you wisdom, a wisdom which surpasses that of anyone who is living." Hence the renowned wisdom of Solomon, which has sometimes been called into question, is more than probable. It is in fact wisdom from the Lord. But please observe that Solomon is accorded this surpassing wisdom *in his sleep* (1 Kings 3.5-15). My dear friends, do you grasp the point of this verse? While others are zealously doing things completely in their own strength and by their own cleverness, the beloved ones of God are being given wisdom, as it were, in their sleep. That is, they are supplied with wisdom and strength from above.

Someone else has reminded us of the very first sleep mentioned in the Bible and what happened. For this we must go all the way back to Adam. At the beginning God creates Adam; but He cannot find a helpmate for him; consequently God puts Adam to sleep! Please notice, though, that this is not an unproductive sleep; it is not a sleeping which accomplishes nothing. On the contrary, in Adam's sleep much is accomplished. God is the One Who puts him to sleep; and while he is asleep, God is at work. God takes a rib from Adam and *builds*—here again is the very word of which we have been speaking—and builds a woman with Adam's rib!

Oh how beautiful if we can see it. Two contrasting pictures are drawn for us here. In the one case are those people who busily engage themselves in all sorts of undertakings; who, with extremely good intention and infinitely hard work, try to do something for God, but all in their own power and wisdom; and the result is, vanity. In the other case can be found those beloved ones of God, those who truly know God. With them, though, it seems as if God puts them to sleep; it seems as though God makes them rest; and while they enter into the rest of God, *God* does the work. And as they are resting in God, He builds a woman. Now we know that Eve is a figure of the church, she is a type of the house of God. Brothers and sisters, we must enter into the rest of God. And as we continue in His rest, believing and trusting that God has accomplished the work already—that He is the One Who has already done the work—then, at that very moment, in sleep He giveth; and the house of God is verily built.

From the figure of a house, the figure of children abruptly appears—suddenly the picture is changed. We read in verse 3: "Lo, the children are an (inheritance) from the Lord, and the fruit of the womb is his reward." Is there any connection between this and the preceding figure? The previous one concerns itself with building and how to build; now all of a sudden the picture emerges as "children, inheritance, and reward." What have these two ideas to do with each other?

We must not forget that building is not simply an external matter; it is additionally a matter of inward growth. Building here is not something organizational nor institutional but organic; it is the growth of life. The concepts of growth, multiplication, increase, and reproduction are invariably related to life. And "children" are the expression of the growth of life; they are in themselves a demonstration of the increase of life. So that if you meditate sufficiently long enough on these two figures you will come to see that the first concept of *building* and the second concept of *growing* are actually one. It is through the increase of life that the church is built.

When we speak of a house we may be thought to mean a place in which people can live, that is, a habitation; or, the term house may be thought to refer to those who are in the habitation, in short, the household or the family. Once again two thoughts are combined. House may mean on the one hand a dwelling-place or, on the other, may signify those who live in the dwelling place: they become the household of God. Hence we see this matter of the increase of life. Therefore, to the question, How is the church looked upon as being built?, must we not say that it is when there is an increase of life? Is it not when the life of Christ is being *increased* among His own? Then it is that we witness the church being built. It is life, something inward.

Let us next consider "inheritance" and "reward." "Children are an inheritance from the Lord, and the fruit of the womb is his reward." When you inherit anything, do you work for it? Do you earn it? It is obvious by its very definition that inheritance cannot be based upon your work or your merit: inheritance is based upon the work and the merit of the one who gives to you. In a word, it is a gift, it is something freely given. Another has worked, but you are to inherit it free. What then is a reward? "The fruit of the womb is his reward." Do you work for a reward? You most certainly do! If you want to obtain a gift, it is something freely given; but if you want to receive a reward, you must do something to prove you are worthy, that you deserve that reward. Accordingly, we once again observe two thoughts which are joined together: on the one side, gift, the free gift of God; on the other side, reward, as though we must work for it. Children are an inheritance from the Lord and the fruit of the womb is a reward.

Brothers and sisters, how is the life of Christ increased within us? On the one hand, it is the gift of God. Apart from God we cannot make ourselves grow a single inch. It is God Who makes the difference. It is God Who gives the increase: it is His free gift to us which enables us to grow in Christ and to mature. Yet on the other hand why is it that some develop faster while others more slowly? Surely there is no partiality to the gift of God. In the final analysis, it is a matter of our *seeking* Him. Do you seek for life? Are you earnestly desiring after the Lord with your entire heart? If you seek Him with the whole heart you are given the life of Christ in abundance. But if you do not seek, if it is of little or no concern to you whether or not you grow in Christ, if you regard the matter lackadaisically and idly, then can there be any wonder that you do not grow in Christ? Hence what we find in verse 3 are as it were the two sides of one thing: the increase of life is the *gift* of God, yes; yet it appears as if it is also a *reward*, because God bestows upon those who earnestly seek Him.

"As arrows are in the hand of a mighty man; so are children of the youth." Children are portrayed as arrows. If a person is in need of arrows he cannot simply go to the forest and attempt to find them about him on the ground. They have to be made and formed and sharpened. Trees abound. . .and therefore you may easily be able to find wood as material for an arrow; nevertheless, you will have to form it and sharpen it before such material becomes an arrow. Children, we know, need to be, like arrows, disciplined, formed, and sharpened. Much in today's modern method of letting the children alone to grow freely and spontaneously too often results in their developing into wild thorns and thistles and not arrows. Those of us who have children need to see the importance of bringing up our offspring in the nurture and fear of the Lord. Children need to be nurtured and disciplined, children need to be taught and instructed, formed and sharpened before they can become arrows in the hand of the mighty One to be used by the Lord for His purpose.

Is it not the same thing with our spiritual life? Spiritual life, to be sure, is a matter of growth; the life within us obviously needs to grow; but let us not overlook the fact that spiritual life has to likewise be disciplined. A life of flesh which is not trained grows wild. In the same manner must our spiritual life be trained and regulated that it too may not become wild but may be conformed to the life image of Christ. This is the reason the cross must operate in our lives. Much stripping, much straightening, much sharpening is required. The cross has to be applied to our natural man—to our emotion, thought and will—to our carnal energy and strength. We must be disciplined like that. Unless we are disciplined as are the children of youth we cannot be formed and sharpened so as to be arrows in the hand of the mighty Lord and so be used by Him.

"Happy is the man that hath his quiver full of them." If the quiver of our Lord is filled with arrows, happy is He! Our Lord is the mighty Man. And He has a quiver: the church. The church is His instrument and His vessel. But there has to be in it many sharp arrows—those whose life within is disciplined, is increased, is multiplied and matured. A matured Christian is as a sharp arrow in the quiver of the Lord, and He can make much use of it. The reason we are not much used, or not used at all, by the Lord is because we have not yet become arrows. We are too immature; we are too dull; we are not sharpened; we are far too rough. He *cannot* use us. How important, therefore, that we be matured in the Lord. How necessary that we be sharpened and disciplined so that He can use us.

By way of conclusion the writer of this psalm asserts that "they shall not be ashamed when they shall speak with the enemies in the gate." What strength! With matured life as the backing, our speech will be strong and effectual. There is force behind our words. And the force and power is in that maturity of life. Matured life is the provision of the Lord against enemies. Matthew 16 records that our Lord said to His disciples: "I will build my church upon this rock." And He then followed up by avowing that "the gates of hades shall not prevail against it." Here is enunciated by our Lord the fact that a conflict rages in this universe. A conflict rages between the Lord and *His* enemy, the devil. But if the quiver of our Lord Jesus is filled with arrows, then when He speaks He does so with power. He will speak with the enemy in the gate and not be ashamed. The gates of hades shall not prevail against the quiver of our Lord. On the contrary, the *church* shall prevail at the gate. Oh that we may grow in Christ. Oh that we may be built up together in order that the enemy may be defeated and the Lord's Name be exalted.

The second stage of our spiritual experience is a period characterized on the one hand by the working of the cross towards the tearing down of what is of the flesh. It is a destroying of the natural old realm. But on the other hand it is a period distinguished by a definite building up. It is a building up in resurrection life, a being established in the new realm. And in it all it is the Lord Who is doing the building. We are simply cooperating with Him. Furthermore, this matter of building up is more than one of external testimony; it is a matter of internal growth: we must be under discipline, we must grow together, we must be fitted and built up together. Then and only then can we become a corporate vessel and instrument in the hands of the Lord that He may be glorified. May we take to heart the lessons of this song of degrees.

Our heavenly Father, how we praise and thank You for reminding us today that unless YOU build, in vain do we labor in it. Yet how full of praise and thanksgiving we are, because You nonetheless give us rest in Yourself; by our trusting, confiding, and completely committing ourselves into Your hands You are able to build through us until You obtain a house for Yourself and a city for Your testimony. O Father, we pray that the lesson Solomon has learned may also be learned by us. As we offer ourselves afresh, we ask You to discipline us, to chasten us, form and sharpen us as true arrows in Your quiver so that we may serve You and honor You and that You may gain glory in the church. We ask all in the Name of our Lord Jesus. Amen.

Full of the Spirit and Very Fruitful

PSALM 128

A Song of Degrees.

1 Blessed is every one that feareth the Lord; that walketh
in his ways.
2 For thou shalt eat the labour of thine hands: happy
shalt thou be, and it shall be well with thee.
3 Thy wife shall be as a fruitful vine within thine house:
thy children like olive plants round about thy table.
4 Behold, that thus shall the man be blessed that feareth
the Lord.
5 The Lord shall bless thee out of Zion: and may thou
see the good of Jerusalem all the days of thy life.
6 Yea, may thou see thy children's children. Peace be upon
Israel!

A comparison of this psalm with the previous one will distinctly
show that Psalm 128 in several respects is definitely a degree
higher. The thought of Psalm 127 is continued and developed in
Psalm 128 while at the same time advancement is made in the
ascent of the soul towards God. We are instructed by Psalm 127
as to the vanity of our labor if the Lord is not in it. No matter
how we may try to work—rising up early, going to bed late, eating
the bread of sorrows—the net result of it all is vanity, because it
is undertaken in the energy of the flesh. The Lord cannot be in
it. But when we turn to Psalm 128 we discover that the soul can
enjoy the labor of his hands. His labor is recognized, his labor
produces fruit, he may enjoy his work. What can account for this
difference? It is due to the fact that by the time of Psalm 128

the soul is no longer laboring in the energy of his flesh but is working in the power of the Holy Spirit.

In the previous psalm the children are pictured as arrows. If a man has his quiver filled with them he is found triumphant and victorious when he speaks with his enemies in the gate. There the children are presented to us as arrows, objects which are sharp and powerful; and so the impression the reader is left with is one of an atmosphere of *war and conflict*. Arrows are not necessary if one is not engaged in war or in conflict! But in Psalm 128 the children are depicted as olive plants round about the table. How totally different here! All is peaceful and prosperous, contented, satisfied and happy.

In Psalm 127 the psalmist looks upon children, the second generation of them, as an inheritance from the Lord, as a reward from God. But in the succeeding psalm the term used is "children's children": the writer sees beyond to the third generation, just as Jacob foreglimpsed his grandchildren before he went to be with the Lord. It is plainly a degree higher.

The earlier psalm laid stress upon building. By contrast the emphasis here is upon the *way* it is built and upon *what* is being built.

The feeling one derives from Psalm 127 is more or less a negative one. Its repeated terms are negative in tone—"unless" and "vain"; that is, Unless the Lord build the house, it is in vain for anyone to labor: Unless the Lord keep the city, it is in vain for the keeper to watch. Its approach is very negative. It tells us that unless the Lord is in our doings they will end each one in vanity. They must instead originate with the sovereign grace of God. Now I do hope we have learned this lesson. Because though it all may seem highly negative, it is nonetheless a very significant lesson. In all our undertakings and in all our ways, no matter how good the intention nor how diligent the labor, unless the Lord is in it throughout it will be entirely vain if done in the energy of our flesh. That is Psalm 127. But in coming to Psalm 128 you find the approach to be altogether positive. You do not find vanity: you find fruitfulness instead. And this is because the ascending soul is now living and walking and working in the

Holy Spirit. And when this is the case, everything is full of fruits. It brings much glory to the Lord.

Clearly, therefore, we cannot enter into the experience of Psalm 128 if we have not as yet passed through the experience of the preceding psalm. We *must* come out of Psalm 127; that is, we must come out of the realm of the flesh and the energy of the flesh before we can ever hope to enter into the power and energy of the Holy Spirit.

This ninth song of degrees breaks forth with the word "blessed." Whenever we think of this word most probably its meaning is not too definite to us. Actually, the word blessed in the original means "happy." We all know what happy means; so that instead of Blessed we can say: "Happy is every one that feareth the Lord": "Happy is every one that walketh in his ways." Yet we realize that those who do not know the Lord may not agree with this assessment at all. May they not say, Well now, if a person *fears* the Lord he must undoubtedly come into a kind of bondage; and consequently he cannot do what he would like to do, go wherever he would like to go, nor speak as he would like to speak. In other words, to those who do not know the Lord, or to those who are simple and inexperienced, the fear of the Lord seems to them a great bondage and limitation. But to those who do know the Lord, to those who are experienced in His ways, it is quite another story. They know way down in their hearts that as a matter of fact the fear of the Lord is happiness. Many view the fear of the Lord as bondage, the way of the Lord as being hard and dull. To the flesh it is quite so. But it is not that way to those who have genuinely known the Lord.

The joy of *this* world is fleeting, and bitter at the end. But real happiness, real joy, the everlasting and peaceful sort, derives from the *fear* of the Lord. True happiness is only obtained by those who fear the Lord and walk in His ways. The tenor of the whole Book of Psalms is built around this particular premise. If you turn to but the first psalm you will find that it commences with: "*Blessed*—Happy—is the man that walketh not in the counsel of the ungodly, nor standeth in the way of sinners, nor sitteth in the seat of the scornful. But his delight is in the law of the Lord; and in his law doth he meditate day and night."

You will perceive that the entire collection of the 150 psalms is centered around this very principle: How can a man be happy? Whence does happiness come? It comes from *the fear of the Lord*. Proverbs is likewise gathered around this fact: "The fear of the Lord is the beginning of wisdom" (9.10). Thus David and his son Solomon both agree on this principle. Actually the whole of the Old Testament is based upon this premise. But let me also add quickly: the whole of the *New* Testament is founded upon this principle too. The Bible in its entirety bears testimony to this maxim. How can we be happy? Only by fearing the Lord and walking in His ways.

Sometimes we may harbor the thought that fear is unhealthy. Is it not stated in the Scriptures that fear signifies something which is not perfect? Does not 1 John include that verse which reads: "Perfect love casteth out fear: because fear hath torment. He that feareth is not made perfect in love" (4.18)? Brothers and sisters, what this verse says, in one respect, *is* true. Why? Either because you do not know the One with Whom you are dealing—you do not know Him fully—or, because you know you have been found wanting in His sight, therefore there is a fear in your heart; and this fear certainly reveals that you are not perfect in love. But if our love has been made perfect, that is, if we are in this world as He was in this world, then perfect love casts out fear. (See 1 John 4.17) We do not need to be afraid of anything. There is a holy boldness within us. On the one hand, all this is quite true. But in another respect, even in love there *is* an element of fear. It is not, though, in the sense of being afraid to approach God for fear of being judged, but of being afraid to displease Him because we truly love Him. The fear here is not that of a slave, fearful of punishment. No! It is the fear of a *son*: he is afraid he may displease his father. He loves his father intensely; he wants to please him so much; and consequently there arises in his heart a holy fear lest in any way he may disappoint his father. Now a holy fear of this kind is not in conflict with love but rather is complementary to real love.

Often we say the Old Testament gives us the Law, and that law produces or arouses fear; and therefore *fear* in the Old

Testament is the secret of a godly life; but that the New Testament tells us of grace which gives birth to love and that therefore in this case *love* is the secret of godliness. Generally speaking, these are correct. Yet if you really meditate upon the Word of God you will have to acknowledge that even in the Old Testament the fear which is there—which, according to our understanding, is a fear of punishment and of penalty—is *not* what God desires. For in the Old Testament the most important thing is to "love thy God with all thy heart." Love! Love, it says! Even so, the fear of the Lord is there too. And in the New Testament, the same thing. Do not think that because love is emphasized in the New Testament you need not be afraid of anything! you need not be afraid of displeasing God! that because of love you can do anything you wish! Not so, brothers and sisters, not so.

In the New Testament as well as in the Old there is a holy fear which goes together with a holy love. The entire life of Joseph in the Old Testament is an illustration of this holy fear. Said he: "I *dare not* sin against God" (see Gen. 39.9). In his very treatment of his wicked brethren, he confessed: "I fear God" (Gen. 42.18). The life of Paul in the New Testament reflects the same principle. He writes that he buffets his body and leads it captive because he is fearful that after having preached the gospel to others he himself should become a castaway (1 Cor. 9.27). Moreover, the Apostle declares in Philippians that his earnest desire, hope and expectation is, that he may not be ashamed, he may not be ashamed! (see 1.20) A holy fear resides within him. He is afraid of displeasing the Lord. Why? Because he loves Him so much.

Look at the life of Jesus. Isaiah prophesied of Him in the eleventh chapter that the Spirit of the Lord would be set upon Him, the spirit of wisdom and understanding, the spirit of counsel and might, the spirit of knowledge and of the *fear* of the Lord (v. 2). Furthermore, the prophet went on to say that "his delight shall be in the fear of the Lord" (v. 3 RSV). Oh, in the whole life of our Lord Jesus, and because of His intense love towards the Father, there is always within Him a holy fear, the fear of the Lord. How He is apprehensive lest in anything He may displease His Father. "His *delight*," says the Scripture, "is in the *fear* of the Lord." Delight and fear go together.

Now it is interesting to note that this word delight in the original is literally the word scent, fragrance, smell, or savor. His scent, His fragrance is the fear of the Lord. Wherever He goes, whatever He does, with whomever He be, He diffuses a scent, He spreads a fragrance; and that fragrance is, the fear of the Lord. If you meet the Lord Jesus you instantly smell the fear of the Lord, at once it imparts to you a holy fear: you recognize that God must be honored. And this is what is described of our Lord Jesus. A holy fear marks out His love life with the Father. "Happy is every one who fears the Lord." Not fear in the sense of being afraid of punishment as would a slave; but fear in the sense of intense devotedness and love to God the Father as would a son.

Brothers and sisters, is there a holy fear within us? "Happy is every one who fears the Lord; who walks in his ways." If you *fear* the Lord, you will *walk* in His ways. One is the spring, the other is the stream. The fear of the Lord is in our heart; it accordingly expresses itself in our daily walk; and we will walk, not in our own ways, but in all the ways of the Lord. Whether His way is that of the cross with the path difficult and thorny, or whether it is a path smooth and easy, such will not concern us. If the fear of the Lord is in our heart, then we shall walk in His way, no matter what that may be; we will not withdraw from it, because it is His way. Who is he who fears the Lord and walks in His way? He is one who is filled by the Holy Spirit, he is one who is led by the Holy Spirit, he is one who walks in the Holy Spirit. "He who is *led* by the Spirit of God," says Romans, "is the son of God."

We find in this 128th Psalm that the ascending soul has experienced something of knowing the vanity of himself; and out of that vanity—the life of the flesh—he enters into something positive—the life of the Spirit. He enters into the *fullness* of the Spirit. "Abide in me," said the Lord Jesus, "and I in you." Here is a soul who has come out of himself and is *abiding* in the Lord. . . Here is a soul who *listens* to the Holy Spirit. . .Here is one who is *obedient* to the Holy Spirit. . .Here is one who is *filled* with

the Holy Spirit. . .Here is one who is *led* by the Holy Spirit
. . .Here is one whose very *life* is in the Holy Spirit. He has left
the life of the flesh and has entered upon the life of the Spirit.
No longer is he dependent upon himself but he is dependent
upon the Spirit of the Lord. And consequently there is now no
more inability or incompetence to those who are in Christ Jesus,
for what the flesh cannot do, the Spirit has fulfilled. (See Rom.
8.1ff.) The soul's labor is no longer in the struggle of the flesh
but is in the power of the Holy Spirit: " 'Not by might, nor by
power, but by my Spirit,' saith the Lord of Hosts" (Zech. 4.6).
And out of that kind of life, what is the effect? "Thou shalt eat
the labor of thine hands." A life led by the Lord will end in a
work which is of the Spirit of God. The labor of that soul's hands
are fully recognized by God.

We must say once again that it is not the Lord's will that we
should be lazy or passive. Even though it is perfectly true that
regardless how diligent we are or how active we are it will be
vain if it is only done in our flesh; it nonetheless is not God's
intent that we are to be passive and lazy. God works, and He
works *through us;* with the result that the labor of our hands is
fully recognized by God because it is a labor done in the power
of the Holy Spirit—it is *spiritual* work. The work shall indeed
be done; yet this is not all, for we shall also find we can *enjoy*
the fruit of our labor: "Happy shalt thou be, and it shall be well
with thee."

God calls us to work together with Him and for Him. He
summons us to work, but He supplies the power. And after we
have done the work, we are allowed to share in His joy and
happiness. How good it is. Take note of what our Lord Jesus said
when He was on the earth. "My food," He informed His disciples,
"is to do the will of him who sent me, and to accomplish his
work" (John 4.34 RSV). This is the food of our Lord. The Lord
Jesus comes to this world to do the will of the Father; this is His
work. And the accomplishing of it becomes His food, His enjoyment. Hence we see that His *life* in the Spirit must come first,
and then out of that comes His *labor* in the power of the Spirit.
The Person of the Lord must come first, and next the labor. His
life and afterwards His work. What is His work? The will of the

Father. And what is the will of the Father? You will remember that in the very beginning God said: "It is not good for man to be alone." And so He worked to build a woman for the man. So what is the will of the Father which the Lord was born to fulfill? Unquestionably He came to this world to fashion a woman for Himself; and we know that this woman is symbolically the church of God. And this becomes His enjoyment, His food, His happiness, His satisfaction. And it is that work into which we have been called.

We have been summoned into the work of God; we have been summoned to build the church; yet not in our own strength or power. How then is it to be built? The church is to be built up by spiritual life and spiritual work—by life in the Spirit and by work in the power of the Spirit. Then are we allowed to enjoy together with our Lord.

What do we observe next in this psalm? The writer without warning changes the figure of speech. Suddenly he brings in a new thought: "Thy wife shall be as a fruitful vine within thine house; thy children like olive plants round about thy table." Do not think it strange that wife and children are brought into view here. For in the physical world, as is true in the spiritual world, the principle is continually the same. If a man is prosperous it will issue in having a family. He will not be satisfied in remaining alone. Out of his prosperity a family will be gathered, a household will be raised up.

To put it another way, it begins with individuals but invariably ends with a corporate body. Spiritually this is likewise the case. If we are growing in our spiritual life, if the fear of the Lord is within us, if we are walking and laboring in the power of the Spirit, the consequence will be that such a life is bound to affect others. . .there will be a gathering in of other individuals. . . there will be a family life. We will enter into the life of the church. You cannot be spiritual wholly by yourself. You cannot do spiritual work isolatedly. The moment you enter into the life of the Spirit you flow into the life of the church. The moment you begin to labor in the power of the Spirit the building of the church begins to be accomplished—suddenly the family comes into view—all at once the family emerges! It is hence a corporate matter; it never remains individual. As soon as a believer begins to be satisfied with the goodness of the Lord, he will be fruitful and will be reproductive. And the outcome will be a household. This is the way the church is built: spiritual life and spiritual work build the church of God.

"Thy wife" here may also be explained as representing the experimental side of our spiritual life. As one abides in Christ and Christ in him, the natural consequence will be fruitfulness. "I am the vine," says the Lord, and "ye are the branches: He that abideth in me, and I in him, the same bringeth forth much fruit." The wife is spoken of as a "fruitful vine in the inner part of the house." We know that a vine is noted for its fruitfulness. Oh! Clusters of grapes in abundance: food, which is juicy and ready to quench the thirst, which can give strength, merry the heart, and satisfy the soul. A vine! So here is revealed a life in the Spirit which bears *fruit*. And what is the fruit of the Spirit? Love, joy, peace; longsuffering, kindness, goodness; fidelity, meekness and self-control (Gal. 5.22-23). One who lives in the Spirit will become fruitful spiritually. The soul shall not be lacking in spiritual fruit. Such fruitfulness is the expression of the Christ-life within, and this builds the house of God. Within the soul himself there is love, joy and peace. Towards others, there will be longsuffering, kindness and goodness. In relation to God, there will be fidelity, meekness and self-control (by which is meant Spirit-control). These are the chief ingredients for the fashioning of the house of God. Brothers and sisters, are you fruitful in this sense?

"Thy wife shall be as a fruitful vine *within* (i.e., in the inner part of) thy house." Some translate "by the side of thy house." But the first rendering seems to be more accurate, because in the Orient the house is built around a courtyard. So that if you would understand this figurative manner of speech you have to appreciate the way houses are erected in the Orient. In America a yard or a garden is set in front of the house with the house just behind it. In the Orient, however, things are arranged differently. There, the houses or apartments are constructed around a central courtyard. And within this inner courtyard vines are planted. Hence the vine here is not for the public but is protected from possible public abuse. The vine is only for the household. The vine is veiled, so to speak, from the outside world; it is hidden.

This is a most beautiful picture. It is just as we find in the Song of Songs: "her cheeks are like halves of the pomegranate, and they are hidden behind a veil" (4.3 RSV). The fruits of the Spirit—whether love, joy, peace, or whatever—are not expressed in an aggressive manner. On the contrary, these spiritual fruits are hidden, veiled, most gracious and most humble in their expression. The person who possesses these fruits does not assertively proclaim: "Look, how loving I am": "Look, how long-suffering I am": "Look, how meek I am." The one who loves, who suffers, and who is meek is in one respect hidden; he is veiled. Because such fruits are not something of which to make boast: they are something for God and for the household of God. And yet these fruits satisfy the hungry and thirsty hearts. The sentiment is plainly that of the Song of Songs Chapter 4, verses 9 to 16.

"Thy children (shall be) like olive plants round about thy table." "Children" bespeaks the increase of life through reproduction. If you have ever noticed an olive tree when it has become old you will see that young olive plants have begun to emerge from the root; and as they make their way out these young olive plants literally surround the old tree. "Thy children shall be like olive plants *round about thy table*." I believe all parents present readily appreciate how happy and satisfied any parent is when he is gathered with his children around his table: the more they can eat the happier the parent becomes. He may have to work that much harder, it is true; nevertheless, as he looks upon them eating around his table how satisfying to his heart it must be the better their appetite is!

Such is the picture which the psalmist is attempting to draw— of a whole family gathered around the table enjoying the abundance provided by the father. What contentment, what satisfaction, what joy! Just to look at the way the children eat and drink makes a parent feel happy and purposeful. The father realizes that today it is he who is feeding them, but that one day *they* shall be able to bear fruit themselves, they also shall produce other olive plants and become blessings to others too. Those who live and labor in the power of the Spirit will bear fruit. They will reproduce; there will be increase of life; there will be other olive plants. You may have to feed them, and yet a day will come when they in turn shall feed others. How satisfying that must be!

Now we know that in the Scriptures wine and oil always appear together: the grape of the vine for wine and the olive plant for oil. These two elements are spoken of together by the writer of this psalm. In the Old Testament, the blessing of the Lord is seen in His blessing of the corn and wine and oil. Whenever the Israelites offered to God, their tithe was the tenth of wine and the tenth of oil. In the New Testament, we have the story of the good Samaritan. When he met the waylaid man who had been beaten by the robbers and left half-dead, how did he serve that man? He poured both wine and oil into his wounds. Wine in the Scriptures represents the love of God: "Thy love is better than wine," says Solomon (S.S. 1.2). The love of God is like wine which heals, which makes our hearts glad. Oil represents the Name of the Lord: "Thy name is an ointment poured forth" (S.S. 1.3). Oil also symbolizes the Holy Spirit. Why? Because the Lord, physically speaking, is not present today. His Name is with us, but who is taking His Name, and who is using His Name? The Holy Spirit. The Holy Spirit is the oil: He makes good to us everything which the Name of our Lord includes. The Name of our Lord is an all-inclusive Name: it embraces all His work which He has done as well as all that He Himself is. And the Holy Spirit is today making good of that Name to everyone of us. That is the oil.

Here, then, is a soul who is filled with the love of God, who is spreading the love of God; and thus is he able to quench the thirst of the needy. Here is one, too, who has the Anointing upon him. Because the Holy Spirit is with him, the Name of the Lord is with him too and he labors under the anointing of the Spirit. And so he is able to help many people. The soul in Psalm 128 is one whose life is distinguished by both love and the Holy Spirit. His is a fruitful and reproductive life. Little wonder, therefore, that he is a person who is used by the Lord to build His church.

How is the church of God built up? It is accomplished by those whose hearts are filled with the love of God and who are anointed by the Holy Spirit.

In setting down the next verse, verse 4, the psalmist begins with the word, "Behold"—"Behold, that thus shall the man be blessed that feareth the Lord." He wants us to notice the spiritual significance of such a life. He wants us to be attracted to it. Hence the writer warns us to pay attention to it, to take serious note of this fact, that only the God-fearing man can truly be the happy man.

"The Lord shall bless thee out of Zion." Zion, as we have indicated previously, is where the King resides; it stands for authority. He who is living, walking, and working in the Holy Spirit is one who is vested with the authority of God. And this authority is used not for destructive purposes but for a positive building up. This authority is not exercised in haughtiness and in pride but is exercised in humility, lowliness, and love. Nor is this authority wielded in order to be served, but for the purpose of serving. And thus such blessing of the Lord out of Zion brings multiplied blessings to Jerusalem, that is, to the church.

"And may thou see the good of Jerusalem all the days of thy life." Brothers and sisters, do you want to see the good of Jerusalem all the days of your life? Do you want to behold the church being built up and blessed by God? You can, you verily can. And how? Only if we live and labor in the Spirit; only if we ourselves are those who are blessed by the Lord out of Zion. The good of Jerusalem cannot come about by our passively looking upon the church and weakly saying: "May the good of Jerusalem come upon you." No, no, no! It is an *active* participation: we are being used by God to bring in the good of Jerusalem; through the overcomers, the whole church of God is blessed; and we shall see it all the days of our life.

"Yea, may thou see thy children's children. Peace be upon Israel!" Oh, it is during this stage of Christian experience that the ascending soul enters upon a life in the Spirit. He is anointed by the Spirit. And he is being used by God towards the building of the house, which is here represented by the wife and the children around the table.

Our heavenly Father, how we praise and thank You that Your Word shows us not only the negative side of things—the vanity for those who labor if You are not the Builder—but also the positive side—that You DO build, and that You build IN us and THROUGH us. We pray we may be those who see the vanity of the flesh but in addition see the fruitfulness of Your Spirit in us and upon us. May we behold the goodness of Jerusalem all the days of our life. In the Name of our Lord Jesus. Amen.

The Life of the Spirit v.
The Life of the Flesh

1 *Many a time have they afflicted me from my youth, may Israel now say:*

2 *Many a time have they afflicted me from my youth: Yet they have not prevailed against me.*

3 *The plowers plowed upon my back: they made long their furrows.*

4 *The Lord is righteous: he hath cut asunder the cords of the wicked.*

5 *Let them all be put to shame and turned backward that hate Zion.*

6 *Let them be as the grass upon the house tops, which withereth afore it groweth up:*

7 *Wherewith the mower filleth not his hand; nor he that bindeth sheaves his bosom.*

8 *Neither do they which pass by say, The blessing of the Lord be upon you: we bless you in the name of the Lord.*

The 129th Psalm constitutes the fifth and last in the second series of the fifteen Songs of Degrees. It concludes what the psalmist has been experiencing in the four preceding songs and anticipates with increased faith what is yet to come. His first utterance is the expression of a painful reminiscence: "Many a time have they afflicted me from my youth, may Israel now say—" We are not told who the author of this psalm is nor what the occasion for its composition. If David is the composer, then how appropriate!

153

David above all others is unquestionably one who has had multiplied experiences in this matter of afflictions and he of all people can speak for all Israel. Because the author is found speaking here for the whole of Israel; he is not merely speaking for himself. The writer puts his words into the mouth of the nation: "May Israel now say." Hence this Israel may be a person—Israel a man—or it may be a nation—the people of God. It may therefore be applied to Israel personally or it may be employed in a corporate sense.

We are well acquainted with the history of Israel as a person, how from his youth up he passed through conflicts and afflictions of every kind. We know that this Israel was formerly Jacob. Jacob was only transformed into Israel after a long history of God's dealing with him. He was born as Jacob, a supplanter—one who seemed to know how to seize upon every opportunity and turn it to his own advantage. Now Jacob had a real desire for good things, a desire for spiritual things (for did he not seek to have the birthright which in the Old Testament represented something spiritual?); but he always tried to obtain them in his own way, by his own clever method, and by using his own strength. And as a consequence, he got himself into all kinds of afflictions!

Jacob was clearly a man of afflictions. He seemed to be a man born out of time, because there was in him from his birth an inner aspiration for the rights of the firstborn; yet Jacob was born second to his brother Esau. He should have been born first, for in him constantly was this consuming desire—this compulsive urge—to possess the birthright for himself. And it will be remembered that in order to get the birthright Jacob was willing to give away anything. He one day was cooking a lentil soup which he had made for himself; it was something which could satisfy him; yet because of Esau's birthright he was willing to let that go in exchange for it. Jacob was willing to sacrifice anything and everything if he could but lay his hands on the birthright. Moreover, in order to receive the *blessing* upon the firstborn, he cleverly deceived his father. He was willing to scruple at nothing if only he could obtain the firstborn's blessing. Jacob sought for the right things, yes—but always in the wrong way.

Because he cheated his brother and because he cheated his father, Jacob had to flee for his life. He went to Padan-Aram and sojourned there for 20 years. On the one hand he seemed to be prosperous there, but on the other hand how Laban his father-in-law cheated him as Jacob had cheated others before, how Laban changed his wages ten times, how he had to suffer hardship and numerous afflictions, how unceasing were his domestic troubles, and how he fell into difficulties of every sort.

Jacob was a man who wrestled to the very end with anyone who might get in his way. He wrestled with his brother, he wrestled with his father, he wrestled with his father-in-law. Jacob was indeed a wrestler! Furthermore, he seemed able to always come out on top. He seemed to prevail over his brother and secured the birthright. He seemed to be able to prevail over his father and secured the blessing. He seemed to be able to prevail even over his equally as clever father-in-law and secured a family and many sheep and goats and properties. Jacob always appeared to be able to prevail and to emerge as the winner. But does he really?

Consider, brothers and sisters, how much that man Jacob suffered! He who was the supplanter, he who knew how to seize upon every circumstance and to turn it to his good, was often in trouble. He obtained the birthright, but he was compelled to flee for his life; he received the blessing, but he had to leave his home and hide as a fugitive in the wilderness; he acquired his family and those numerous flocks and herds, but with it all he experienced every sort of domestic trouble and hardship, so much so that if the Lord had not intervened he would have lost everything, as he himself later confessed (see Gen. 31.42). And ironically he ultimately had to share the fruit of the labor of his hands with his father-in-law and even with his brother Esau who labored for it not at all.

Here then was a wrestler, one who strove with anybody and everybody, one who seemed to come out on top every time; and yet upon closer scrutiny it was not actually so. For if the Lord had not been with him he would have lost everything. If the Lord had not protected him, his brother would have killed him. If the Lord had not intervened, Laban would have taken every-

155

thing away from him. So we have before us a wrestler who seemed in every case to prevail; and yet, when he was wrestling with man God was the one who was really wrestling with him.

But we must hasten on to what occurred at Peniel. The experience of Peniel stands as the culmination of every past experience of this man Jacob since his youth. It was not something new. During all these years this kind of encounter had been going on. Even so, Peniel serves to reveal what had been taking place throughout those years. The entire past was consummated at the ford of the Jabbok River. There to the Jabbok comes Jacob with his huge family and with all the possessions he has acquired. Having just been delivered out of the hands of his father-in-law, he now has to face his brother Esau, whom he hears is approaching with 400 men. What a plight! What a situation! He thinks, he plots, he arranges, he maneuvers; he employs every means and method at his disposal.

Finally, Jacob settles upon a plan to divide his family. He sends his people over the ford, but he himself cannot cross over it. He has figured out everything, yet is not certain of anything. Everybody has by now crossed the stream, but Jacob alone remains behind. For some reason he cannot bring himself to cross the river. Does this not perfectly betray his inner situation? Though surrounded by an extremely large family, he is a person very much alone. In this plight he is reduced to isolation, because all his people and his entire wealth have already preceded him across the ford. Somehow he is not able to plunge forward; he instead hesitates, he lingers alone.

But though Jacob is left by himself, it is not for long. Soon a Man, an angel of the Lord, appears on the scene and *wrestles* with him throughout the night. Yet, strange to say, that Man is unable to throw Jacob to the ground. That Man *cannot* prevail against him during the night. It is not until the day breaks— actually, that Man *had* the power in Him the whole night through to prevail but it seemed He did not use His power; He instead held it back until daybreak—it is not until then that the angel of the Lord finally touches the sinew of Jacob's thigh. And at that moment Jacob is crippled for life. Nevertheless, crippled though he is, Jacob continues to hold on to, yes, to cling to, that Man and cries out: "Bless me! Unless You bless me I will not let You go!" The angel of the Lord seems now to have prevailed over Jacob; and yet, if we read the record of Genesis carefully we will find that the Bible puts it this way: The angel of the Lord said to Jacob, "Your name shall no more be called Jacob, but Israel; for you have striven (or wrestled) with God and with men, and have prevailed" (32.28 RSV). This, then, was Jacob's experience at Peniel.

We see that Jacob wrestled with man and seemed to prevail always. But Jacob also wrestled with God, and it seems that someone else—God Himself—had at last prevailed over Jacob. However, the Scripture says of this encounter that once again Jacob had prevailed! Here is the mystery of God's dealing: that when Jacob had wrestled with different people it actually had been God who had wrestled with him. Jacob was such a strong person; he was so clever, so cunning, so oily. Jacob was in addition so patient that even God found it difficult to outlast him and to prevail against him! For Jacob always was one to stand firm, no matter what. He would not budge an inch! He wanted to have *his* way, he endeavored always to find *his* way, he desired to lay hold of everything for *himself*. And hence he appeared to prevail against every man; and yet the fact must not be overlooked that this man Jacob had to suffer terribly because of the apparent prevailing. And it was by means of this very suffering that God had been wrestling with him. God wrestled with Jacob until He was compelled to crush the sinew of his thigh and to cripple him for life.

It should be remembered that in wrestling the most important spot on your body for this sport is not located in your arm; it is upon your thigh. That is the strongest, most strategic area for wrestling. If you can but *stand,* you are able to continue the fight. You will not be thrown off your feet. But at Peniel we see that Jacob, having endured many long years of affliction and suffering of every sort, at last caves in! The Jacob which was so strong in him is at last subdued. He finally gives ground. And as he gives in, as he yields ground, God declares: "You today have prevailed. You had not prevailed before, in either wrestling with man or with God. You may have thought you had prevailed, but in reality you suffered defeat. But today, when really defeated, you have prevailed."

Do we now apprehend the mystery of God's dealings? Jacob's prevailing lay in his defeat. In those times when he thought he had succeeded he actually had suffered defeat—he had to run for his life, he got himself into trouble; he fell into every kind of affliction. But when he finally acknowledged himself as defeated, he at last gave in, yet clung to God and said, "Without your blessing, Lord, I cannot go on anymore." To which God replied, "You have prevailed, not only over man, but also with God. And because of this your name shall henceforth be Israel, a *prince* of God."

"May Israel now say: many a time have they afflicted me from my youth: yet they have not prevailed against me." How true this was in the case of Jacob! From his youth up was he afflicted many a time; but even so, "they have not prevailed against" him. Just exactly why, though, have these afflictions—through individuals, situations, and events—*not* prevailed against Jacob? Why have they *not* crushed him beyond restoration? Not, certainly, because of the cleverness, the cunning, or the strength of Jacob. Yes, he had all that, it is perfectly true; and these qualities would appear to account for all his apparent success; nevertheless, these native talents and abilities only served to involve him in more trouble and suffering.

No, we have to probe deeper and realize that had not the Lord been with Jacob his seeming victories would have ended up in defeats. Jacob gained the birthright by seizing upon his brother's weakness, he obtained the blessing of the firstborn by cheating his father. But had the Lord not helped him out, he would have been killed by his brother. Jacob lost everything when he left home, but the Lord stood with him and promised him a great deal. And though Jacob possessed wives, sons and daughters, and many flocks and herds and properties, nevertheless, had not the Lord intervened, he would have lost everything once more. In other words, these circumstances could afflict Jacob but could never prevail against him, could never overwhelm him beyond restoration, solely because the Lord had been with him and had interposed on his behalf. And God had been using these many afflictions to transform a Jacob into an Israel—and that constitutes real prevailing, that becomes a genuine victory.

Brothers and sisters, in a sense, this holds true for every one of us. We have within our heart a desire, a longing, an aspiration after spiritual things. God has put such a desire in us. Now if we do not have a desire within ourselves for God and for things spiritual, then may I say I fear we may not be saved at all. If we are saved by the grace of God, if we have been redeemed by the precious blood of the Lamb, then that life which is within us must carry with it a desire and a longing for God and for things spiritual. How sad it is to see so many of the Lord's people with little or no desire for God and for His affairs. I do not believe this was the case in the very beginning of our Christian life. Most likely when we were newly converted there *was* such a desire, there *was* such a longing and aspiration within us for God; but somehow, we too often lose that desire. Yet every child of God is born again with a desire like that which was in Jacob, a longing for the birthright, a yearning for the blessings of God, a desire for things spiritual, an aspiration for spirituality. Such a desire as this must be in each of our hearts, and the stronger the better. Do we have such a longing within us? This should be the inborn condition of each one of us when we are born anew.

However, even though the desire is there—even though the desire is right—even though it is correct for us to long for God and proper for us to seek after the birthright and the blessing of the birthright, even so, we, like Jacob, attempt to fulfill this desire of ours in the wisdom and energy of our flesh. Dear friends, do you long after God? Why do you desire after Him? Are you stretching out for spirituality? Why do you want to be spiritual? Are you earnestly aspiring to the birthright, that is, the right of the sons of God? But why are you seeking for that right? Do you desire after God for God Himself? Or do you long for God in order that He may bless you? In other words, even in our desiring after God and desiring for spirituality it may be we have an ulterior motive. We genuinely desire these good and commendable things. But why? Quite plainly, it is for ourselves.

Self is still at the center. Nothing is wrong with the desire, true; but the motive behind the desire is not pure. We say we seek after God, that we aspire after spirituality—this is thoroughly right and proper. But how do we come by these things? By what means do we obtain them? Will we go about achieving them in our cleverness and by our strength? We say we love God, but how do we in actuality love God? We love Him, not in His way but according to our way. We think God should be served in this or that manner, and that is how God is going to be served! We do not wait upon the Lord and serve God in His way. We instead try to serve Him in the energy of our flesh. Rather should we see the futility of the flesh and depend upon the power of the Spirit of God.

Our emotion, our will, and our mind seem to be stretching out for God and for the things of God. But how our emotions need to be purified; how our mind needs to be renewed; how our will needs to be redirected. In all of this fleshly activity, self is still at the back of all the searching, the seeking, and the striving. But thank God, God is wrestling with us. When we, like Jacob, wrestle with man, and with circumstance, and with environment, and try to get on top of everything, God behind the scene wrestles with us. We may prevail, but it is merely the prevailing of the flesh. It is achieved at a great price in terms of many afflictions. God brings us into the "many afflictions" that through them He may deal with the Jacob in us. God wishes to purify us from our selfish purposes and activities.

Like Jacob, our prevailing over men and circumstances is not through our selfish and tricky ways, but will be through God's prevailing over us by disciplining us and bringing us under His wing. God is attempting to bring us to a point where we see, as Jacob finally did, that we have to give in; that there is not strength left in us; that unless the Lord bless us, everything else is vain. Our prevailing over God is in our being overcome by Him and in our clinging to Him for His blessing. Like Jacob, our prevailing lies in our defeat, in our being crippled, in our being reduced to weakness. And out of such weakness a prince of God is produced.

Let me ask you, Have you been brought to this point? Probe a little into your own experience. Why is it that God has allowed so much suffering and affliction to cross your path? How is it that your apparent victories consistently turn into plain defeats? That at one moment it seems you are on top, but the very next moment you must flee for your life? You apparently have taken *it*, only to find that it has taken you—you do not really prevail in a given situation. Have you ever paused to inquire after the meaning of all this? God has been dealing with you, many a time, from your youth, until you be matured. Brothers and sisters, what is youth? Youth here symbolizes the strength of our flesh; while maturity stands for the strength of God's Spirit. God is transforming us. God is purifying us. God is allowing every one of these sufferings to traverse our path that we may perceive and understand that it is never in our cleverness nor in our strength that we can prevail; but that it is only in our defeat—it is only in our giving in to God—that we really do prevail and grow into maturity. For this, God permits us to be afflicted. Our way is hard and thorny. Many a time are we reduced to desperation, to zero, in order for us to experience how the Lord comes in. As we decrease, He is increased in us. As Jacob disappears, Israel appears. Oh, that we may be able to see this!

Turning now to the next portion of the psalm, we find that the writer has created a most singular metaphor to describe his many afflictions—"The plowers plowed upon my back; they made long their furrows." Have you ever seen a farmer plowing in the old-fashioned way? He uses an extremely sharp steel plow, and as the farmer plows his field this instrument of steel knifes its way into the ground, turns up the clods of soil, lays bare the field, and makes long open trenches. It is a telling picture of the dealings of God. Dear friends, how often our very soul is as the ground of a farmer's field. How often God allows different people and circumstances and events to come into our life. And these cut into our soul like a steel plow in the ground—they dig deeply into our back and make deep the furrows: they cut, they turn up, they lay bare the soul and make our soul to bleed.

It once was said of Joseph that "his soul entered into the iron" (Ps. 105.18 ASV margin Literal). That fits closely the experience being described here. The cross cuts deeply and enters into our soul, disturbs us, and lays us bare and bleeding before God and man—revealing what are our thoughts, manifesting what are our feelings, and uncovering what is in our volition. The iron and steel has made its way into our soul. What a painful experience it is; and yet we know, do we not, why the farmer plows the field and makes long and deep those furrows? It is not for idle pleasure that he does this! The farmer does it with a purpose in back of it all. He plows the field and makes open the trenches and cuts deep the furrows with the idea of sowing seeds and with the hope of eventually reaping a golden harvest. Ploughing is for planting and for harvesting. The deeper and longer the furrows the better it will be for planting more seeds and reaping a greater harvest.

Oh that we may see that this is not something negative but is an act performed for a positive purpose. How often do we brood over our afflictions! How often do we pity ourselves! How often we sit about and cry! How often we say why? why? why? Why does God allow these things in my life? Why is it that my seeming victories end always in defeats? Why? Brothers and sisters, the answer lies right here: God plows our soul in order that He may sow His eternal seed in abundance and that He may garner a golden harvest out of our life. Was this not true of Jacob, for out of his many and deep afflictions, all Israel eventually is developed. Look at the dignity he possessed at his old age—able to bless the Pharaoh of Egypt and to worship God on the staff of his crippling. It is most positive indeed in purpose.

The psalmist then turns around to speak of the wicked and his end. "The Lord is righteous: he hath cut asunder the cords of the wicked." The Lord may permit the wicked to prosper and to prevail for a time; the wicked may be able to extend and bind his cords around the righteous, but it cannot be for long; for the Lord is righteous: He will cut asunder the cords of the wicked! We cannot be sure whether or not this is a continuation of the earlier metaphor. If it is, then we can correctly conclude that the cords spoken of here represent the ropes which tie the plow to its victim—that is, to the cow. In the olden days, when plowing, the farmer attached his steel instrument to the cow by means of ropes. So the writer declares here that these ropes or cords are broken—they are cut asunder; in other words, we are *set free.* Dear brothers and sisters, it is very true that God may allow the wicked to have a hold upon your life and to make you miserable; but it is only for a period of time: one day God will sever the cords which bind and will as a matter of fact set you free!

"The wicked" in this second series of the Songs of Degrees represents our flesh. Hence do not look for the wicked in others: the wicked is our flesh: and the flesh, however it manifests itself, is wicked in the sight of God. How the flesh has control over our soul and makes our soul a victim. Because of our flesh, we have to suffer and suffer and suffer. Why do we so often need to suffer? It is because of the flesh, the flesh which is behind our emotions, our will and our mind; and because of that we have to suffer. Nevertheless, it is but for a time: when the work of God is fulfilled in us He will *cut* the cord and set the spirit free!—free for God and free for His purpose! The spirit has gained the ascendancy.

Verse 5. "Let them all be put to shame and turned backward that hate Zion." Zion we have said before stands for the authority and the throne of God. The flesh is certainly not subjected to God, nor can it be subjected to the law of God. It on the contrary rebels against God's authority. Our flesh *hates* Zion; but it shall be put to shame and turned back. "Get thee *behind* me, Satan: for thou savourest not the things that be of God, but the things that be of men" (Mark 8.33).

Verse 6. "Let them be as the grass upon the house tops, which withereth afore it groweth up." It is helpful if we know that in the Orient the roof of the house, the housetop, is flat. Moreover, it is made of mud. The people beat the mud until it becomes thoroughly hard; and that becomes the roof of the house. Now because it is made of mud, sometimes grass will grow and emerge very quickly on the housetops. However, even though there may be grass which suddenly sprouts upon the housetop, it just as rapidly withers on the spot because there is no supply. The shoots of grass wither very quickly. It is not necessary to even pluck them from the housetop. This is a perfect depiction of the flesh, of the life in the flesh. Peter reminds us of how "all flesh is as grass, and all the glory of man as the flower of grass. The grass withereth, and the flower thereof falleth away: But the word of the Lord endureth for ever" (1 Peter 1.24,25). All the works of men, Paul reminds us, are as grass—"wood, (grass), stubble—each man's work will become manifest" (1 Cor. 3.12b,13 RSV).

At times we may think the flesh is as powerful as were the Anakim giants in the land of Canaan but that the spirit is as a grasshopper by comparison. This however is due to our lack of vision. If we have a more excellent spirit, if we have God's viewpoint, we will realize that all flesh are as the grass upon housetops. Whereas grass should be on the earth or in the meadow, that is to say, at a low place, we find in this case that the grass has lifted itself up to the housetops. Now is not the flesh just like this grass? Does not the flesh likewise try to lift itself very high above everybody? Is not this precisely what the flesh tries to do—to get on top of everything? It is high above all! Yet this very elevation becomes its annihilation. The moment of its greatest height in glory and honor is the moment of its most terrible downfall and destruction. Both grass and flesh alike shall wither. The shoots of grass are superficial and are prone to die, because of a lack of supply. So too will be the flesh, for if we "make no provision for the flesh" it shall soon dry up. The flesh, like the grass, should be underneath and not be above: this is the only rightful place for the flesh: for only then may it continue and thus be useful. If the flesh remains low it may remain longer; but should it attempt to push itself up, it cannot help but wither and be brought to naught.

Verse 7.   "Wherewith the mower filleth not his hand; nor he that bindeth sheaves his bosom." The condition of the wicked is such that it flourishes fast, but it dies fast too. It seems to gain the upper hand, yet there is nothing to fill the hand of the mower. There is not enough grass for one to hold on to and cut—it is entirely withered. It can neither fill the hand of the mower nor fill the bosom of him who bindeth his sheaves: in short, there is nothing, absolutely nothing! Nothing to fill the hand, nothing to satisfy the bosom! Brothers and sisters, flesh and its every work is vain. . .it has nothing to satisfy your heart. . .it is vanity of vanity. There is no fulfillment, there can be no realization:

it all ends up in nothing. Nothing in your hand, nothing in your bosom. Vanity is written upon the flesh. Because that *is* the life of the flesh.

Finally, in verse 8, we read: "Neither do they which pass by say, The blessing of the Lord be upon you: we bless you in the name of the Lord." You recall in that lovely story of Ruth (2.4) of how, when Boaz came to his field, he said to his reapers, "The Lord be with you." And his reapers responded with, "The Lord bless you." This was the custom in the East at that time. Whenever anyone was having a harvest and his reapers were busy harvesting in the fields, those who were passing by would invariably say, "May the Lord bless you! Bless you with His abundance, bless you with His riches!" For the life of the flesh, however, there *cannot be* such blessing of the Lord.

This entire psalm has shown to us, therefore, the tremendous contrast between a life in the Spirit and a life in the flesh. The life in the flesh may seem to be in ascendancy for a time, it may seem to prevail like Jacob for a while; but remember, in Jacob's very prevailing was his defeat, in terms of suffering and affliction and trouble. The life in the flesh will always end up in emptiness, in frustration, in dissatisfaction, in non-fulfillment, in no blessing, in nothing, in a word—vanity. By contrast, though, the life in the Spirit is a life which *really* transcends; it is a life which truly prevails, prevails with God and with man. It is a life that makes use of all the sufferings and afflictions and turns them into glory. It is a life which is fruitful, purposeful, blessed of the Lord, a life which brings glory and honor to God. May this be our life before the Lord, may we be found among those whose life is in the Spirit.

Our Father, we pray You will open our eyes to let us see the utter vanity, futility and emptiness of the life of the flesh. We pray we may be willing to submit our- selves to Your dealing; that we may be purified and transformed; that in our very defeats we may prevail, and be turned from a Jacob into an Israel. We ask You to speak to each one of us and to all of us. We pray that Your Spirit will work this out in our lives for the glory of God. We ask all in the Name of our Lord Jesus. Amen.

The Stage
of
UNION

Brokenness

PSALM 130

A Song of Degrees.

1 *Out of the depths have I cried unto thee, O Lord.*
2 *Lord, hear my voice: let thine ears be attentive to the voice of my supplications.*
3 *If thou, Lord, shouldest mark iniquities, O Lord, who shall stand?*
4 *But there is forgiveness with thee, that thou mayest be feared.*
5 *I wait for the Lord, my soul doth wait, and in his word do I hope.*
6 *My soul waiteth for the Lord more than they that watch for the morning: I say, more than they that watch for the morning.*
7 *Let Israel hope in the Lord: for with the Lord there is mercy, and with him is plenteous redemption.*
8 *And he shall redeem Israel from all his iniquities.*

This eleventh song of degrees inaugurates the beginning of the third and concluding stage in the Christian's experience towards that unitive life with God. The seeking and ascending soul during the first stage of the journey has moved from that which is earthly into that which is heavenly. During the second stage he has moved from that which is carnal or soulish into that which is spiritual. But at this moment he begins to enter upon the third and final stage of his experience, which is, to be united with God in a fuller way.

As we read and consider this song a question will most likely arise. Since this ascending soul has passed through those experiences of the first and second stages then surely he must have been delivered from sins and transgressions; if he is not sinless and perfect, at least he is freed from the bondage of sins and transgressions. How is it therefore possible for this eleventh song to exude such a heavy sense of iniquities?—so heavy in fact that it can almost be classified in the same category as is Psalm 51, a penitential psalm. Is it because that soul has backslidden? Or is there something else which is before us? I believe this is a matter we need to consider very carefully before the Lord.

The sentiment of this song is very well conveyed by these words: depths, cry, iniquities, who shall stand?, forgiveness, wait, hope, mercy, plenteous redemption. If you were to read the biographies of those rare souls who follow the Lamb whithersoever He goeth, you would find in their experience something very similar to what is described in this song of degrees. Such an experience has been termed by some as "the dark night of the soul." It is a phenomenon which stands at the threshold of a life of union with God. It is an event which is terrible in itself. Yet, if a person successfully passes through this experience he enters into the liberty of the sons of God. And it is just such an experience as this which is here unfolded to us in the 130th Psalm.

Before we go into this subject, however, I think I must call your attention to one point. And that is, that if your spiritual walk has not yet taken you to this stage, do not claim that such an experience will never occur, and be not frightened by the prospect of such an event. As the Lord leads you in your ascent towards Him you will pass through stage after stage, experience upon experience. And this will be one experience which, if you are earnestly following after the Lord, you sooner or later must certainly pass through. And the Lord *will* get you through into the liberty of the sons of God.

In the preceding psalm we considered at great length the experience of Jacob at Peniel. And about this Peniel experience of Jacob wrestling with the angel of the Lord and being transformed into Israel we said that it was the *consummation* of all his past experiences, of all the previous dealings of the Lord with that man Jacob. In one respect Peniel brought the span of years past together into one crisis. By that one crisis, though, it not only concludes what has gone before but brings in what lies ahead. In other words, the previous song has actually advanced a little further beyond what marks out the second stage of spiritual experience, for this particular event at Peniel speaks of the crippling of Jacob—the crippling of the natural man, or, to use another expression, speaks of the breaking of the backbone of the fleshly life. It is a very definite event, an experience which tears down Jacob and brings in Israel, a life of union with God. Hence we may place such an experience at the end of the second stage—that is, at the conclusion of the stage of enlightenment—or place it at the beginning of this final period, the stage of full union with God. So in a sense the experience of Jacob at Peniel stands at the threshold of the third and final stage.

During the second period of our Christian life the Lord deals with us concerning the expressions and the activities of our soul. He deals with our mind, our emotion, and our volition. He is dealing with our energy, the energy and activities of the flesh. *But,* very little is touched concerning the *life* of our flesh. The activities have been dealt with but the life of the flesh, which is self, has actually not been crippled yet, it has not yet received a drastic blow. Such a work must be done during the third stage or at the beginning of that stage.

What are the characteristics of the dark night of the soul? Let us not forget that this thing happens only to those who have already tasted the illumination, enlightenment and emancipation of the second period of Christian experience. We recall that during the second period the soul is set free from the ties of the world and enters into light: he receives much vision, understanding and revelation from the Lord. He bathes himself in the full light of the Holy Spirit. But the soul may also be required to endure afflictions, and many afflictions at that; the soul, as we saw in the preceding psalm, may have to experience the plowing of the plower upon his back which makes deep and long the furrows; he may pass through many times of darkness just as a seed must which is buried beneath the earth; he may encounter countless periods of affliction as, by all appearances, the seed does which decays and dies.

Nevertheless, one thing is very certain: whether there be

171

afflictions or there be periods of darkness, within his heart that soul *knows* the Lord is with him: he knows the Lord has never forsaken him: he knows that though there be affliction in his body and agony in his soul, nevertheless, in his spirit there is confidence, there is fullness of light, there is fullness of faith, there is the sustaining power of the presence of the Lord, and he knows the Lord will not permit any temptation to him more than the soul can bear (1 Cor. 10.13). Brethren, afflictions are nothing if the presence of the Lord is with you. Darkness is *never* darkness if the Lord is with you. During the second period the soul may pass through many "dark" events; even so, he has an inward registration that the Lord is working. There is within the ascending soul the awareness of the presence of the Lord—he knows that the Lord is with him. And *that* makes the burden light and easy.

Consider the life of our Lord Jesus. While on this earth He went through many afflictions. Oh! What afflictions, what tribulations, what sufferings He endured! But as He went through all of them He was comforted by one very precious thought: the *Father* was with Him, He was pleasing the Father and the Father was pleased with Him. And because of this fact, no matter how great the problem nor how difficult the way, there was strength within Him which carried Him through. But the moment arrived when our Lord Jesus had to go to the cross. And during those first three hours of Calvary, how men crucified Him, how men mocked Him, how they derided Him—Oh! how hell raised itself up against Him! Nonetheless, throughout these times our Lord Jesus could still say, "Father, *forgive* them, for they know not what they are doing." The Father was ever present with Him, giving Him support, providing Him strength, making His burden bearable. And He was comforted.

But what happened at noon time? The sun abruptly hid itself; darkness prevailed over the land; and during those last three hours, even our Lord Jesus must cry out: "My God, My God, why hast *Thou* forsaken Me?" It was at that moment that our Lord entered into the dark night of the soul! He tasted the bitterness of being forsaken *by the Father:* He was made sin for us: He tasted the bitterness of hell and hades! And this made the burden almost unbearable: He was broken in His heart. But thank God, towards the end, the Son can say, "Father, into Thy hands I commit My spirit."

This in part explains what is meant by the dark night of the soul. At the very beginning you were troubled by the world and the things of the world. Yet the Lord has delivered you; you are now above. You have revelation, you are bathed in full light. You are continually rejoicing in the Lord. And you are going forward: the Lord is leading you on and on. But as you are progressing in such a positive manner, as you are enjoying the presence of the Lord, as you are thinking that everything is now all right, that you are going onward and making great strides, and there seems to be no limit: at that very moment, suddenly! you are plunged into the depths. And with no reason. Abruptly, the sun is hidden. Without warning, a pitch-black cloud comes upon you. All at once the thunder rolls and the lightning strikes. And suddenly you stand quivering and trembling, naked and bare under the apparent anger of the Lord—stripped and alone. But what makes it even worse is, that the soul entertains the presumption that he must have somehow greatly offended the Lord. And right away you discover you are the greatest. . .sinner. . .in the world.

In spite of all former experiences, in spite of every evidence of the past grace of the Lord, in spite of the fact you have come a long way, you will still come to a point when the Lord seems to be withdrawn from you, when the grace of God seems to be withheld from you, and you are left totally alone! It is like our Lord's experience on the cross during His last three hours, when He was compelled to cry "out of the depths" that terrible cry of inner loneliness. Outward sufferings, mental anguish, become unbearable because the inward support is yanked away. God has hidden His face from you. And immediately you see yourself as the greatest sinner in the world. Oh the awfulness, the terribleness, the horridness of this *self* of yours: there *is* no good in you.

The sense of iniquity is greatest to those who have known the Lord the intensest. Here in Psalm 130 the consciousness of iniquity is so great that that soul is overwhelmed. If the Lord should withdraw Himself and withhold His grace from him, what can be left but that simple, naked, sinful self of his! This soul stands before the Lord in utter darkness, trembling with fear. He realizes how sinful he is, that there is no good in him. He deserves more than his share of judgment. The very spring of the natural man is now being touched and has been found to be defiled. And so he cries out. He cries: "Lord, who shall stand? If Thou shouldst mark iniquity, who can stand? I am *born* in sins; I am *reared up* in iniquity; there is nothing good in me. If Thou shouldst mark iniquity, who can stand? Even the heavens and the earth are unclean before Thee (see Heb. 9.23). I deserve everything. I deserve to be judged. And condemned. And yet, I look to Thee for forgiveness. I know there is forgiveness with Thee." Not the forgiveness of our various sins; it is the forgiveness even of *this sinful man*. This is the soul's feeling at that awful moment. He is conscious of nothing else but the greatness of his iniquities. Who can stand if the Lord should inquire of us? The soul is literally crushed under such burden. This is tasting the bitterness of death, of hell and of hades. Our naked sinful self—the life of the flesh—is fully revealed. It causes that soul to abhor himself and makes him very afraid of himself.

Oh, this is the experience of a soul's dark night! In the depths, the sense of inward iniquity is so keen that it can easily overwhelm the soul. Many rare saints who pass through such an experience even doubt that they are saved. The soul goes through desolation and despair. Everything seems to be lost: their very salvation seems to be called into question. The revelation of self, the very life spring of the natural man, is so appalling that the soul loathes himself. He feels God is more than justified to forsake Him, to withdraw from him, nay even to condemn and judge him.

But has God really withdrawn Himself? Has he really forsaken us? Not in the slightest. This is only the way we feel. On the one hand, the soul accepts what comes as fully justified; on the other, he is crying out for forgiveness. Yet the soul may find difficulty in getting his voice heard because he is at the bottom of the depths, but again this is purely his own feeling. God allows this that we may know ourselves that there is no good in us. He permits it in order that we may realize that without Him we cannot live. We can only live by Him and in Him. And as our soul cries out, He hears. The Lord *does* hear. There *is* forgiveness, there *is* mercy, there *is* plenteous redemption.

Such an experience at this time is somewhat similar to the experience of Jonah. Jonah was swallowed by a big fish. And while he was in the darksome belly of that fish, he cried: "Oh Lord, I am cast into the depths; I am cast out from the sight of God! My soul fainteth! But as I faint I *cry* unto the Lord *and* He hears me. Salvation is of the Lord." Jonah prayed and was sure of salvation. Dear friends, when you are thrown into an extremity so deep that it seems your cry cannot possibly reach to the Lord, remember, if you cry, he hears; you will learn afresh that He has never forsaken you nor has He left you. He has plenteous redemption.

In the greatest moment of agony over his own iniquities, therefore, the soul in Psalm 130 could still look up and be assured by the faith within him that there is forgiveness with the Lord. This forgiveness is more than that of sins we commit in the beginning of our Christian life. It goes far deeper; it in addition is a forgiveness of the person himself who commits all those sins and iniquities. Moreover, such all-embracing forgiveness as this does not usher in a life of lasciviousness or looseness of conduct. What it brings in is the fear of the Lord—"there is forgiveness with thee, Lord, that thou mayest be feared" (v.4).

We do not know who wrote this song of degrees, but it would not be any surprise to us were David the author. For he had encountered many dark moments. How frequently David was plunged into the depths: depths of blackness, of desolation, of despair. How often David was pushed to the furthest extremities of life—sometimes through his own fault and sometimes not. For example, the experience recorded in Psalm 51 is due to his own fault. He is reproved by Nathan for what he did with Bathsheba. How he pours out his inner feeling. He is broken by God, his very bones are crushed. But thank God, together with a brokenness of that sort, his spirit is also crushed and so is his heart. He knows God will not take pleasure in outward sacrifices: "The sacrifices of God are a broken spirit: a broken and a contrite heart, O God, thou wilt not despise" (v.17).

Thus this was a "depth" which could be traced to his own fault. But at other moments the "depths" may be due to the faults of others, as is confirmed by Psalm 34. On the occasion told of there, David had to alter his behavior before Abimelech by pretending to be mad. And why? It is the fault of Saul. Because of his valor against God's enemies, David draws down upon himself the jealousy and wrath of Saul. He has to flee for his life. Even as a fugitive in the court of a Philistine king, he is not safe. He is compelled to feign madness. And what do we find David saying? "The Lord," he says, "is nigh unto them that are of a broken heart; and saveth such as be of a contrite spirit" (v.18). David is not bitter in his spirit. On the contrary, his spirit is broken and contrite. David is broken to the point of contrition, to the point of softness and tenderness. And hence he finds the Lord to be near to him. Oh, how frequently David was cast into the depths! Yet the spiritual lesson was the same for David whether the circumstance was due to his own fault or that of someone else: God has allowed these things to come into his life to gain but one end, which is, that David may be reduced to nothing in himself that he may have a broken spirit. Read Psalm 34, read Psalm 51, and what do you find? It all comes down to one issue. "Lord," prays David, "You will not despise the broken heart. A broken and a contrite spirit is what You delight in." This is the sacrifice which God is willing to accept.

Brothers and sisters, the one element which hinders our union with God is a hardness of our heart and of our spirit. Such a condition is ours quite naturally. Even at the genesis of everything, after Man had first sinned, Adam blamed Eve and God, and Eve put the blame upon the serpent. How we hold on to ourselves! We want to maintain our integrity, even though there is hardly any integrity to be maintained. We may have experienced the *activities* of our flesh being dealt with, but this self of ours continues holding on to its integrity. We will not let go of ourselves. Everything else can go, but self, the I, cannot go. For if *I* go, there is nothing left. Pride lies behind this hardness. And should our environments remain smooth and should we be continually dwelling on the mountain tops, these factors shall only serve to strengthen our hardness and the harshness we show towards others; for we shall become very self-righteous and quite self-dependent. Yet this is the sure way to be rejected by God. A seed which is intent upon protecting its integrity—the wholeness of its shell—will never multiply into many grains. (John 12.24). Such a seed may be good to look at, but it can never be useful in feeding hungry souls.

God so loves us, however, that he casts us into depths of all kinds. He plunges us into low, humiliating, dark, impossible positions. And by so doing, we are reduced to weakness, to helplessness, to extremeties so that a brokenness of spirit may be engendered. Sad to say, though, the results do not always end up in that fashion. Look at Pharaoh, how he was hardened through the repeated hand of God. Woe to those who are hardened still further under the disciplinary hand of God; but blessed are they who under God's discipline are softened and mellowed. Instead of finding fault with others, with environments, with God even, such a soul begins to see the greatness of his iniquities. How he has missed the mark, how he has gone astray! He is humbled before God, he is broken in his spirit. And he covets the forgiveness which comes from God. The depth has done his soul real good.

May I inquire, Have you been broken? Has your *self* been broken? Have you been brought to such a point that, having been cast into the depths, you are shown your iniquities and you let go of yourself and confess, "O Lord, there is nothing in me. It is all broken. I cannot stand on my right. I have no right to claim. I deserve more than I have been dealt with. O, sinful I!" Have you come to *that* position? Is brokenness the mark of *your* life?

Let me say again that only brokenness can bring us to the threshold of a life of union with God. It cannot simply be a few cracks in the shell! Many Christians *have* been cracked; some fissures have indeed left a mark in their life. But this is not enough. To be united with God in a fuller way our whole being— this self of ours—must be broken. . .shattered to pieces to such an extent that it cannot be restored. Jacob's thigh was radically touched by God and so he was crippled for the remainder of his life; he was forced to lean upon a staff; his leg could not be restored. There must come into our life a very definite experience —whether or not it occurs once or occurs gradually, that is not the point—but there must come into our life this experience of being broken *beyond repair* before God: broken in the sense that we have no strength, crushed in the sense that we can no longer demand our right, in the sense that there is no righteousness in us, in the sense that we are *utterly* ended. . .and that God is our beginning.

Verse 1 to verse 4 of this psalm details the calamity of the soul. The soul, as we have just seen, has entered into the depths and in that extremity learns the lesson of brokenness.

From verse 5 to verse 8 we have described for us the calmness and the comfort and the consolation of the soul. As this soul is plunged into deep waters and it is revealed to him concerning his iniquities, he begins to abhor himself to such a degree that he *dare not* fight against God. His only attitude is: I wait—"I wait for the Lord, my soul doth wait" (v. 5). Though deliverance does not come at once, for the Dark Night is long, he can still wait patiently for the Lord. The natural man, however, cannot wait: you cannot wait if your self life is not broken. You instead want to take action. You want to fight against someone, fend off something. You want to protect yourself. You want to maintain yourself intact by being delivered out of the depths as soon as possible. You cannot wait! You will argue and murmur instead. You will do anything and everything except wait. By contrast, though, this soul is waiting before the Lord. He is not trying to tell the Lord what He should do. He is not telling Him that he has had enough. He is not dictating to Him to push the clock forward in order to shorten the Dark Night. On the contrary, he commits himself to the Lord and *waits* upon the Lord. He is content to stay in the night as long as He wishes. He does not want the time to be shortened even for a second. He may not be immediately delivered; he may remain in the depths for some little while; and yet, he has learned brokenness; therefore does this soul wait patiently before the Lord. "I wait, my soul doth wait."

The soul has returned to quietness. "In returning and rest shall ye be saved; in quietness and in confidence shall be your strength." Isaiah 30.15. "They that wait upon the Lord shall renew their strength; they shall mount up with wings as eagles; they shall run, and not be weary; and they shall walk, and not faint." Isaiah 40.31. The struggle and the unrest are past. The soul returns to wait upon the Lord because he has learned the lesson of brokenness.

Moreover, it is a waiting with *hope*—not a waiting without an end, but with hope: "I wait for the Lord, my soul doth wait, and in his word do I hope." But this hope is not wishful thinking. It is a hope founded upon the solid Word of God. He remembers the promises of the Lord. He knows that heaven and earth may pass away, but every jot and tittle of the law shall be fulfilled. Although his environment may continually appear to be adverse and opposite, nevertheless the Word of the Lord stands forever. As he is therefore in the depths, and as he is patiently waiting, the Word of God comes to him, the promises of the Lord: "I will never forsake you"—"I will not leave you as orphans"— "I will build my church." In addition, the Lord promises forgiveness and love. And hence all these promises form the basis for the hope of this soul, who waits and hopes in the Lord.

But let us take note that the writer of the song does not wait passively, as though giving himself up to the whims of fate. Not at all. He waits actively. He waits with anticipation, with expectation, with patience, with assurance. For he is awaiting the dawn (v. 6). Though the night is long and the darkness seems to deepen, yet in his heart—where faith has now gained the upper hand—he knows that the morning is coming. And so he waits and waits yet longer for the dawning of the morning. What is morning to him? The Lord Himself. The Lord shall appear as the dayspring or sunrising (Luke 1.78), refreshing the soul with its healing power. The *Lord* is morning to him. *With* Him, the soul can enter the day. But *without* the Lord, it is dark night to the soul. And though he may not even feel the presence of the Lord—that feeling having been taken away from him—still, by faith he knows that the Lord is near and that He is coming soon. He waits with hope.

"My soul waiteth for the Lord more than they that watch for the morning: I say, more than they that watch for the morning."

Who are these watchers for the morning? Perhaps they are those sentinels who are stationed about on the walls of Jerusalem, guarding the city during the night. And in their long vigil, how they grow tired and long for the dawn. For when the morning is come their duties are done; they are released and can hasten away to rest. How *much* these watchers watch for the morning. Those who are diligently seeking the Lord, those who enter into the depths for the sake of the Lord, those who keep long vigil for the church and for the kingdom of God, how they long for the morning to arrive when they can be released from their duties!

These watchers for the morning may also symbolize the priests in the temple. The temple priests, we know, always assigned one of their number to climb in the dark of night to a high place and there to stand and look and look and look. Look for what? Look for the morning! When he sees the sun's rays strike, when he glimpses the streaks of sunlight appearing above the hills of Moab, then he cries aloud: "The morning has come!" And when *he* cries, immediately thereafter all the activities of the temple begin. The morning sacrifice will be offered; the incense will be burned; the hour of prayer has come. Every activity of the temple has commenced. Most likely this is the case here.

If you are one who loves the Lord dearly, if you are searching and seeking and running after Him, then you can be likened to those who are standing on high and awaiting the coming of the dawn. Yet not because you expect to be released from your duty, but because you know that when the morning comes that then your real worship and duty begin. Oh how you look forward to the day when you can worship the Lord without any restraint, with no limitation. We shall worship Him as we ought. We shall serve Him as we ought. The night is gone and the morning has come. Now this is the spirit of waiting which is found in the heart of that soul. And not for himself alone; it is for all Israel: "Let Israel hope in the Lord: for with the Lord there is mercy, and with him is plenteous redemption." This the Lord will do not only for that individual soul but also for the whole of Israel.

Oh brothers and sisters, the reason the Lord allows us to taste of the depths and the extremities and to learn the lesson of brokenness is in order that through our brokenness the mercy, lovingkindness, and plenteous redemption of the Lord may be manifested, spread, and passed on to the church of God. And the consequence will be that the Lord "shall redeem Israel from all his iniquities."

Our heavenly Father, how we praise and thank You that Your purpose is beautiful, loving, adoring, perfect, complete. How we praise You: it is Your will for us to be united with You in one spirit: it is Your will for us to be conformed to the image of Christ. And because of this, You are willing to expend time and trouble and even be misunderstood by Your own in plunging them into the depths. Oh how we thank You: You deprive us, You strip us, You bring us into desolation and nakedness, into an abhorrence of our self, into brokenness—a brokenness beyond salvaging in order that You may fashion a new vessel and fill it with Yourself. How we praise and thank You for the morning when we shall serve You as we ought and we shall worship You as we love to. We pray in the Name of our Lord Jesus. Amen.

Humility

1 *Lord, my heart is not haughty, nor mine eyes lofty: neither do I exercise myself in great matters, or in things too marvelous for me.*

2 *Surely I have calmed and quieted my soul, as a child that is weaned of his mother: my soul is even as a weaned child.*

3 *Let Israel hope in the Lord from henceforth and for ever.*

Although this psalm is extremely short, within it lies the deepest of spiritual lessons. I believe it is clear to every one who reads this psalm what that important lesson is. It is the lesson of humility. The very brevity of this psalm manifests the genuineness of its author's humility. One who is truly humble does not speak too much: he in addition speaks very little of himself: the humble man neither boasts nor vaunts. Whatever is solid emits but a small sound; a drum, by comparison, beats loudly because it is hollow inside. Only those who are empty within are those who make the greatest noise. Hence this song by its very structure exhibits the essence of humility.

It is indicated here that this is a song of degrees. And it can certainly be said that this song is one step in advance of the preceding one. The earlier psalm teaches us the lesson of brokenness. This psalm, though, teaches us the lesson of humility. Out of brokenness there comes forth humility. And that is the *only* way to humility. A person can never have real humility if he has not gone through the experience of brokenness. This, however, we will touch upon later.

You will note that this song is attributed to David. David of all men was one who passed through much suffering to have learned the lesson of this psalm. David was a person who learned humility in his life. Recall, if you will, how, when he was young, David was overlooked and neglected by his father. For when Samuel came to anoint from among the sons of Jesse one of them to be the King of Israel chosen by God, his father Jesse gathered all his sons *except* David, as though to say that only from among *these* sons could there possibly be one who would be anointed. David he left in the field. He was despised and neglected by his own father (1 Sam. 16.11).

Recall, too, that when war broke out between the Israelites and the Philistines, David's three elder brothers joined the army and were subsequently stationed at the front. Shortly afterward David was sent by his father to look into the welfare of his brethren. But his eldest brother Eliab reprimanded him by saying to him: "I know thy pride, and the naughtiness of thine heart"! (17.28) Yet is it not an axiom of human nature that we always measure others by what we ourselves are? David's brother Eliab said to him, "You are proud!" But we sense that David's brother was guilty of that very fault. King Saul too was one who ill-treated David. For after David had been used mightily by the Lord to defeat Goliath and the Philistines and was brought into the court of Saul and was doing well, Saul became extremely jealous of him. So that David began to be hunted down like a partridge on the mountains by jealous King Saul (26.20).

We must bear in mind that when David was young he had been sent to tend a few sheep; but already he had become a mighty warrior (1 Sam. 16.18, 19). Think of that! A mighty warrior looking after a few sheep! What kind of life must that be!?! What frustration must that be! And when he came into the prime of his life he became a fugitive. Fleeing for his life, David had to hide away in caves; he regarded himself hounded as a dead dog and chased after as a single flea by his enemies (1 Sam. 24.14). Hence we find during the early life of David that he was crushed and broken and treaded upon *repeatedly*, so much so that he became a man of brokenness. The Lord allowed these things in his life in order that he might have a spirit of brokenness. And that out of that brokenness he might possess a spirit of humility. David became a humble man, a man of genuine humility.

We know of course that David twice fell terribly in his life. During the entire span of David's life there were but two occasions recorded in which he displeased the Lord greatly. Once, he fell in the matter of Bathsheba—the sin of the lust of the flesh. Even so, notice his reaction towards the discipline of the Lord. In reading the 51st Psalm you will discover that he learned through his fall this one precious lesson, the lesson of humility: how he felt himself *broken* before the Lord: how he was *contrite* in his spirit. Study his reaction to the Lord's discipline. When the chastening hand of the Lord was heavy upon him—the child born of his lust was dying—he fasted and lay on the floor, hoping the Lord might be merciful to the child; but after the child was dead, David rose up, washed himself, went to the tabernacle, and worshiped the Lord.

Throughout this entire episode we observe that David was broken before the Lord. And out of his brokenness, a humble spirit emerged. He was not rebellious, he was not hardened; he instead was submissive, he instead was meek and lowly, he was yielded before the Lord. Yet because of the serious circumstances surrounding his sin, the hand of the Lord must perforce still weigh heavily upon him: his own son Absalom rebelled against him: David once again had to flee for his life. And as he was leaving Jerusalem and was climbing the Mount of Olives a man by the name of Shimei came forth from the other side and threw stones at him and cursed him. David's general wanted to go over and kill the man. But observe how David refrained from avenging himself on Shimei. Said David, "Let him stone me and let him curse me. The Lord asked him to do it. Perhaps He will look upon my affliction and be merciful to me and relieve me of this curse." (See 2 Sam. 16.10-12) In this very reaction can be detected a man who is humble before the Lord.

As we stated earlier, David twice fell terribly. The second instance was towards the end of his reign. You will remember that David was agitated to *count* the people of Israel. God had continually promised that His people would be as the stars of the heaven and as the sand of the sea. God, in short, had promised *countless* people. Nevertheless, David began to number them. He wanted to see how many he had. But what was the motive behind it? It was pride. Pride and nothing else lay behind it. What David should have done was to believe that the Lord had given him countless subjects: he should have trusted in the promise of the Lord. Instead, he grew proud: he wanted to number them to see how many there were (2 Sam. 24). But what do the Scriptures say about David after he numbered the people? The Scriptures relate that David was pricked in his heart (v. 10). David began to see the error of his way; and consequently he humbled himself before the Lord.

Brethren, we need to see another important lesson in all this. Although humility marked out David throughout his life, yet towards the end of his reign he fell greatly in this very respect. It is really ironic: Moses for instance, who was the meekest of all men—God Himself declared it to be so—got severely angry one day! And as a result, what happens to our image of Moses? It is spoiled! Something of this nature occurs quite frequently, does it not? Very often the greatest temptation for a person who is marked by a special feature of Christ lies in this very regard. The greatest danger to a man possessed of the greatest virtue is to act opposite to what he by that virtue is. This shows us we have nothing whereof to boast. We need the mercy and the grace of the Lord *all* the time. Moses was the meekest; nonetheless he was disqualified from entering the Promised Land because during that one careless moment he misrepresented God. Moses represented God in His meekness, but he *fell* in this very respect. By the same token, David represented Christ in the matter of humility, and yet, here he was, indulging in pride by counting his people.

Despite this, however, David is still a man of humility; because, how he reacted! The moment he realized what he had done, he humbled himself before the Lord and confessed, "Lord, I am wrong, I am wrong." And shortly afterwards he confided, "Lord, I am willing to be under your hand of discipline." (See 2 Sam. 24.14) He humbled himself before the Lord; he knew the Lord was merciful. And we remember the story: out of this very experience the site of the temple was chosen (v. 18ff; cf. 2 Chron. 3.1).

In great contrast to David was Saul. Saul started out as quite a humble man, or at least he appeared to be so. I believe anyone who reads the early account of Saul will declare, "He most surely was a humble man!" In Saul's first encounter with Samuel, Samuel eyed him and asked, "Who is it that all Israel is desiring? Is it not *you*?" And how did Saul react? Saul replied with, "No, no, no! I am of the smallest of the tribes of Israel. I am but a Benjamite. And in the families of the Benjamites, my family is the *least*." (See 1 Sam. 9.20, 21) Oh how humble he was! And again, when he was chosen King they could not *find* him! He was there, but they could not locate him. Why? He had hidden himself among the baggage (10.22). A very humble man. And when he was anointed King the sons of Belial despised him. They protested against him: "How shall *this* man ever save us?" They did not want him to be their king; consequently they despised him and brought him no gifts. But Saul minded this not in the slightest; he was as one deaf (v. 27 ASV margin). Here he was, even ready to forgive those who despised and rejected him.

We would naturally conclude from all this that Saul was a very very humble man. But as time went on, what do we see happened? We learn that Saul forgot his past self, he became an arrogant and proud and hard soul. He puffed himself up and sought after vainglory. What haughtiness he displayed in advancing his own judgment instead of the judgment of the Lord. He became a proud and jealous Saul. The higher he climbed the prouder he became. Now had Saul changed? Those who look at outward appearance will say, Yes—Yes, of course he had changed. But the Lord, Who looks upon the heart, knows this is but a natural assumption: for Saul had *not* changed, and that, as a matter of hard fact, was really the trouble. Even if in the beginning he appeared to be humble and acted in a humble way, yet in actual truth his heart was proud: he was merely hiding his pride *under* humility! It was false, not real. The haughtiness of his heart was only revealed long afterwards. And when the Lord's hand finally came down upon him, how he rebelled against that hand. He was hard to the very end. Not so, with David. His kingship did not spoil him in the least. David was a man whose spirit had been broken long before and who was therefore humble before the Lord.

May I say, that *humility is not natural to us*. In this world of men we may find some who appear to be more humble than the others; but the truth of the matter is, humility is not a virtue of the flesh. To put it bluntly, when we appear to be humble *naturally*, it is merely pride in disguise. Humility is solely the nature of Christ. It is absent in the man of the flesh. No matter how much we may appear to be humble, within us we are proud. The more humble we appear to be, the more arrogant is our spirit. Humility comes from Christ. Humility is the *nature* of Christ. It is His very character. You remember that familiar portion in Philippians, Chapter 2.5-8. There we are told how our Lord Jesus—Who is God Himself, Who is equal with God—emptied Himself of everything: He poured out Himself completely: He took upon Himself the form of a bondman, a *slave*: and being in the form of a man, He humbled Himself and became obedient to the Father, obedient even to death, the death of the cross. From the very beginning to the very end of His life, there was one facet about the Lord Jesus which distinguished Him from all other men: for while all other human beings were proud and arrogant, he displayed the beauty of humility. Here was One, the Son of Man, Who was humility incarnate. How humble He was. Of Himself He testified, "I am meek and lowly in heart." And His testimony is true.

How can the humility of Christ be ours? Or, to put it another way, how can Christ be *our* humility? What is the secret of having Christ in this way? Let us not forget this fact that we have Christ in us: Christ dwells in us in all His humility. Nevertheless, why is it that it is not a daily reality to us? Why is it that even we who belong to Christ, we who *have* the life of Christ, do not exhibit His humility but on the contrary display arrogance and pride? Why? Simply because the road to humility leads via the route of brokenness. If we are not broken in our spirit before the Lord, then the humility of Christ has no way out of us.

Humility, to be understood correctly, is not something we

can take upon ourselves by attempts at making ourselves lowly. The more we try to be humble and the more we try to create humility in our lives, the prouder we become! Instead of giving other people the impression of our lowliness, we leave them with the impression of our own superiority: "I am more humble than you are!" It is consequently not something which can be manufactured: it is something which must come naturally. And how? Through brokenness. Hence Psalm 130 precedes Psalm 131, for unless there is brokenness in our life there cannot be any humility. Lowliness stamps the life of those who are in union with God. If illumination, understanding, enlightenment, vision, and knowledge characterize a child of God who is in the second stage of the spiritual ascent, then humility distinguishes that one who is in the final stage of spiritual experience, that is to say, in the stage of union with God.

Let us now come to this psalm of David's which is before us. We do not know the occasion which inspired it. For myself, I can only hazard a guess. King David, you will recollect, prepared a tent on Mount Zion. He afterwards went out to bring the neglected ark into Jerusalem. And as he was removing the ark towards Jerusalem, David leaped and danced before it with all his might. But as the ark came into the city, David's wife, Michal the daughter of Saul, looked out of her window and beheld David doing these things, and she at once despised him in her heart. Upon David's return home to bless his household, Michal came out to meet him and angrily said, "How the King of Israel made himself mean and low today in the eyes of the handmaids of thy servants!" But King David replied, "It was done before the Lord!—I played before the Lord! And I will make myself *yet more vile* than by what I did before. Moreover, I will be base in my own sight!" (See 2 Sam. 6.14-22) Oh how we can see the humility of David *before the Lord*. Can it then be that this was the inspiration for the writing of this psalm? I do not know; but it may very well be so.

"Lord, my heart is not haughty, nor mine eyes lofty: neither do I exercise myself in great matters, or in things too marvelous for me." David is addressing himself to the Lord. And in this opening verse he tries to give expression to his inner feeling of lowliness in three different ways. He touches upon three organs: one is the heart, the second is the eyes, while the third is the mind: neither in his heart nor in his eyes nor in his mind is there any trace of arrogance or pride.

The heart is the seat of our moral and spiritual being. Out of the heart issues *everything* in our life (Prov. 4.23). Now as David was examining himself before God, he honestly could say, "My heart is not haughty." Can we say that? Can you and I affirm, "My heart is not haughty"? Can we declare as did our Lord Jesus, "I am of meek and lowly heart"? Are we so humble, so meek and lowly, before the Lord? Are we so soft and tender and gentle before Him? Is there any haughtiness or pride, any uplifting of ourselves before the Lord? If we remember ourselves all the time, we will be proud and haughty. But if we do not even notice ourselves, if our heart is filled instead with Christ, we will be humble indeed. What great contrast, then, is Isaiah 14, where it speaks of Lucifer—Satan the enemy of mankind. In *his* heart, what did he say? Was he not always saying, "I, I. . .I, I, I?— *I* will raise myself high above the stars of God; *I* will set *my* throne there; *I* will be in the assembly on the mount; Oh, *I* will be equal with God!" Haughtiness, pride, the uplifting of himself! Brothers and sisters, is that our spirit? Or is there in our spirit that meekness, that lowliness, that humbleness which confesses, "Lord, I am nothing."

What *is* humility? Humility is nothingness. Humility is self-abnegation. Humility is the absence of self. If we are thinking of ourselves in terms of I, I, I—Oh how I am humble—Oh how I am meek—Oh how I am lowly—then I am afraid that this very attention which is drawn towards that I is itself a sign of pride. Remember, humility is self-lessness. The reason humility stamped the life of our Lord Jesus is because He was self-less. He never thought of Himself; He never tried to make Himself humble or to make Himself appear as nothing. He did not need to; because, before God, He regarded himself as nothing already: "I can do nothing of Myself: I cannot speak, I cannot do: Not Mine, but the Father's will." In the entire life of Christ you cannot detect the slightest evidence of self at all: only God. *That* is the key. No self! Humility is just natural to Christ!

Ah, but with us, how different. In our heart there is reserved a very large place for I, myself—what I am, what is going to happen to me, what I can get, what I want, what satisfies me, what hurts me—I, I, I—I want to be this, I want to have that. Because self occupies such a large area in our heart, it is *impossible* for us to be humble. Because of His selflessness, Christ died on the cross for us. But with us the process is reversed. How can we be selfless? How can this self life of ours be dealt with? Brothers and sisters, this self of ours can only be dealt with by our dying on the cross. See the reversal of the process? Christ is selfless, so this takes Him to the cross where He dies for us: we, though, take upon ourselves His cross and die on it to *make* ourselves selfless. We therefore say that humility comes from brokenness, and brokenness issues from suffering—even the sufferings of the cross. If we do not allow the cross to work deeply in our lives so as to break this "I" of ours down, then humility is beyond us.

"Lord, my heart is not haughty." No pride here, no arrogance, no hardness. Only softness, meekness and submissiveness, only yieldedness and lowliness before God. God can now do anything he wishes: we are like soft and tender clay in the hands of the Potter: He may mold and fashion us and do anything He likes with us, without our resisting or without our rebelling. Is this so with us in *our* heart? When the Lord allows something to happen in our lives, when we go through some trial or affliction, oh how our heart rebels against the hand of the Lord! How we become hardened because of it! But what does David say? "My heart is not haughty." Here is a heart which is humble before the Lord.

"Nor my eyes lofty." You know, our eyes are related to our heart: what is in our heart is disclosed through our eyes: eyes are the reflection of our inward condition—windows which reveal our inside. So that if you are haughty in heart, your eyes cannot help but be lofty. You look down upon everyone else. You conceive yourself to be somebody. You feel you have accomplished something. You therefore look at others through lofty eyes. And this simply reveals that there is no humility in your heart. But dear friends, in order to correct this flaw, let us not try to deal with our eyes first but let us try to deal with our heart first. In the early days of my Christian life I came to realize the need for humility and so I made the error, as most others do, of trying to deal with my eyes. I tried to walk with my eyes looking downward upon the earth and not looking elsewhere: I tried to be humble that way. But do you know that when my eyes were directed towards the earth my heart was uplifting itself clear to the third heaven? How useless! We have to deal with the *root* first, and that is the heart. As we allow our hearts to be dealt with, our eyes will not be lofty.

"Neither do I exercise myself in great matters and in things too marvelous for me." This passage has two different translations. One is: "Neither do I exercise myself in great things, in things too marvelous for me." Which is to say, that his mind is being exercised about matters that are *way above* him. Now if the heart is the seat of purpose and the eyes are its expression, then the mind is its activity. What occupies *our* mind? Are we trying to penetrate areas too wonderful and too great for us? Or are we willing to leave some things to God? And the other translation is: "Neither do I walk about in great matters and in things too marvelous for me." But whichever rendering it may be, of one thing we can be sure: Here in this psalm is a soul who is *not* exercising himself or walking about in great matters and in things too wonderful for him. "Well," you will say, "but that is bad. Is it not right for us to look into great matters? Is it not correct that we should search out the deep mysteries of the Lord? Is it not proper that we should so search and seek that we may find? For if we do not exercise ourselves in these great and wonderful matters then we remain here and do not progress to there." It is needful for me to say in reply that this is just not so.

We must keep in mind that this soul who is ascending has by this time reached the third stage of his Christian experience. During the second stage he was brought through a period of great light; he received vision, illumination and understanding from the Lord; and he actually seemed to be able to understand the mysteries of God. Oh! he was brought into great matters and into many things very wonderful. Naturally when anyone is in that stage his desire will be to have more, more, and still more!

191

He will seek for increased explanation and penetration into the profound secrets of God. But the Lord has dealt with that soul here. The Lord has crushed him, has trodden upon him, the Lord has broken him down in such a way and he has arrived at such a stage that he can currently say, "Lord, I do not exercise myself in great matters, nor in things too marvelous for me. If you grant me these things, I gladly receive; but if you should not, I am content. I am content to be left unknown and not knowing. I will not agitate and become restless, because I want to *prove* the secret of God."

What a contrast many other Christians present, who, having gone some distance with the Lord, arrive at a point where they become restless. *Their* cry to the Lord is, "If You do not show me Your secret, I shall be restless!" Oh, they just want to know the secret of the Lord. And should the Lord not reveal His secret to them, then they become agitated and disturbed! Not so with one who has learned the lesson of brokenness. With him there is no agitation, no unrest, no anxiety nor fret. He is willing to go without explanation, trusting in the love and faithfulness of God. He will say, "Lord, I am but a child. If You want to show me something I am here to listen; *but* I will not exercise myself, force myself, make myself labor for *great* things—as though I am great, or for *wonderful* things—as though I am wonderful. No, I am nothing but a child." In the stage of union the soul can rest in not knowing why. The "whys" are answered by Who. We know Whom we believe, and know what we have entrusted to Him towards that Day. The mind is at peace and rest.

Dear people, are we in such a state? Do we have such an attitude? On the one hand it is not wrong to search and to seek; on the other hand it is a right spirit which can say, "I do not exercise or walk around in great matters. I am content to be small, I am content to be insignificant, if that is what God wants me to be. I am not trying to ask or to seek or to exercise or to labor for anything for myself. I leave it entirely with the Lord." Is your soul condition in this way? If so, what a rest that is, a soul which is at rest indeed.

But what is the secret of this soul? What is David's secret? How is it that his heart is not haughty, that his eyes are not lofty, nor his mind exercising itself in areas too wonderful for him? How can he have come to that place? Verse 2 unfolds the secret. "Surely I have calmed and quieted my soul, as a child that is weaned of his mother: my soul is even as a weaned child." How beautiful! David has calmed and composed his soul as a weaned child with his mother. We know a child needs milk for his sustenance. It is right for a child to seek his mother's breast for his supply, because this is how he can live; otherwise he dies. There comes a stage, however, when a child must be weaned. The child is growing up; he needs something different; he needs solid food to sustain his developing, growing life. Unless such nursing condition changes to something else, the child will never be able to eat solid food so necessary for growing to maturity. He has to be weaned. But we know it is very difficult to wean a child. I think all mothers can testify to that. How the mother has to resort to different tricks. Sometimes she needs to put something bitter like pepper upon her breast; sometimes she has to refuse the child's insistence upon having the breast. And it is all too true that the child will cry, the child will struggle, the child will fight. And much misunderstanding will ensue. The child will think that the mother is cruel, that the mother is hard and harsh. He will verily misunderstand his mother. So that during the process of weaning, it becomes difficult for the child and the mother alike. The child cries, and the mother cries too.

Even so, mothers, what can you do? You *have* to do that. And after a certain period, the child finally accepts the weaning. But brothers and sisters, please notice that after this happens, the child—the weaned child—may contentedly lay upon the breast of his mother, and there he can look up at the face of his mother and converse with her in a more advanced way. Moreover, they can give mutual love. No longer a one-sided love, but love flowing from one to the other and is returned in kind. He is no longer a child seeking milk; he is growing: he is becoming a son: he is becoming one who can have fellowship with his mother, one who can share the burden of his mother: he is becoming one who is growing into responsibility, into fellowship, into usefulness. A weaned child lying upon the breast of his mother means a closer relationship between the two. No longer does the child seek for milk; he has been weaned. He has accepted this discipline, and so the soul is composed and at rest. There is now no more misunderstanding, no more struggle, no more hard feeling.

Brothers and sisters, we are not only to be weaned from the milk of this world; from that we certainly must. In this respect many Christians are still babes: they are still supported by the milk of this world. Take the world's milk away from them and they will cry, they will struggle, they will fight; they will think that God is too harsh. Have you ever heard of cases like this? People will come to you and complain: "What, a Christian cannot do this, a Christian cannot do that? God is too cruel—He is too hard!" They must have the milk of the world. But this has nothing to do with the passage presently before us, because this psalm is speaking of the advanced stage in our Christian experience. Hence, not only are we to be weaned from the milk of the world, but even from the milk of God!! We are exhorted to leave the beginnings of *Christ* and to proceed onward into that *maturity* which is in Christ (Heb. 5.12-6.1).

We cannot remain babes who have to be continually fed with milk, that is, the beginnings of Christ. It was exhorted of the early Christians: "Let us go on, let us go forward! Let us be weaned from the milk." We cannot remain as babes: we need solid food. We must grow: in responsibility, in understanding, in fellowship, in usefulness. Dear brothers and sisters, are we weaned from the beginnings of Christ? Are we weaned from the blessings of God? God may withhold His good things from us; but we can *rest* in Him, because we want God—the God of blessing—and not the blessings of God. As young Christians, it is true that without the blessings of God we cannot live: God blesses this, God blesses that. If God blesses, we are happy. If God does *not* bless, then are we saddened and we cry out! However, we have to come to a point when God can withdraw His good supply from us and yet we can still rest upon His breast and look up at the face of Jesus and be content—simply and solely because He is there. God can take away every one of His blessings: nevertheless, if only *He* is there, that satisfies the soul. The soul is at rest, resting on the love of God, even when deprived of His blessings. The soul no longer seeks God's blessings, but God Himself. It is no longer the grace of our Lord which satisfies, but it is the Lord of grace Himself that satisfies.

"A weaned child upon his mother's breast." This reminds us, does it not, of John, the beloved disciple, leaning upon the breast of his Master and conversing with Him? That is precisely the condition of the soul here. Even as John leaned upon Jesus' breast and asked questions, so our soul can be united with God in the Spirit, and there is communion and fellowship. Emotion, thought, and will are all under discipline—weaned not only from the worldly supply, even weaned from God's good supply. God may withdraw any good thing from him, yet the soul can rest in God. Nothing today can disturb the soul, not even the lack of spiritual blessings so-called. Only a weaned child can come into the initial stage of sonship. He then has a right of his own, he becomes a person in himself.

The soul has by this time accepted the deeper working of the cross. And the spirit has gained the ascendancy and is in control. The soul has been put under yoke and becomes a willing steward: "Father, not my will, but Thy will be done" will be the continuous prayer of such a soul. Then humility becomes supernaturally natural: you do not need to *make* yourself humble, nor to remind yourself *to be* humble, for you *are* humble. Everything which flows out of you bears the stamp of humility. It pervades your whole being. It will thereafter be difficult for you to be proud, though there will always be the possibility. This, then, is the expression of a life of union with God.

Verse 3. The earnest teaching of this humble soul is: "Let Israel hope in the Lord from henceforth and for ever." The soul that is weaned even from the blessings of God is one who hopes only in the Lord: Christ in you, the hope of glory. He has l-o-n-g since given up hope in himself. He does not even hope in the blessings of God: he hopes only in the Lord Himself: he wants the Lord and the Lord alone. He will not hope in anything or anyone else anymore. Christ has thus been incorporated and constituted in the life of this soul and such is the hope of glory. This is truly a life of union with God. And because *he* hopes in God, this soul exhorts all Israel—he exhorts the entire church—to hope in the Lord, from henceforth and forevermore; because that is the one thing which is true, which is real, which is solid. It is only when Christ the Lord is developed in us that we have hope. Let this, then, be our attitude always.

May this very short song teach us this basic, yet highly important lesson of humility.

Our Father, how we praise and thank You that You exhibit before us humility in the Person of Your Son, our Lord Jesus. How we praise and thank You that You have put Your Son, the very embodiment of humility, in us TO BE our humility. Lord, we do cry to You how so often this self of ours stands in the way of the display of Your lowliness in our lives. We cry to You, May Your cross truly work in us. Oh, we cry to You, that as we are put through afflictions we may be those who are beyond humiliation because we are low before You. We ask that Your humility may mark our life. We pray we may be as a weaned child upon Your breast, in union with Yourself. Make it so, by Your Spirit. In the Name of our Lord Jesus.   Amen.

Mutual Desire and Fulfillment

1 *Lord, remember David, and all his afflictions:*

2 *How he sware unto the Lord and vowed unto the mighty God of Jacob;*

3 *Surely I will not come into the tabernacle of my house, nor go up into my bed;*

4 *I will not give sleep to mine eyes, or slumber to mine eyelids,*

5 *Until I find out a place for the Lord, an habitation for the mighty God of Jacob.*

6 *Lo, we heard of it at Ephratah: we found it in the fields of the wood.*

7 *We will go into his tabernacles: we will worship at his footstool.*

8 *Arise, O Lord, into thy rest; thou, and the ark of thy strength.*

9 *Let thy priests be clothed with righteousness; and let thy saints shout for joy.*

10 *For thy servant David's sake turn not away the face of thine anointed.*

11 *The Lord hath sworn in truth unto David; he will not turn from it; Of the fruit of thy body will I set upon thy throne.*

12 *If thy children will keep my covenant and my testimony that I shall teach them, their children shall also sit upon thy throne for evermore.*

13 *For the Lord hath chosen Zion; he hath desired it for his habitation.*

14 This is my rest for ever: here will I dwell; for I have desired it.

15 I will abundantly bless her provision: I will satisfy her poor with bread.

16 I will also clothe her priests with salvation: and her saints shall shout aloud for joy.

17 There will I make the horn of David to bud: I have ordained a lamp for mine anointed.

18 His enemies will I clothe with shame: but upon himself shall his crown flourish.

This is the longest of the Songs of Degrees. The previous one is quite short, and its very shortness fits perfectly the spirit of that song, which is the spirit of humility: a humble man does not speak much, especially of himself. Psalm 132 on the other hand is extremely long by comparison; and yet its very length seems likewise fitting. The sentiment of this psalm is the sentiment of one who longs after God and desires very much to satisfy His heart. At the same time this song also reveals how God too desires to satisfy—He desires to satisfy the heart of that seeking soul. In other words, the 132nd Psalm expresses a *mutual* desire and a *mutual* fulfillment; and whenever this is the case, a song is bound to be long!

We must not forget that these last few psalms form the expressions of a soul who is being united with God in a fuller way. When a person is in close union with God he desires Him and what He wants above all things else. And when a soul is in this state he will discover that God assumes exactly the same attitude towards him, that is, God seeks to satisfy him, to perfect him, and to complete him. In short, the ascending soul has reached such a degree of union with God that there develops an intense desire on *both* sides to complete the other. Such desire is always the expression of deep, deep union. And this is what we find in Psalm 132. Hence, its unusual length.

At the very outset of this soul's ascent we learned that his greatest longing after God was that he might dwell with the Lord. How this soul from that moment onward begins to move. He journeys towards Jerusalem until at last he arrives in the city where the house of God is. As his love for the Lord increases, his desire and love for His house increases too. A definite ascent can be detected in these Songs of Degrees even with regard to one's concern for the house of the Lord. During the first stage of his walk with God a person yearns to go to God's habitation. During the second stage he longs to build the habitation of God. And when entering upon this final stage, not only does he long to build the tabernacle of God but he also longs to search out a place for locating it. Our love towards God can therefore be measured, or can be expressed, in terms of our corresponding love and concern for His house.

Who exactly wrote this psalm we do not know. It might have been David during the time when he brought up the ark of the covenant into the tent he had erected on Mount Zion in Jerusalem. Or it might have been written by Solomon at the time he consecrated the temple he had built for God. Or it might have been set down by some unknown author who wrote after the spirit of David and Solomon. As we have indicated repeatedly, however, the most important matter is not *who* but is *what*—what we can learn in terms of the spiritual lesson which is communicated to us through the psalm.

It becomes quite clear in the course of reading this song that its background has to do with David's desire to build a house for God. We know that David even when only a youth tending the sheep in the fields of Bethlehem was all out in his heart towards the Lord. It is a most inspiring sight, is it not, to behold a man or woman in the days of youth whose heart is wholly set upon the Lord? That was the case with David. While he was shepherding those sheep in the field he heard about the ark of the covenant of God. The psalmist exclaims: "Lo, we heard of it at Ephratah." Most likely Ephratah was the same place as Bethlehem, because we find in Micah 5.2: "Ephratah-Bethlehem." (See also Gen. 48.7 and 1 Sam. 17.12) When David was young he heard about the ark of the covenant of God in Bethlehem. He had not yet had the chance to *see* the ark; but he at least had *heard* of it. And having heard about it, David's young heart went out to the ark of God.

We know that the ark stood as the symbol of the Lord's presence with Israel at that time. It consequently must have occupied a most prominent place in the hearts of all who loved the Lord. And so David's heart desired after the presence and the glory of the Lord. He heard how the ark of the covenant of the Lord had led the people through the wilderness into Canaan: what the ark had done for the Israelites in leading them across the river Jordan: how the ark had been stationed in the tent of Shiloh: how it had been captured by the uncircumcised Philistines: how God's glory had protected His ark in the land of the Philistines until it was returned to the Israelites: and how the ark had finally come to be stationed at Kirjath-jearim in the house of Abinadab. All of this did David hear as a youth. And whenever he heard about the events surrounding the ark he could not put them from his mind and heart: he meditated deeply upon these events: and thus his heart went out to the ark.

"We heard of it" is then followed by: "We found it"—"We found it in the fields of the wood." We know that the "fields of the wood" has reference to Kirjath-jearim ("the city of woods or forests"): the ark had been abandoned in a wooded place, forgotten. Saul, who had no love nor concern for the Lord, had *never* consulted the ark during his time; the ark had been completely forgotten by the nation (1 Chron. 13.3). It had to be searched for and found; for having been neglected and forgotten in the wood, it was no longer in a prominent place. David diligently sought for the ark. He was one of the faithful whose desire was to go to where the Lord was and to worship at His footstool (v. 7 of this song). He heard of it; he sought after it; and he finally found it. Whereupon it became his desire to remove the ark to Zion. It was his longing that God should be honored, should be consulted, should be worshiped—and in the right way, in the right place. All this was to be found in the heart of David.

David has been called by the Scriptures "a man after God's own heart," for he possessed the same heart-desire as that of God. He wanted nothing but God and God's interest and purpose. He desired the presence and the glory of the Lord more than anything else. Brothers and sisters, is this the same with us today? Is it true that God, God's interest and God's purpose are all that we desire on earth? Is He the supreme focus of our mind? Is He our heart's love? And do we desire to satisfy His heart? Do we long to find a place for Him and to build Him a house? If so, then we are men and women after God's own heart.

While wandering in the wilderness and hiding in caves David was not occupied with thoughts of himself; he thought preeminently on God. His concern was: God did not have a permanent place. And how he longed that he might establish for Him a place on earth and a habitation among His people. How he yearned that he might build God a house. David was not thinking continuously of himself, "Oh! that I might have a permanent residence. Oh! that I might dwell in peace and security." On the contrary, as he walked in such a wandering state, David was preoccupied with God: if he was wandering, how much more must the Lord be wandering among His people—if he was fleeing for his life, how much more must the Lord be neglected and turned out by His own people.

Remember what God said when David expressed his ambition to build Him a house? God said, "From the day when I led my people out of Egypt, I have been wandering all the while; I have been living in tents and in tabernacles; I have *never* dwelt in a house of cedar." (See 2 Sam. 7.6, 7) While David was in battle fighting his enemies, he was dwelling in a tent. His thoughts again turned towards God and how he wished he could find a place of permanent rest for the Lord: "Oh, that the day may come when there shall be peace, and God shall rest in peace among His people." Moreover, after he finally ascended the throne of Israel and was in a house of cedar himself, he felt uneasy because the ark of the covenant still rested in a tent.

The supreme thought, desire and longing in the heart of David always and everywhere was the same: a house for the Lord. Observe his actions in connection with the ark. He had long contemplated the ark during his days of wanderings and adversities. And as soon as David was anointed King over all Israel, the first action he took was to capture the city of Jerusalem from the Jebusites and to make it the capital. We have to ask ourselves why David did this. Was it purely political? Not at all. There has to be a deeper motivation behind it than that. The reason his first act as King of Israel was to capture the city of Jerusalem was that somehow David seized this city for God Himself. Recall how in the book of Deuteronomy the Lord through Moses had told His people that when they entered the Land of Promise He would appoint a place of *His* choice, and *there* His ark would be set; and *there* the tribes of Israel must go up and worship Him, because that would be the place of His appointment. Yet we know too well that when the Israelities entered the Land a tent was erected at Shiloh and the ark was placed there. Later, the ark was shifted to Gibeah, next it was removed to the land of the Philistines, and ultimately it was left at Kirjath-jearim. But all these places were temporary. A permanent place, the site of God's appointment and of God's choice, was yet to be selected. But where was this place to be? "The Lord hath chosen Zion; he hath desired it for his habitation," announces this song of degrees (v. 13).

We do not know how, but in some way David himself received a revelation from God. He well knew that God needed a place, a site where He would set His ark; but somehow he got an impression, somehow he received a revelation, that of all places Jerusalem was to be that site. And hence we notice that the very first deed David performed as King was to take Jerusalem for the Lord. He made it the capital not so much for himself but more so for God. Jerusalem was to be the center of Israel's worship and service. Note in addition that as soon as he gained control of Jerusalem the second thing he did was to remove the ark of the covenant to Mount Zion in Jerusalem, to the tent which he had prepared (1 Chron. 16.1). How he gathered all Israel for this purpose, and how he humbled himself and rejoiced before the Lord.

And after he removed the ark to Jerusalem, the next thing David wanted to do was to build a *permanent* house for the Lord. His wish was well-pleasing to God, for He reciprocated by promising David a house and a throne everlasting. And although he was not permitted to build the house—because he was a man of war—even so, David's son was later to build it. And though he did not have the privilege of erecting it himself, he was nevertheless given revelation as to the spot and the design of the temple (see 1 Chron. 28.11-19). Moreover, despite all his afflictions David nonetheless made preparations for the house of God. Oh! because of his love for God, he prepared a great number of materials for the building of God's temple. Afflictions could not deter him.

"Lord, remember David, and all his afflictions." I ask you, Can God ever forget our affliction? Never! You do not need to remind the Lord of that! Yes, God can, and God will, forgive and forget our sins and transgressions; but He will never forget our affliction. But let us be quite precise as to the nature of the affliction mentioned here. For it is not the many tribulations of David in the ordinary sense which are in view. The affliction spoken of in this song is of a very special caliber. It is an affliction *for the sake of God,* an affliction due to one's *love* towards God. Because of his intense love for the Lord a person suffers for that very reason. In short, the soul *troubles* himself; and he is willing as well to *be* troubled for the sake of his love for God. Can God, then, overlook such an affliction? God will never forget anything which has love for Him involved in it. The Lord remembers every tiny little thing if it is done or is endured for the love of God.

David troubled himself—much. Said he: "I will not allow myself to sleep, I will not permit my eyelids to close, I will not come into my house, I will not go up to the couch of my bed." David troubled himself! Someone may quickly retort: "Well, but it is so unnecessary; nobody forces him to do all this, and to command him—'David, do not go to your house and be at ease. David, do not go to your bed and rest. David, do not close your eyelids and sleep.'—Nobody ever compels him." Quite true! It was David indeed who forced himself and stirred himself up. This was something out of David's own heart of love for the Lord. He would not give himself rest; he would not allow himself sleep; he afflicted himself; he was willing to go through any suffering for the sake of his love for God. Oh, *this* is the affliction in view here. And God on His part will never forget such affliction.

Brethren, how willing we are to trouble ourselves for the sake of satisfying our own desire. We are disposed to go through lots and lots of troubles merely for the sake of satisfying ourselves. But who are those willing to bestir and trouble themselves and go through affliction for the sake of God? Who are they? Have you ever bothered yourself in this way? In the days of adversity or in the days of prosperity, when in trial or at peace, what is your thought, what is the one consuming passion of your heart? Are you thinking of God, are you concerned with His interest and His purpose, are you taken up with His house and His rest among His people? Have you ever made yourself restless, sleepless, because God's purpose remains unfulfilled among His people? because His heart is as yet not satisfied? How easy we are to be satisfied when *we* are satisfied! We forget God's need, God's purpose. But for a man who is united with God in one spirit this will be the unmistakable sign—that he is concerned at *all* times for God and His interest.

The intensity of David's love for the Lord is fully disclosed in verses 2 to 5. "How he sware unto the Lord and vowed unto the mighty God of Jacob." I am easily reminded of the experience of Jacob. As he fled from his home, Jacob rested his head upon a stone one night in the wilderness. And there at Bethel God granted him a vision. God revealed Himself to Jacob and gave him great promises. After he awoke, though, Jacob was afraid. For, he said to himself, "surely God was in this place, and I did not know it!" And then he vowed a vow. He said, "If God does what He has promised, if God is good to me as He has said, if He brings me back to my father's home in peace, then I will use this stone as a pillar for His house: I will build God a house and serve Him" (Gen. 28).

We indeed find Jacob vowing a vow to the Lord here, but oh how it was done out of a bartering spirit. He would build a house to God, yes; but God must first do all these things to him. He acted out of a spirit of bargain—not too noble. Not so with David. David also vowed a vow. But David vowed before the Lord out of *pure love*. He did not ask for some blessings first, but was willing instead to trouble himself to the uttermost for the sake of God. Said David, "I will build His house. I will not give myself rest and sleep until I find out a habitation for my God." How could *he* rest if God had not found His own rest among His people? Hence he bestirred himself to search out a habitation for the mighty God of Jacob. He would fulfill what his fore-father had only promised. Yet not in the spirit of barter, but in the spirit of love—because he loves Him. Because David loves Him, therefore he wants the Lord to come to rest. Oh dear friends, this is truly a man after God's own heart.

The desire of David was to find God a place and a habitation (v. 5). He longed to be able to speak as did Moses centuries before when the ark was set forward: "Rise up, Lord, and let thine enemies be scattered." And likewise speak when the ark came to rest: "Return, O Lord, unto the many thousands of Israel." (Num. 10.35,36) David wanted to have the place and the tabernacle ready for the ark to arise to its rest. In other words, David longed that God at last could arise and go into His rest (v.8 of this song). And he longed, too, for God to be served and worshiped in the proper way—"Thy priests (to) be clothed with righteousness" and "Thy saints (to) shout for joy" (v.9).

David's desire was fully accepted by the Lord, for his desire coincided exactly with the Lord's desire. What David had chosen was chosen by Him, what David had planned was intended by Him. David took Jerusalem, and *his* very taking of that city proved to be the place of *God's* choice. David desired to build God a house; and *his* very desire was *God's* desire. And God accepted this and acknowledged that David had received revela-tion: "For the Lord hath chosen Zion; he hath desired it for his habitation. This is my rest forever: here will I dwell; for I have desired it" (v.13-14).

Furthermore, after the house had finally been built by David's son, God accepted the prayer of Solomon by saying: "I have hallowed this house, which thou hast built, to put my name there for ever; and mine eyes and mine heart shall be there perpetually" (1 Kings 9.3). What a thing of beauty! To realize that the very desire of David proves to be the very desire of God, the very choice of David proves to be the very choice of God! How happy if all *our* desire and effort will result in this way. David and God are united in one thought, in one desire. It is not that God purposed one thing and David purposed another, that God chose one thing and David chose another. No. On the contrary, we see how both God and David are united in one thought, in one heart, in one spirit.

Because of this union of God and man together, what will be the effects? What will be the consequences when the Lord dwells among His people and is at rest with them? From verse 15 to verse 18 three things are mentioned. *First.* "I will abundantly bless her provision: I will satisfy her poor with bread." *Abundant blessing.* Brothers and sisters, in this life of union with God, there will be no lack in anything: all the poor and needy ones shall be satisfied with bread. When a soul is fully united with God—in heart and in spirit—he is abundantly blessed by God. That soul is filled with the riches of Christ, the provisions of the Lord; there is no lack of bread, no lack of nourishment at all to his soul.

Second. "I will also clothe her priests with salvation; and her saints shall shout aloud for joy." *Full salvation.* It is distinctly more than what is found in David's prayer. In verse 9 the prayer of David had been: "Let thy priests be clothed with righteousness." And God's answer is: "I will clothe her priests with *salvation.*" Salvation is greater, includes far more than righteousness. Again, David's prayer had been: "Let thy saints shout for joy." And God's answer once more is: "Her saints shall shout *aloud* for joy." Not simply shout for joy but shout aloud for joy. You know, God invariably grants more than we ever ask for; His answer always surpasses our request.

And *third.* "There will I make the horn of David to bud: I have ordained a lamp for mine anointed. His enemies will I clothe with shame: but upon himself shall his crown flourish." *Superior power!* Horn symbolizes power! strength! The divine life generates divine power, as shown in the horn of David which buds. No one can stand against it; and he who is anointed shall shine for the Lord. All of this issues from a life which is in union with God.

But I have purposely left until last those two verses in 11 and 12: "The Lord hath sworn in truth unto David; he will not turn from it; of the fruit of thy body will I set upon thy throne. If thy children will keep my covenant and my testimony that

I shall teach them, their children shall also sit upon thy throne for evermore." Prior to God's acceptance, in terms of fulfilling and blessing, of David's desire and prayer as seen in the later verses, God showed David that He could not be outdone. For let us not forget that after David had expressed to the prophet Nathan his desire to build the Lord a house (2 Sam. 7.1-2,5), the Lord answered David through Nathan on this wise: I will not in any way be surpassed by my servant David! David wants to build Me a house? Wait a minute! I first want to build him a house. David wants to find a place for Me? Hold on now! I will first find a resting place for him and for all Israel. Just as soon as David had uttered his heart desire towards God and His house, God immediately stepped in and said: Just a moment, David! I had long been thinking of *you* and *your* house and *your* throne. I will establish your house, and I will establish your throne. And your house and throne shall be permanent if your descendants hearken to me. All this we can see in 2 Samuel 7.4-17. Here before us, then, is God's house and David's house. God's rest and the people's rest. God's place and a place for Israel. God's throne and David's throne.

Dearly beloved, what do we see exhibited here? What were God and David doing? Do we not perceive in this how the Lord and David were vying with each other in seeking each other's good? Is it not a remarkable display of that union of which we have been speaking? There is God's servant David who with his whole heart is trying to satisfy God, is trying to please God, is trying in a sense to complete Him. And there too is God, attempting with all His might and love to equally—yea surpassingly—satisfy David, to establish David, to perfect him, to complete him. Oh! how they vie with each other to complete each other! Now that is mutual desire and fulfillment. That is true union.

How the desires of both man and God are here merged together! For David's house shall be God's house and God's house shall be David's house. David's throne shall be the Lord's throne and the Lord's throne shall be David's throne. In establishing the house of David the house of God is secured. In establishing the throne of David, the throne of God is set. Why? because the house of David and the house of God are one; and the throne of David represents the throne of God. These two elements become harmoniously united into one: in the establishing of David's house the house of the Lord is built: in the establishing of the throne of David the throne of the Lord is set among the people of Israel. God thus finds that His need is met in man, that is, in man's desire after God's own glory. In fulfilling man and perfecting man God finds His rest. Hence of the man David, only one element was required—a desire; whatever else remains to be done is accomplished entirely by God Himself.

Brothers and sisters, what can we do? We can do absolutely nothing. There is but one thing which God wants us to have, and that is, a desire and a longing for Him, a heart and a concern for the Lord and His interest, for the Lord and His house. And if we have this, the rest is undertaken by the Lord Himself: He established David's house in order that Solomon might build the temple: He established the throne of David in order that the throne of God might be manifested among the nations: all things are accomplished by the Lord. The only element required of us is simply to have a heart and a desire for Him as did David.

Is David's desire our desire? Then we too shall be men and women after God's own heart. Does this one issue—that God may rest among His people—occupy our hearts? Is this the one concern which occupies our being? Many seek their own interests, but David sought the interest of the Lord. Do we have such an interest and such a desire as did David? Are we genuinely concerned with God and His house? Such is the feeling and the sentiment of this psalm. And this represents a soul who is in genuine union with God. It is not merely something which is in our emotion; it is something which is far down deep in our heart and in our spirit—that we long for nothing but God Himself. Now if this be the case with us, we shall find that God desires nothing but us too.

Surely it can be said, therefore, that the soul in this psalm has so entered upon the third stage of his ascent towards full union with God, that he can truly proclaim: "I am my beloved's, and his desire is towards me" (S.S. 7.10).

Our Heavenly Father, how we praise and thank You that You surpass us on all occasions: when we shower but a little love upon You, how You do pour forth Your GREAT love upon us; when we are but a little bit concerned with Your interest, oh how MUCH You are interested in us; when we desire after You, You desire us even MORE. Oh, we do praise and thank You that You are the Conqueror; we would be the conquered and we gladly would be conquered by You. Oh, we worship You. We pray that this life of union—in spirit, in heart, in desire—may be true of every one of Your children. Whom do we have in heaven but You; Whom do we desire on earth but Yourself! May it be so. May it ever be so. We ask in the Name of our Lord Jesus. Amen.

Body Life a Blessing

1 *Behold, how good and how pleasant it is for brethren to dwell together in unity!*
2 *It is like the precious oil upon the head, that ran down upon the beard, even Aaron's beard: that went down to the skirts of his garments;*
3 *As the dew of Hermon, that falls upon the mountains of Zion! For there the Lord has commanded the blessing, even life for evermore.*

In the psalm before this we saw how one who is touched by God's love and who therefore loves God expresses that love towards Him: he prepares for God a dwelling place. What is meant then by being touched with God's love? What is the meaning of loving God? Well it is most decidedly not being simply ardent emotionally towards God, for the love of God is deeper, far deeper, than our emotion. In loving God David comprehends God's heart and takes God's satisfaction as his satisfaction. He unreservedly offers himself, willing to disturb his own self that God may be satisfied. Now the soul who expresses himself before God in this manner is without question one who truly loves God. And this is in fact what we saw as we considered together the previous psalm.

Our present psalm advances yet another step or degree. If Psalm 132 speaks of loving God, Psalm 133 speaks of loving the brethren. The First Epistle of John unfolds to us how we ought to love our brethren if we truly love our Father God. This commandment, writes the Apostle, is received from the

Lord Jesus; namely, that whoever does not love his brother whom he *has* seen cannot love God Whom he has *not* seen (4.20). This is a most natural sequence. Brotherly love is but a continuation of God's love or love towards God. Should anyone love the Father he invariably will love the Father's children. If he is so concerned with the affairs of God that he is willing to sacrifice himself for satisfying the Lord, surely he will also be interested in his brother's need and seek to perfect that brother through self-sacrifice.

In Psalm 132 we see how David prepares a resting place so that the God Whom he loves may find rest in a home on earth. In Psalm 133, we see how brethren in the house of God dwell together in unity. If God can find no rest among men, how can we ever have rest and peace? But if God enjoys a rest among His people the consequence will be that God's people will find rest among themselves. Hence loving God forms the center while loving the brethren forms the circumference. What therefore happens at the center (Psalm 132) shall soon be happening at the circumference (Psalm 133). Such is the most natural sequence.

How can we love one another? How can we dwell in unity? The secret lies in loving God. Should we be constrained by the love of Christ to rise up and love our God, we shall naturally love the brethren. Hence unity with God in love is the secret, whereas unity among the brethren in love is the secret made public. We can therefore say that Psalm 133 marks a further ascent beyond Psalm 132.

This psalm bears the title of A Song of Degrees of David. It is David's song. David had experienced much in his own house which was quite opposite in character to the sentiment reflected in this psalm. I would imagine that as David began to set this song down he must have been full of many feelings. For we know that in his father's house the brothers were *not* in harmony. That household had eight sons, but they could not dwell at all in oneness. Even though David had been anointed as King by the Lord, he was nevertheless despised by his brothers, because they simply could not reconcile themselves to this fact. When he was sent by his father to the battlefield to see how his brothers were faring, he was wrongly accused by his eldest brother Eliab, who blurted out with: "I know thy pride, and the naughtiness of thine heart; for thou art come down that thou mightest see the battle" (1 Sam. 17.28). His brothers could not accept God's choice of David and hence were envious of him.

Take a look at David's own house. He had many sons and daughters, yet these children of his could not dwell in peace and unity either. They fought against one another. The bitterness between Absalom and Amnon, who could never get along with each other, ended with the first killing the second. Solomon and Adonijah too strove against one another. They each one sought to succeed their father David upon his throne. No peace existed between them because they sought for one reason or another to cut each other down. And so the brethren did not dwell in unity even in the house of David.

How strange that in this world of ours brothers in the flesh rarely dwell in peace and oneness. It is extremely rare to find such a happy scene according to flesh and blood. How tragic. Kinsmen according to the flesh ought to love one another and to live together in unity, but how often we find in human families that the brothers are jealous of each other and cannot live in peace. The house of Jacob can serve as another example. Jacob had twelve sons. The ten older brothers counseled together to sell their younger brother Joseph to the Midianite traders, even though they frequently quarreled among themselves. Even our Lord Jesus was confronted with brotherly hostility while on earth, for His brothers according to the flesh did not understand Him nor would they believe in Him. Time and again they gibed at Him. (This was of course later corrected in the Spirit.) Brethren should verily love one another and dwell together in harmony, yet how frequently this just is not the case. It is indeed to be sorely lamented.

Probably, out of his unhappy and bitter experience, David longed all the more for that oneness which was of the Spirit. He experienced those happy occasions of seeing Israel gathered as one in bringing up the ark of Zion, of finding Israel one in offering gifts towards the building of the temple. Moreover, David also observed how all the male adults of the twelve tribes gathered thrice a year at Jerusalem and celebrated the Feasts according to the Word of God. Together they assembled and lived in harmony, praised God and shared the sacrifices they offered, and were greatly enriched through mutual fellowship. They were together for some time and enjoyed its every moment. What a lovely scene to witness! How peaceful and harmonious! David was deeply touched by such events. And so, perhaps under the pressure of these two contrasting scenes which he had witnessed, David may have been moved by the Spirit of the Lord to compose this brief—yet very lovely—song. Psalm 133 consequently celebrates and describes the blessed event of the people of Israel dwelling at Jerusalem in unity.

But though the Israelites did dwell in oneness at Jerusalem thrice a year, their days together were nonetheless not for very long. After a particular festival of a few days length had been concluded, they were again scattered each to his own place. Many unpleasant things would subsequently happen among them. One tribe would strive against another tribe, and ten of their tribes would fight against the other two tribes. Their abiding together in unity had been extremely short-lived; it was far from permanent.

Even so, David turned out to be a prophet here. Because as he was composing this song David saw, through the spirit of prophecy granted him, One Who is a greater than David, One Who should one day sit on his throne. At the time when this greater than David shall come, that is to say, when the Lord Jesus shall come, a unique phenomenon will appear on earth: all who are redeemed by and belong to Him shall truly dwell in unity, for they shall become one body and live and express this body life. Hence this psalm is likewise prophetic. It foreshadows a day when God shall obtain a body for His Son Jesus Christ, and in that one body all the members shall dwell in unity and look after one another in love so that the Name of God may be glorified.

We will recall that as the day of His earthly departure was approaching, our Lord prayed earnestly for those Whom He dearly loved. It was the one supreme prayer of His life, and in it He had but one request before the Father. It expresses the very reason why He had come to this earth. "Holy Father," He prayed, "may (they) be one, as we are. . .May (they) all be one; as thou, Father, art in me, and I in thee, that they also may be one in us: that the world may believe that thou hast sent me" (John 17.11,21). Oneness, as we see from this prayer, is the mind of the Lord. What kind of oneness is this? Not, certainly, an outward sort, but one which is inward, not a superficial kind but a oneness which is genuine. Our Lord desires all of us who belong to Him to be one just as He and the Father are. The oneness of the Father and the Son is not an external kind; it is internal and in the Spirit. Only a unity of this nature is perfect unity, only oneness of this kind is perfect oneness.

We must truly offer our thanks to God, for our Lord gives to us His glory that we all may be one. But of what does this glory speak? Does it not speak to us of His life? The life of our Lord is glorious. Where there is death, there is shame. That is why people use all manner of means to hide this shame. Why are the dead dressed up? Why are magnificent tombs erected? They are attempts at covering up shame, because death is shameful. But life? Life is glorious. Where there is life there is glory. Oh, beloved, the glory of our Lord is in His very life. He gives His *life* to us; He gives Himself to us; *He* is in us and we are in Him. And such union is oneness indeed: for the Lord is in you and the Lord is in me, glory is in me as well as in you; and the glory of this life has joined us together in Christ. Therefore we need not try to manufacture a oneness outwardly, because resident within us already is this glory of life, and that life is one.

But having come into possession of this life of oneness, we must now express it in a practical way. Never is it the Lord's thought that we should only possess this oneness inwardly in spirit without there being any outward manifestation. If there is no expression how can there be any testimony? Let us remember what our Lord prayed—"that they may be one, even as we are one: I in them, and thou in me, that they may be made perfect in one; and that the world may know that thou hast sent me, and hast loved them, as thou hast loved me" (John 17.22-23).

The reason our Lord gives us His glory, life and the one

Spirit is that through this one life and Spirit we may testify to the world that we are genuinely different. What is infinitely rare in natural relationships is an absolute must in spiritual relationship. The world has been full of strife and discord, but the children of God can manifest tremendous harmony. The world has been marked by unbrotherly conduct, yet the brethren of our Lord can display the highest degree of brotherly kindness. And the effect? The world is compelled to acknowledge this manifestation of the one life of God on earth, because with natural men such unity as this is impossible. And so they are moved to repent and to receive Jesus as their Savior. Such is the testimony of oneness.

In the early church one hundred and twenty believers gathered together with one accord in prayer. Subsequently, on the Day of Pentecost, the Holy Spirit descended and baptised them into one body. Thereafter, the Lord added many to their number. On that first day alone three thousand were saved. And what does Acts 2 then tell us? Those who believed shared one life and had the Spirit of unity in them; they also assembled together without discrimination, maintaining with one heart the Apostles' teaching and fellowship, the breaking of bread and the prayers. The Lord added to their number one by one those who were being saved. Still later, five thousand more were saved after God had performed a miracle through Peter and John. Think for just a moment. During that period there must have been nearly ten thousand believers in the church at Jerusalem! But what does the Bible say about them? Oh! Just observe! They "were of one heart and of one soul: neither said any of them that ought of the things which he possessed was his own" (4.32)! What were they doing? They were abiding together in oneness. And such an expression of unity enabled them to bear a strong testimony in Jerusalem.

Hear what Paul exhorted his fellow-believers in the church at Corinth:

> I beseech you, brethren, by the name of our Lord Jesus
> Christ, that ye all speak the same thing, and that there
> be no divisions among you; but that ye be perfectly

joined together in the same mind and in the same judgment. For it hath been declared unto me of you, my brethren, by them which are of the house of Chloe, that there are contentions among you. Now this I say, that every one of you saith, I am of Paul; and I of Apollos; and I of Cephas; and I of Christ. Is Christ divided? (1 Cor. 1.10-13a)

He appealed to them by the name of the Lord Jesus Christ that they all speak the same word and agree in heart.

In his letter to the church at Ephesus Paul is again found beseeching the brethren: "Walk worthy of the vocation wherewith ye are called, with all lowliness and meekness, with long-suffering, forbearing one another in love: endeavouring to keep the unity of the Spirit in the bond of peace" (4.1-3). Paul said almost the same word in his letter to the Philippian church. He encouraged the believers there to fulfill his joy by being "likeminded, having the same love, being of one accord (and) of one mind" (2.2).

God's will is that we may be one. He desires us to dwell together in unity. Oneness is the spirit within, living in harmony is the expression without. Since we are one in life, we ought to be one in the expression of that life—we ought to live together in unity. The unity of the Spirit, which is the seven "ones" spelled out in Ephesians 4.4-6, has been given to us that we may live accordingly. If we move out of this unity of the Spirit we are certain to move away from the unity of dwelling together in love. If we keep the unity of the Spirit we shall soon find ourselves living realistically in the body. A body life will be manifested. A life, not of uniformity, but of unity. A life with all the members functioning coordinately to the self-building up in love.

This realization of the body life is one of the characteristics of the third stage of our Christian experience. During the second stage one may in very fact be given vision concerning the church, one may even be used by the Lord towards its building; but only in the third stage does he come into the reality of a body existence. The natural life—this self life of ours—must be dealt

216

with first before the life of the body can ever be realized. There are many of the Lord's own who have truly tasted the reality of the body in life!

Hence the stress of this psalm is not on doctrine but on experience. It does not treat of that inward oneness which God has already given us; rather does it emphasize the outward testimony of living. We ought not merely to *sing* of oneness; we must additionally *live* this oneness. This is what God genuinely desires of those who are His.

This priceless little song of David's begins with "Behold!" We know whenever a word like that is employed in the Bible it signifies that what follows is something worthy of our attention, not at all to be overlooked. The psalmist wishes us to view a rare scene, an event seldom observed upon the earth. It is a picture of brethren living in unity. And so the psalmist cries aloud: "Behold, how good and how pleasant it is!" Yet no attempt is made to tell the measure of "good" and "pleasant," for these are indescribable. He can only say "how" good, "how" pleasant. An undescribed description is the highest form of description. It is not only indescribable; it is in addition something which has to be experienced for one to ever know its full goodness and pleasantness. He has shown us how good and how pleasant it really is.

What God in His Word judges as good may not be the same as what we usually consider. And by the same token what we consider as good may not be recognized as such by Him. What are the things which God reckons as good? Whatever satisfies God's heart and fulfills His purpose, whatever comes out from Him, constitutes His work, returns to Him, and glorifies Him is a good thing in the eyes of God. And such a good even surpasses the "good" once proclaimed by God over the old creation.

When God created all things at the beginning what did He announce after His first day's work? God said, It was good. (He did not assert it to be good on the second day.) He said it again on the third, the fourth, and the fifth day. And He saw that it was *very* good on the sixth day. Finally on the seventh day, He rested. As God reviewed His work of creation, He saw that it was good.

217

Why? Because He created with a purpose, and whatever realized that purpose satisfied His heart and was accounted good.

Let it be recognized, however, that this "good" was yet but a hope. After God had created the heavens and the earth and man, He expected man to fulfill His will; He accordingly saw that it was good. Here was the anticipation of a future, the possibility of a satisfying of God's heart. Unfortunately, this "good" was soon spoiled. The "good" degenerated into "bad", *very* bad it may be said. God could no longer pronounce "good"; He had rather to say that it was corrupted, corrupted beyond salvage. Praise God, though; for in spite of such irreparable corruption God did not faint nor lose heart. He proceeded to work anew. God's Spirit works on just such corrupted flesh as are we. He re-creates us in Christ that we may be a new creation, because "if any man be in Christ, he is a new (creation): old things are passed away; behold, all things are become new" (2 Cor. 5.17). And as God presently views His new creation in Christ, He exclaims, How good it is! But this is now far more than expectation; this is *realization*. It is no longer anticipated good, it has become good realized. Consequently, the "good" of new creation surpasses even that of the old creation.

What is meant by being "pleasant"? "Pleasant" conveys not only the feeling of soothing comfort and joy; it is additionally employed in Hebrew to convey the sense of a harmony of music such as is heard from a symphony orchestra. Here is a conglomeration of many and varied instruments—some with high pitch, others with low pitch; some that are loud, others which are soft; some which have a melodious ring, others which exude a dull ring; and when all these are played under the baton of the music director, they present a sound of perfect harmony. Such a blending as this is what is here meant by being "pleasant." Suppose a discord suddenly sets in, someone, say, conceives the idea of independently playing his own tune. At once the pleasantness of the music is spoiled. Only what is harmonious renders a true sense of pleasantness, peacefulness and satisfaction. (See 2 Sam. 1.23.26; Ps. 81.2; S.S. 1.16, 7.6—where the thought conveyed by the word "pleasant" carries with it the idea of agreeable, harmonious, in unison.) The same word

218

is used in the Hebrew for the pleasantness inspired by the sight of a cornfield (Is. 32.12) or by the sweetness of honey (Prov. 16.24): harmonious, abundant, sweet. Furthermore, it should be noted that the first instance in Scripture where "good and pleasant" have been used together is in the description given of the garden of Eden (Gen. 2.8-9). But the scene before us here is even far more beautiful than that of the very first garden of God.

Beloved, *what* is so good and pleasant to look at, to behold, that it can satisfy God's heart? "Behold, how good and how pleasant it is for *brethren to dwell together in unity!*" That's it, brethren in unity! And this to the beholder is a symphony, an artistic display, a treat. Who are these brethren? Those who possess the same life of Christ, all who are born again of the same parenthood—God the Father, those who have the same Holy Spirit indwelling them: these are the brethren.

How does God desire us brethren to live on earth? He wants us to dwell in unity. The word "dwell" connotes much more than simply coming together on the Lord's Day, singing, praising, and listening, and then bidding farewell to one another. Everyone is courteous, friendly, and polite (yet are distant and cold underneath); each puts on his Sunday best (and yet hides all his corruption). Since the time is short, the contact is casual. It is confined merely to external intercourse, handshaking and smiles. Everybody returns home peacefully. Can this be dwelling together? Certainly not. For if it is, then there is no fellowship, no display of life, no beauty, no harmony in it at all. It is instead dead and social in nature. There is no distinctive quality about that, for such a situation can occur anywhere in the natural realm. It can bring in no honor and glory to God.

What, then, is the scriptural meaning of "brethren dwelling together in unity"? To dwell means to reside permanently. Since they dwell together, they must live in close and prolonged contact, being knitted together and fitted together as one, under a single roof. Now we usually say that familiarity breeds contempt. In such a close situation we tend to become careless. We will begin to see each other's faults, we will become bold at striking out at others. Our flesh is laid bare, the wall of

219

presumption and pretense is let down. And so it becomes easy ground for contention and strife to develop. The spiritual application can therefore be seen rather easily, which is: that we, as the redeemed of the Lord, possessing one life and one Spirit, ought to live harmoniously, fellowshiping constantly and encouraging one another frequently. The Lord has given us the unity of the Spirit by which we are able to live in one accord, being tempered together as members of one body, having the same mind, the same opinion, the same judgment, the same purpose, being of one heart and soul, being one in affection and love, and one in work and labor.

Now the beauty of it all is that every one of these natural consequences of a life lived in the flesh can be overcome because the very life of the flesh—self—has been dealt with. In its place the Spirit rules, and the Spirit is one. It is the Spirit of love. And love covers a multitude of sins and shortcomings. It is love which will now govern our actions. Moreover, there is also coordination and mutual service. The closer together the brethren are, the deeper will be their unity in the Spirit. They become more like each other as they each are becoming more like Christ. This is God's doing, and it brings in His glory. This will be a testimony towards God, because the world will recognize that God has sent His Son into the world. For how else can such unity be explained? And oh, were the children of God to dwell in such unity as this, how good and how pleasant must be their testimony!

But the problem lies precisely here. We are well able to keep peace and maintain an appearance of unity if our meetings are occasional and our contacts are casual—if, in short, there is no conflict of interest and no chance of rubbing each other the wrong way. But if, to worship and to serve God, we are actually being thrown together into close proximity to one another, and as one family and as one body we begin to encourage and to help one another, then we shall observe many problems commencing to arise among us. Being so close and involved we cannot help but begin to rub against one another. We start to voice our different opinions and right away difficulties begin to abound.

It is admittedly not easy for any one of us to dwell together in unity with others, becoming harmonious as a symphony orchestra whose varied musical instruments merge into one perfect blending of sound. Have you ever experienced what I sometimes do when having a meal? At times while eating too fast and too much I inadvertently bite my tongue or else the inside of my cheek. How painful it becomes for the moment! Why should such a thing happen to me? Because my teeth and my tongue or cheek live too closely together. So that when I am not careful, difficulty arises. But God be thanked, my tongue never attempts to strike out in vengeance on the basis of being ill-treated by my teeth. It never decides to leave me; for if that were to happen, I would be left dumb.

Here we may learn something. How very wonderful that God places within us a beautiful life, a harmonious life—that Spirit of oneness; how equally wonderful for Him by means of various circumstances to throw us together that we may be beaten and re-shaped into one, and so serve Him with one accord. Naturally there will be times when we disagree and when we jar one another adversely. Yet praise Him, the life He has given us overcomes all these discordant elements. However much we may be disturbed outwardly, within us we have a life that transcends all.

Doubtless we must accept the dealing of the cross. For if the self life remains intact the brethren cannot dwell in unity. Men are divided by their self life. Whenever my self comes to the fore, whenever I live out from the self, at that very moment I am not dwelling in oneness with my brethren. Beloved, no two "selfs" can ever be harmonious; in the realm of the "self" there can never be unity.

Let us thank God that we belong to Him and are willing to accept the cross. Whenever I chafe and irritate my brother, the Lord's life in me on the one hand lays hold of me by showing me how the love and unity in the Lord transcends everything, while on the other hand I am constrained to accept the cross.

Paul exhorts us in Ephesians 4 to lead a life worthy of the calling in which we have been called. How? The first ingredient is: "with all lowliness." Now there is no place else where lowliness is demanded of us more rigorously than in the church. The spirit which prevails in society is one of self-importance. Everybody is Number One. None yields to the other. Such self-importance, it is true, has its effectiveness in society, but it poses one of the great difficulties in the church. For brethren to dwell in unity, the first requirement is lowliness. What is lowliness? It means selflessness, or self-abnegation. How extremely anxious people are today to save their face. Yet how far better it would be, dear brothers and sisters, were we to have no face to save in the first place! In the church we must learn to be selfless—never defending ourselves, never standing up for ourselves and never striving for ourselves.

The second ingredient necessary to have for abiding in oneness is "meekness." A humble person is a meek person. He will never hurt others nor oppress people. He will not insist on carrying out his opinion nor compel others to yield to him.

And the third ingredient is "patience, forbearing one another in love." Our action towards people is meekness while our re-action towards them is patience. Nevertheless, how frequently we reason that since he has treated *me* in such and such a manner, I must deal back in kind. Not so, brethren. If you are treated with violent oppression, you must react with patience, forbearing one another in love. For the brethren to dwell in the church in harmony, it is important to "forbear one another in love, eager to maintain the unity of the Spirit in the bond of peace." Do we not see that its demand is most exacting? It demands that this self of ours be broken, without which brethren cannot possibly dwell in unity.

What are the marvelous consequences if brethren dwell in unity together? David weaves together two similes to describe such unity and its blessings. First, "it is like the precious oil upon the head, that ran down upon the beard, even Aaron's beard: that went down to the skirts of his garments." We all know from the Old Testament that God commanded Israel to prepare holy anointing oil.

Take thou also unto thee principal spices, of pure myrrh five hundred shekels, and of sweet cinnamon half so much, even two hundred and fifty shekels, and of sweet calamus two hundred and fifty shekels, and of cassia five hundred shekels, after the shekel of the sanctuary, and oil olive an hin; and thou shalt make it an oil of holy ointment, an ointment compound after the art of the apothecary: it shall be an holy anointing oil. (Ex. 30.22-25)

As we can readily see the spices which went to make up this anointing oil were all of the finest, and were therefore most costly. Each time this oil was to be blended it was manufactured in an immense quantity, never in small amounts. Historians tell us that 750 ounces of solids were compounded with five quarts of oil. In the use of it, sometimes it was sprinkled with the finger or merely applied lightly. But when it was used in the anointing of the high priest, it was so profusely applied that when it was poured over the high priest's head so much was poured out that it would flow down upon his beard and breast, and even down to the hem of his garments.

You may perhaps ask why such a waste? For it may seem to some as though it is not only a wasting of the oil but is also a spoiling of the priestly robes. Yet God's thought is always higher than our thought, and His way higher than our way. Do you not recall how even after the tabernacle and all the things therein had been set in order and the priests chosen, that everything still remained dead until the anointing of the furnishings and the priests? But when finally the anointing came, the whole tabernacle was instantly quickened into life, with all the services under the anointing becoming alive to the satisfaction of God's heart.

We have the record of Aaron being anointed as the high priest. He at first is clothed with the high-priestly robes and thereafter anointed with oil. (See Ex. 29.5-7, 40.13; Lev. 8.12) The most lavish use of the holy oil is upon Aaron. The tabernacle and all its furniture are anointed by the oil being sprinkled thereon, but only upon *Aaron's* head is the oil poured out in abundance. There being no record of any subordinate priests ever having been anointed in this way, we can confidently believe that every succeeding high priest had to be inducted into the high-priestly office in the same manner. We definitely know that after the Captivity there was no more such anointing, because the art of making this holy oil was eventually lost. And this fact only serves to heighten even further the singular relationship between the oil and Aaron. Hence this oil is very dear, not only because of the costliness of its exquisite ingredients but also because of the exclusive use to which it was put.

Aaron is of course a type of Christ as high priest, although Christ is of a higher order (Heb. 7). The oil of gladness is poured upon His head (Ps. 45.7). Now at the time of His baptism it is true that our Lord was anointed with the Holy Spirit, but the anointing was for the purpose of His ministry upon the earth. At His ascension, however, the Lord Jesus was anointed by the Father with the promised outpouring of the Holy Spirit for His ministry in heaven as the Great High Priest. Christ, which name means "the Anointed One," has been anointed to be our High Priest and is today serving in the true sanctuary and in the true tabernacle. As God poured out the oil of the Holy Spirit upon the ascended Lord the Spirit began to flow down upon His beard and on down to His body. Here we see the Head and the body joined together under one Anointing. At Christ's ascension the Father anointed Him with the Holy Spirit, Who flowed on down to His beard. I believe the experience of the Day of Pentecost answers to this running down upon the beard which we see in Psalm 133. But the oil of the Holy Spirit continues to flow, it runs down upon His body; that is, the Spirit flows down to the church which is Christ's body. And the anointing of the Spirit is still running today: the Spirit flows down to the very hem of His robes. In other words, the Anointing shall ultimately reach the uttermost part of the body of Christ. Now we today are His body and we have been joined in one to Him Who is the Head. Consequently, in His being anointed we too have been anointed.

One Anointing, one Spirit covers the entire body. We receive the outpouring of the anointing of the Holy Spirit because Christ received His anointing. Is Christ anointed? Then we are anointed too: anointed for true service in the true house of God: anointed for priestly ministry under the Great High Priest. Before being anointed we were dormant, but after the anointing we were quickened. We serve God by serving one another. We serve under one Anointing, and so we serve coordinately. As we brethren dwell together in unity, we are therefore united in Spirit and each of us occupies his own place in the body. The anointing oil flows freely and flows upon us all. Everyone is energized by the Holy Spirit to serve.

Beloved, are you filled with the Holy Spirit? Have you received the outpouring of the Spirit? Have you been anointed with the holy oil? The simple fact is, if you submit yourself to the Head and are rightly joined to the body—if you dwell with your brethren in unity—the oil will most assuredly flow down to you as well as flow through you to others. But if you and I are at odds with each other and we do not take our proper place in the body, then the Holy Spirit is restricted by us in His flow and the ministry in the body is accordingly hindered. But what riches of ministry must there be if we brethren dwell together in unity! If all of us allow the cross to do its necessary work, we can and will abide together in oneness and thus the Spirit of God will flow among us. Every brother or sister will be anointed with the Holy Spirit and will serve livingly. And how good and how pleasant such a condition as that will be!

The pleasant state of brethren dwelling in unity is also likened to "the dew of Hermon, that falls on the mountains of Zion! For there the Lord has commanded the blessing, even life for evermore." Mount Hermon, one of the highest mountains in its area, is located in the northern part of Palestine, and reaches at once to the height of nearly ten thousand feet from a platform scarcely above sea level. "This platform," wrote Henry Baker Tristam in 1867,

> is for the most part an impenetrable swamp of unknown depth, whence the seething vapour, under the rays of an almost tropical sun, is constantly ascending into the upper atmosphere during the day. The vapour, coming in contact with the snowy sides of the mountains, is rapidly congealed, and is precipitated in the evening in the form of the dew, the most copious we ever experienced. . . .No wonder that the foot of Hermon is

clad with orchards and gardens of such marvelous
fertility in this land of drought.

Thus the dew is formed by the condensation of vapor as it
ascends from the warmer valleys below to the cooler mountains
above where Mount Hermon is. The dew afterwards descends
upon the lower lands and brings with it moisture and life to
the vegetation. And because of its heaviness, the dew almost
looks like rain as it habitually falls from Hermon's heights. With
the result that the vegetation in the lower regions is exceedingly
luxuriant.

Now in relation to Hermon, the mountains of Zion are much
lower hills by comparison and are located to the south. We do
not know whether or not the wind can actually carry the dew of
Hermon that far; it really matters little, however, since this is
but figuratively presented in Psalm 133. Hermon in the Scriptures represents *heaven* (see for example in S.S. 4.8 where it
stands for the heavenly position). Zion, on the other hand, speaks
of the place where God reigns on *earth*, which is the church. So
that what is being said here is that the refreshing dew of
heavenly life shall abundantly descend from where God is to
where the people of God are; that is, it shall fall upon the church.
Upon Zion, upon the church of God, is the sole place where
"God has commanded the blessing, even life for evermore." But
only unity of the brethren is that condition of the church which
can bring down this abundant blessing from heaven. And if
such a good and pleasant condition does exist in the church, then
the heavenly blessing shall indeed descend and fill every brother
and sister with fresh life and vital energy.

Dear brethren, how precious this must be. If by the grace of
God and for His glory we can dwell in unity—having been joined
together by one life and now willing to let the cross deal with
our "self"—all the ministries within the church will be spiritual
and heavenly, and the life of the church will be fresh and
overflowing in abundance. How goodly is this picture! And
how its outworking must surely satisfy God's heart. If we love
God, we must seek after this experience. I personally believe
that in these last days God is anxious to obtain for Himself a
people who shall dwell in unity and live out the body life. So

shall the world come to know Christ the Head, and also us who belong to God.

Dear heavenly Father, how we praise and thank You for giving us one Life to share and one Spirit to live. We are truly one body, being members one of another. We pray we may dwell together in unity as You have desired us to live, that love may prevail in our midst, and that the cross may be borne with joy. Oh that we may experience Your Anointing together and prove the abundance of Your life in the body May the world be compelled to acknowledge "how these people love one another" and thus may know that You, Father, have sent the Son and You have loved us as You have loved Your Son. To You be all the glory. We ask in the Name of Your dear Son, our Lord Jesus Christ. Amen.

Ministering Unto the Lord
Through the Night

PSALM 134

A Song of Degrees.

1 *Behold, bless ye the Lord, all ye servants of the Lord,*
   which by night stand in the house of the Lord!
2 *Lift up your hands in the sanctuary, and bless the Lord!*
3 *The Lord that made heaven and earth bless thee out of*
   Zion!

We have now reached the last of the Songs of Degrees. Of this little song Martin Luther once remarked: "I take this psalm to be the conclusion of those things which were spoken of before." I believe this to be true. In our several considerations together, we have seen that this series of fifteen songs began with a soul who, belonging to God, begins to long after Him. He desires to dwell in the temple of God so that he may be freed from the bondages of the world and that he may seek the Lord with a pure heart. Step by step, degree by degree, he has been making his ascent. To reach his goal the mounting soul must climb up many rungs, each of which is indispensable and very crucial: being released from the entanglement of this world, he is cleansed from sin; being exposed to God's light, he recognizes that there is no good in him, that is in his flesh, and thus he accepts the dealings of the cross; being illumined by God, he receives revelation as to the eternal purpose of God; being broken in heart and humbled in soul, he is enabled to fuse a deeper union with the God Whom he loves; and so he ultimately commences to live the life of the body as was mentioned in Psalm 133. And so we may say that these Songs of Degrees can represent in sequential fashion the ascent of the Christian soul in his spiritual mounting towards God. These songs began with a longing for peace and have their end in a union with the God of peace. They had their start in Meshech and in the tents of Kedar but they conclude with Jerusalem and its temple. Their commencement was a prayer; their conclusion is praise.

Let us now come to this last song of degrees—Psalm 134. In the preceding song the *unity* of the body was portrayed for us. But what the psalmist desires to communicate to us in this concluding psalm concerns the *ministers* in the body. We shall observe them ministering to the Lord until the day breaks. They are actively employed in serving God and men while waiting themselves for the return of the Lord. They serve in the spirit of rapture. And they shall be the first to meet the dawn, for they are awake and waiting.

We all know by this time that the people of Israel gathered to Jerusalem three times a year for prayer, worship and sacrifice in God's temple. And so some interpreters say that Psalm 134 actually constitutes the last song sung by the pilgrims as they finally ascend to the temple. They had traveled from afar, usually arriving in Jerusalem at the time of the evening sacrifice. And hence they there and then would address themselves to the priests who were serving in the temple, who would in turn respond to their greetings with blessings. Others say, though, that this song was used as the pilgrims began to leave for home, after having been in Jerusalem for some time. While they were departing for home, their hearts still lingered in Jerusalem. How they wished they could dwell there forever, that forever they could abide in the house of God and worship Him. This, however, was not permitted by circumstance and environment. They must return, yet they did not want to leave in the morning. They probably stayed on in the temple, therefore, till the evening sacrifice had been offered. The sky had grown dark, the door of the temple by this time was closed, the lamps were now lighted, and the guards had taken up their posts upon the temple wall.

Slowly the pilgrims descended the Jerusalem hills for the journey back to their homes. How reluctant they were to leave;

hence they no doubt gazed back from time to time. They would look back and upwards after taking but a few steps. They beheld the night scene of Jerusalem, with the temple guards standing at their stations under the light of the lamps. And as they viewed this scene, they could not help but shout from below, "Behold, bless the Lord, all you servants of the Lord, who stand by night in the house of the Lord! Lift up your hands in the sanctuary, and bless the Lord!" What they meant by this was: "We are now departing, we cannot stay on in the house of God; we therefore entrust to you this matter of ministering to the Lord. May you all minister well! You servants of the Lord, you who stand by night in the house of the Lord, bless the Lord! Lift up your hands and bless God!" They lovingly exhorted the guards to be faithful in their tasks, wishing they themselves could fulfill the work. Since they could not remain forever, they had to delegate to these who could the duty and privilege of serving the Lord through the nights.

How these people of Israel loved God and loved His house. How they wished those servants of the Lord not to watch the night merely in appearance. They wanted them to fulfill their duties on the one hand but to give thanks and praise from their hearts on the other. The word "bless" in the original we know means "happy." You who are servants of the Lord must make Him happy! You must satisfy God's heart! You should not merely perform your duties, you must love your God from the depth of your heart! There you must pray and worship and bless, that the Lord may be satisfied and glorified!

Now as those Israelites who were leaving exhorted these servants of the Lord, as they lovingly commended them to duty, in return the latter responded by shouting from above, "May the Lord bless you from Zion, He who made heaven and earth!" As if to say, "You are now returning home. May God Who created heaven and earth bless you out of Zion! May the authority, glory and blessing of the Lord be with you! May you take all these back with you!" These servants of the Lord bless the pilgrims with the blessing of the Lord of Zion. Their blessing is authoritative, that is, there is the power and the reality of the blessing. This is priestly ministry—serving God and serving men. Only those who serve the Lord with faithful hearts can bring down the blessings of Zion to others. Their fellowship with the Lord brings to others the authority and glory and blessing of God.

Oh how glorious and wonderful this picture is! What a fitting conclusion it is. Whichever may be the occasion—whether the pilgrims have just arrived at the goal, or as is most probably the case, the pilgrims have fulfilled their desire—in any event this psalm celebrates a happy conclusion. They came to the feasts by ascending steadily; now in returning, the grace of God follows them home. This, then, forms the background of this the last of the Songs of Degrees.

Today our situation is different from that of the Israelites. They could not remain long in Jerusalem nor dwell in the house of God. They must return to their dwelling places, for they had other responsibilities awaiting them there. Their coming to the feasts was occasional; therefore they delegated the service of the Lord to the priests and the Levites who served in their stead. Even though their hearts were full of longing, they had to return home. But today, are we not all the servants of the Lord? Does not the Bible tell us that we who believe in the Lord are every one of us a priest? We all abide in Jerusalem, in the house of God. Not, of course, in the material and physical sense. We who belong to God worship Him together in the church with our brothers and sisters. We need not ever leave God's house, for God is in our very midst, God Himself is our home. Others may come for a visit and then go away to their dwellings, but we are here permanently, for the Lord is our house, the church is our home.

We are like Mary Magdalene. On the day of the resurrection of the Lord Jesus, she went to the tomb but could not find the body of Jesus. She assumed that someone must have taken the body away. Peter and John too came, and they looked into the tomb. But when they could not find the body of Jesus they returned to their homes. Mary, however, stood weeping outside the tomb. Others could go home without the Lord, but she could not, for *the Lord* was her home. Without the Lord, she became homeless. Her home was not a house, but the Lord Whom she loved.

Beloved, our Lord is our home, the church of God is our dwelling place. If we miss the Lord, we become homeless; if we miss the church, that is, if we are out of fellowship, where can we go? Thank God, this need never happen; for the Lord is in us, and we are in Him. Nothing can separate us from the love of God in Christ Jesus our Lord. Let us thank God also that we are among the brethren, and the brethren are among us. We are one big family which *cannot* be destroyed.

Physically speaking we gather for but a brief span of time. After a while we must return to our places of abode. We too have many things to do: some of us are studying, some are working, some are occupied at home. But thank God, spiritually speaking, we are in the Lord and the Lord is in us. We will never lose each other's presence. In addition, we are members one of another in the church. We belong to the same family and shall never be separated. As we cannot be separated from our Lord, so we shall not depart from God's house.

Our present situation far surpasses that of the Israelites. In our day every brother or sister is a servant of the Lord. All minister to God. Whatever may be our earthly profession, we only live on earth for the Lord and for serving His purpose. Our earthly occupations are solely for the maintenance of our existence in order that we may better serve our God. We all are God's servants and we dwell in His house which is the church.

Spiritually speaking, we are in the evening hour—now is the nighttime upon us. Why do I say that? Because our Lord Jesus, Who is the Sun of righteousness, is not here, just as the day is no longer here but turns into night when the sun goes down. But praise be to God, His Word tells us that "the night is far spent, the day is at hand"; "for yet a little while, and he that shall come will come, and will not tarry" (Rom. 13.12; Heb. 10.37). Only in this little while do we watch the night in God's house. We stand, watch, serve, and testify for the glory of God. Through prosperity and adversity, through the sunshine and the darkness, we remain in the house serving the Lord.

As we all realize, though, it is not easy to watch the night. It is a very trying period, especially late in the night when the watchers can sometimes fall asleep. People would like to return home and to sleep. But the faithful of the Lord shall take their places in the house of God and serve. They shall take up the long vigil of the night. They shall guard the interest of the Lord. They shall lift up their hands in prayer and praise. They shall minister to the satisfaction and pleasure of the Lord. And they shall bring down the blessing of the Lord to His people. Let us therefore watch and pray. Every one of us must do his part. We must worship and serve our God in the church for we are all God's servants.

But let not our service be of outward appearance. Please note that a servant of the Lord can fulfill his duty merely in a legal way. He may be a guard or a watcher, and he may be faithful in carrying out his duty, but his heart may not be upon the Lord. How easy for a servant to be occupied with his job, or even make ministry so much the thing of his soul that the Lord is crowded out of his heart. This will be simply an outward service without the reality of a spiritual ministry. He may do his job well, he may perform his tasks very correctly, but the Lord has not been satisfied. The Lord requires of his servant more than the exactness of service. He demands a heart-love towards Him. The lesson of the letter to the church in Ephesus (Revelation 2) is that of the absolute necessity of the first love. And this is what the pilgrim psalmist in this song exhorts God's servants to have. The word which permeates and lingers long in this psalm is "Bless." The pilgrim exhorts the servants to bless the Lord: Make the Lord happy! It betrays the fact that his own heart is filled with this very desire to bless the Lord, to make the Lord pleased, happy and satisfied.

Consequently, if ever we serve God in the church we must love Him with our whole heart. What can satisfy God's heart? Love alone can. Oh brothers and sisters, in what way can we satisfy God when we are serving and worshiping in the church? How can we make Him happy? By doing everything *from the heart!* How glorious it is if we each perform our part of service in unison with others and lift up our hands in prayer with hearts full of first love! Our hope is that everyone will lift up his hands and bless God. That everyone learns how to pray in the church. All must offer their mouths to pray and to praise.

What a ministry it must be when the servant executes his duty with the spirit of praise! This is serving the Lord and not simply serving the house (see Ezek. 44). And by this means shall the heart of God be satisfied.

What will happen if we serve God in this fashion? "May the Lord who made heaven and earth bless you out of Zion!" If we love and serve God in this way, He shall pour down His blessing upon us from Zion, which is to say, from His throne. "Surely goodness and mercy shall follow me all the days of my life: and I will dwell in the house of the Lord for ever" (Ps. 23.6).

Now is the song concluded. How lovely is this song! How precious is its theme! May we all do our part in the church, having our hearts filled with the love of Christ that we may be built up together in love. May God be glorified and may we be blessed!

The race of God's anointed priests
    Shall never pass away;
Before His glorious face they stand,
    And serve Him night and day.
Though reason raves, and unbelief
    Flows on, a mighty flood,
There are, and shall be till the end,
    The hidden priests of God.

His chosen souls, their earthly dross
    Consumed in sacred fire,
To God's own heart their hearts ascend
    In flame of deep desire;
The incense of their worship fills
    His Temple's holiest place;
Their song with wonder fills the Heavens,
    The glad new song of grace.

    —GERHARD TERSTEEGEN, 1697-1769
    Tr. Unknown

Watch! for the morning is breaking,
  A moment, and He will be here!
The mists and the shadows are fleeing,
  The darkness will soon disappear;
And He, for Whom Ages have waited,
  The Lord Who has tarried so long,
Will come in an outburst of glory,
  A moment, and we shall be gone!

Watch! for the morning is breaking,
  A moment, the crown will be won!
A moment, and we shall be with Him,
  A moment, the journey is done!
Lord, keep us each moment unsleeping,
  And count us all worthy to be
In that noble band of Thy watchers,
  Whose *life* is a vigil with Thee.

—MARGARET E. BARBER, 1866-1930

To my high school sophomore English teacher, Jessica Rewitz.
Thank you for believing in a girl who couldn't do the same for herself.
I did it.